TEACH YOURSELF BOOKS

FRENCH GRAMMAR

Jean-Claude Arragon, M.A., L es L, MIL

NTC Publishing Group

Long-renowned as *the* authoritative source for self-guided learning – with more than 30 million copies sold worldwide – the *Teach Yourself* series includes over 200 titles in the fields of languages, crafts, hobbies, sports, and other leisure activities.

Printed in England by Clays Ltd, St Ives plc.

Contents

Introduction

When we speak or write our own language, we make up sentences, which are, in general, understandable by all those who are familiar with the language. Such sentences are not built haphazardly. The words appear in a certain order and, like the pieces of a jigsaw puzzle, occupy a specific place in the overall pattern. This means that our minds have discovered the acceptable (and unacceptable) ways of speaking and writing. In other words, we have worked out the grammar rules of the language, and if we hear a child or a foreigner say *I has done that or *I very like it, we know instinctively that those phrases are not acceptable (although they may still be understandable), because they break the rules which our brain has worked out, even though we may not always be able to state why this is so or exactly what the rule is. Similarly, when learning another language, we have to acquire the vocabulary and the grammar of that language in order to build up a store of knowledge which will enable us to understand and to communicate. This can be done in different ways with varying degrees of success. One way, perhaps the more effective, is to spend long periods of time in the foreign country, but this is not always possible. Another way is to learn every word and every grammar rule you need mechanically, but this is very tiresome and, unless you are blessed with a superb memory, very frustrating. Yet another, and perhaps more practicable method, is to build up our knowledge of words and structures by becoming *actively involved* in the learning process and in the discovery of the rules, as we did when we learnt to speak our own language.

Looking back over our formative years, it may seem that doing so was quick and easy but this is not so! Long before we even began to talk, our brain was doing an amazing amount of 'detective work' using the language information which was coming to our ears, 'examining' it, piecing things together, mastering sounds, phrases, sentences, making up its own rules and later inflicting the results of all those thoughts on other people. That is precisely what you must learn to do once again. However, instead of having to work out all the rules by yourself, you will have this book at your elbow. The book is, in

---

*Here and throughout the book an asterisk (*) is used to denote an unacceptable utterance.

essence, not very different from a recipe book. It will give you a list of the 'ingredients' you need (grammatical words) and the order in which to use them to turn your efforts into acceptable and palatable recipes (sentences). But it is essential that you experiment on your own: you must prepare your own sentences from the 'ingredients' used in the examples given, using the latter as models. Teach yourself to listen or look for similarities or differences in any new material you come across. Compare words, phrases, sentences. In that way, you will develop positive attitudes which are the key to linguistic success. And whenever you *discover* a rule, however small, you will have made excellent progress because that is a rule you will not forget!

The aim of this book, therefore, is to help you improve your skills in French through active participation. It would be unfair to claim that you will find all the answers in it. However, an honest attempt has been made to present the main rules of French grammar in a clear and precise way. The vocabulary used in the examples is largely based on *le Français fondamental*, a list of the 3000 most commonly used words in the language. In this way, useful memory space will not be taken up with seldom-used items. It is hoped that by so doing, the author will have provided a useful tool for the beginner and at the same time encouraged more advanced learners to develop and refine the knowledge already acquired.

NB: Whenever a very important or problematic point is encountered in the course of the explanations it will appear in a boxed section which will be immediately recognisable. Particular care should be taken to remember the context of such sections.

The book is designed to be read through once to get 'the feel of the language' and then returned to as often as necessary, to learn a specific point, to refresh your memory, or to check on one of your own 'theories'. Let us take an example of this 'theory-building' which is so crucial to the learning process. If you come across phrases like the following:

Voici la voiture rouge.   *Here is the red car.*
Voici le chat noir.   *Here is the black cat.*
Voici les pommes vertes.   *Here are the green apples.*

you should examine them carefully. This examination should enable you to formulate the following theories:

Theory I: The word **voici** can be used with a masculine noun (**le chat**), with a feminine one (**la voiture**) or with a plural one (**les pommes**). Therefore it could mean either *here is* or *here are*.

Theory II: Words expressing colour (**rouge, noir, vertes**) all appear after the name of the thing or being they refer to. Therefore, this seems to indicate that, in French, adjectives of colour follow the noun they refer to, whereas in English they are placed before it.

Theory III: The adjective **vertes** and the noun **pommes** both have an **s** in the plural. Therefore it could mean that

(*a*) French nouns take an **s** in the plural (which is similar to English);

(*b*) French adjectives take an **s** in the plural (which is totally different from English).

If you check in the relevant sections of this book, you will find that theories I and II are absolutely correct, but that III is incomplete and needs to be refined further.

The more you become accustomed to looking at the language in this way, the more rewarding your learning will be and the quicker your progress.

Finally you should remember two crucial points:

1 A language is a living thing; grammar rules are there to capture its individuality and its vitality, not to destroy them.

2 Every language has its own identity and you must not try to 'bend' the rules of French to fit those of your own language.

If this book helps you to gain greater confidence in the use of French and a clearer view of the way the language operates, it will have more than met its goal.

1 The Development of the French Language

The present state of the French language is the result of a long and complex evolution and of numerous external influences. At various stages in its history, France was invaded by different ethnic and linguistic groups: Greeks, Romans, Celts, Franks, Arabs . . . and each of those groups left its mark on the country and its language. There is little doubt, however, that the most profound influence of all was exerted by the Romans and by their language, Latin, both in its classical and popular forms. However, the words and grammatical structures borrowed from Latin were modified to fit the needs and the patterns of the developing French language, thereby contributing to its originality. Some of the original features of French are given below.

The gender of nouns

French nouns are divided into two gender categories: masculine and feminine. To the learner, the division may sometimes seem arbitrary or even amusing, but there are reasons, obscure though they may be, for the classification. At this stage, it would not be helpful to go into those reasons. For those who have studied Latin, however, it may be helpful to know that borrowed masculine and neuter Latin nouns are masculine in French whilst borrowed feminine Latin nouns have retained their original gender.

Although there are useful rules which can help you recognise the gender of certain nouns, the best method is to learn any new noun with a word which will give an indication of its gender. That is why every new noun should be associated with the singular form of its definite (*the*) or indefinite (*a*) article. Unlike their English counterparts those words carry information about the gender of the noun that follows.

Thus you should learn:

not: voiture	*but*: **la voiture**	*or* **une voiture**
car	*the* (fem.) *car*	*a* (fem.) *car*

not: sac   *but*: **le sac**   *or* **un sac**
　　 bag   *the* (masc.) *bag*   *a* (masc.) *bag*

This is very important and may save you a great deal of trouble at a later stage.

Gender and number agreements

Since French nouns are divided into two gender categories, masculine and feminine, it is logical that words related to those nouns should also bear the mark of the noun's gender; that is why it is vitally important to know what the gender of a given noun is; failure to do so would result in a cascade of mistakes.

Compare: le grand homme brun   *the tall dark-haired man*
and: **la** grande dame brune   *the tall dark-haired woman*

The above examples clearly show that, whereas in English the definite article *the* and the adjectives *tall*, *dark-haired* are the same in the masculine and in the feminine, it is definitely not so in French.

French nouns can, whenever necessary, bear the mark of the plural. This also occurs in English. However, there is a striking difference between the two languages in this respect: the plural form of an English noun nearly always sounds *different* from the singular one:

　　a wall ⟶ *walls*
　　a home ⟶ *homes*

The plural form of a French noun nearly always sounds *exactly the same* as the singular one:

un mur ⟶ **des murs**　　 ⎱ the **s** is not
une maison ⟶ **des maisons** ⎰ sounded

It is therefore vital that some other signal or 'advance warning system' be present to indicate whether the noun is in the singular or the plural. This is done with the help of a category of words called determiners; the definite article **le**, **la**, **les** (*the*) and the indefinite article **un**, **une**, **des** (*a, some*) belong to that category.

Compare: **la** grande dame brune   *the tall dark-haired woman*
and: **les** grandes dames brunes   *the tall dark-haired women*

The *only* difference in sound between the two comes from the definite article **la/les**.

This explains why, in French, determiners cannot usually be omitted.

Vowel removal (or elision); liaison

In certain circumstances, some vowels (**a**, **e**, **i**) are removed at the end of a given word and are replaced by an apostrophe (') which is a marker used to signal the elision. The reason is that French does not usually permit a 'clash' of vowels between two adjoining words. So, if such a clash is likely to occur because a word beginning with a vowel or a 'silent' (mute) **h** follows another word ending with a vowel, the last vowel of the first word disappears and is replaced by '. Therefore:

*le enfant becomes **l'**enfant   *the child*
*le hôtel becomes **l'**hôtel   *the hotel*

NB   Vowels cannot be removed from the end of nouns, adjectives, verbs, adverbs (important grammatical words); they can only be removed from *specific words* like the definite article, pronouns or the preposition **de** (*in*, *at*, *from*) for instance. In the case of the definite article, the result of this process is that the reduced form **l'** no longer carries any gender information. That is why, when learning new nouns, you should replace **l'** by the appropriate indefinite article **un**, **une** (*a*).

Thus you must learn:

not: **l'**orange   *the orange*   *but*: **une** orange   *an orange* (fem.)
not: **l'**acteur   *the actor*   *but*: **un** acteur   *an actor* (masc.)

The need to eliminate the 'vowel-vowel clash' across word boundaries, has also led the French to make use of liaison (or word-linking). As we have already seen, certain letters at the end of a word are not sounded; this may result in the occurrence of a 'clash'. To avoid this clash the French *either* sound the last letter of the preceding word:

Compare: un peti**t** homme   *a small man* – the **t** is sounded
and: un peti**t** garçon   *a small boy* – the **t** is not sounded

or they modify the preceding word whenever possible:

Compare: **ce** garçon   *this boy*
and: **cet** enfant   *this child* – **ce** has become **cet** to avoid the clash

For a fuller treatment of this point, you should refer to Appendix I, where you will also find a list of words beginning with 'non-silent' (aspirated) **h**, before which vowel removal or elision does *not* occur.

The 'tu' and 'vous' forms

In French, there are two ways of addressing a person: you can either use the **tu** (*thou*) form or the **vous** (*you*) form. Most English people seem to have great difficulty in deciding which to use. The rule is in fact quite simple:

tu is used between relatives or close friends but not normally with strangers or passing acquaintances. There are, however, some exceptions:

(*a*)   members of a close-knit group, students for instance, use the **tu** form, even though they may not know each other; in this case the **tu** form creates a bond between members of the group;

(*b*)   the **tu** form can be used with a complete stranger as a mark of contempt. Parisian taxi-drivers use this quite often!

vous is used in all other cases. It should not be seen as a sign of stand-offishness, but as a *mark of respect*. The best thing to do is take your cue from the French: if they use **tu** with you, you may use it with them, if not use **vous**.

Sentences and their components: the jigsaw puzzle

Sentences in French, as in other languages, are made up of sections called clauses or phrases, which in turn are made up of words.

To the beginner it may be useful to consider the French sentence as a linear jigsaw puzzle, each word representing a piece of the whole pattern, for which the right place must be selected. In English, you know instinctively how the pieces fit together. It is crucial for you to realise that they may not fit the same way in French:

| Compare: | (Le | — | beaujolais | nouveau | est | arrivé. |
| and: | (The | new | Beaujolais | — | has | arrived. |

| or: | (Voici | le | — | chat | noir. |
| and: | (Here is | the | black | cat. | — |

| or: | (Je | le | vois | — |
| and: | (I | — | see | him. |

You must therefore beware not to impose upon French the rules of your own language.

The pieces of the jigsaw puzzle (words) are not all alike in shape or status, but they all have a specific role to play. Because of this, they have been grouped in grammatical categories; it would be extremely awkward and wasteful to try and explain grammatical rules without using grammatical words. Grammatical categories are recognised the world over and used in the teaching and description of all languages. Therefore, if you wish to consult a dictionary, or other reference books, you will have to become familiar with a few 'technical' words. After all, when you go to an ironmonger's, it is easier to ask for 'a screw' than for 'a tapering cylindrical piece of metal with a spiral ridge running on its outside and a slotted head, for fastening pieces of wood or metal together'!

Below is a list of the grammatical categories which will be examined in subsequent chapters. Rather than presenting the categories by order of importance it has been decided to introduce them to reflect, as far as possible, the order in which they would occur in a sentence.

Determiners

A determiner is an element which occurs before the name of a thing or being, and gives some useful additional information as well as (in French) giving advance warning of the *gender* (masculine or feminine) and/or the *number* (singular or plural) of that name. In English, determiners do not have exactly the same role.

Compare: **le** sac   *the* bag – masculine

la carte   *the* map/card – feminine

les visiteurs   *the* visitors – plural

The main categories of determiners are:

(*a*)   the definite article: **le, la; les** (*the*);

(*b*)   the indefinite article: **un, une; des** (*a; several*);

(*c*)   the partitive article: **du, de la, des** (*a certain amount of*);

(*d*)   the possessive adjective: **mon, ma, mes** (*my*);

(*e*)   the demonstrative adjective: **ce, cette; ces** (*this/that; these/those*);

(*f*)   the exclamative adjective: **quel, quelle, quels!** (*what(a)*!);

(*g*)   the interrogative adjective: **quel, quelle, quels?** (*what/which?*)

(*h*)   the indefinite adjective: **quelques, plusieurs, certain(s)** (*a few, several, certain/some*);

(*i*)   the numeral: **un, six, dix, cent** . . . (*one, six, ten, a hundred* . . .)

Adjectives

Adjectives are words which are added to the names of things or beings, to give details about (some of) their characteristics.

le **vieux** monsieur **barbu**   the *old bearded* man.

la **petite** maison **blanche**   the *small white* house

Some adjectives can be found before the noun, some after. This is not a matter of choice; there are definite rules governing the position of adjectives: adjectives expressing colour are placed *after* the noun and not before it as in English. Adjectives are also found after a small number of verbs such as: **être** *to be*, **devenir** *to become*, **sembler** *to seem*, **paraître** *to appear*, **rester** *to remain*:

Il est **riche.**   *He is rich.*

Elle devient **belle.**   *She is becoming beautiful.*

> In French, as already mentioned, adjectives agree in *gender* (masculine/feminine) and *number* (singular/plural) with the name of the thing(s) or being(s) they qualify. This is *not* the case in English.

le **grand** garçon   *the big boy* – masc. sing.
la **grande** fille   *the big girl* – fem. sing.
les **grands** garçons   *the big boys* – masc. plur.
les **grandes** filles   *the big girls* – fem. plur.

Nouns

Nouns are the words that name things, or beings, for example le **bois** *wood*, la **table** *table*, un **docteur** *a doctor*, des **touristes** *some tourists*. Nouns are usually divided into two categories:

(a)   *common* nouns, like those above;
(b)   *proper* nouns, i.e. those naming countries, rivers, mountains, seas, etc., or giving the surname or name(s) of people. They begin with a capital letter:
La **Tamise**   *the Thames*,   les **Alpes**   *the Alps*,
Léonard de Vinci   *Leonardo da Vinci*

Pronouns

A pronoun is a word which can replace a noun or a noun-phrase (determiner + adjective + noun). It is very useful because it allows us to avoid tiresome repetitions.

Le pauvre homme n'est pas malade, **il** est mort!   *The poor man is not ill, he is dead!*

Tu vas au cinéma ce soir? J'**y** suis allé hier!   *Are you going to the pictures tonight? I went there yesterday!*

In the above sentences, **il** represents and replaces **le pauvre homme** and **y** represents and replaces **au cinéma**.

Verbs

Verbs are words which express an action or a state:
les enfants **chantent**   *the children sing/are singing* (action)
le professeur **est** malade   *the teacher is ill* (state)

Adverbs

Adverbs are words or expressions which indicate where, in what manner, when, how often, etc., an action is (was, will be . . .)

performed. They are used to modify the sense of a verb, or of another adverb; they can also modify the sense of an adjective.

L'autobus *roule* **vite**.   *The bus is going fast.*

L'autobus roule **très** *vite*.   *The bus is going very fast.*

L'autobus est **très** *rapide*.   *The bus is very fast/quick.*

The use of bold italic indicates which word the adverb modifies. Adverbs, unlike adjectives, do not normally vary in gender (masculine, feminine) or number (singular, plural). There are only very few exceptions to this rule.

Linking words

They connect together words or phrases in the speech chain. Among those, we find:

(*a*) *Prepositions* like **à** *at/in*, **de** *of/from*, **dans** *in*, **sur** *on*, **devant** *in front of*, **pour** *for*, **contre** *against*, etc. They are used to link two words or phrases, and they clarify the relationship (generally of purpose, space or time) existing between the two:

Ils attendent **sur** le quai.   *They are waiting on the platform.*

Êtes-vous **pour** ou **contre** cette idée?   *Are you for or against this idea?*

Ils se préparent **à** partir.   *They are getting ready to go.*

(*b*) *Conjunctions* like: **ou** *or*, **mais** *but*, **et** *and* which are used to link two phrases of equal status:

Ils ont accepté **mais** nous avons refusé.   *They accepted but we refused.*

or like: **bien que** *although*, **parce que** *because*, **pour que/afin que** *so that*, etc. which serve to introduce a phrase (sometimes called subordinate clause) which will 'complete the picture' as far as meaning is concerned. Those words establish a relationship between two sections of a sentence.

L'accident s'est produit **parce qu**'il allait trop vite.   *The accident occurred because he was going too fast.*

Je te le dis **pour que** tu ne sois pas surpris.   *I tell you so that you won't be surprised.*

Note: Words in this category do not vary in gender or number.

Interjections

These are small words, which are used to convey a feeling, a command, or a noise.

Ouf! nous l'avons échappé belle.   *Phew! we had a narrow escape.*

Clac! la porte se ferme.   *The door closes, bang!*

Registers and styles

When we speak (or write) our own language, we use a wide range of words and expressions (register) arranged in a certain way (style). Register and style are strongly influenced by the circumstances in which we speak or write. We do not express ourselves in the same way when addressing a close friend or a relative, a stranger, a superior or a subordinate. Our expressions can be colloquial, familiar, normal, formal, etc. Using the wrong type of language in a given situation could amount to committing a serious social gaffe.

Let us take as an example the following questions:

1   What can I do for you, sir?
2   What do you want, mister?
3   What can I do you for, squire?

It will be immediately obvious to a native English speaker that although all three expressions are aiming to elicit the same information, they contain important overtones and cannot be used at random.

If it is normally easy to 'gauge' the appropriateness of a given register or style for a particular occasion in one's native tongue, it is extremely difficult to do so in the case of a foreign language. In any case, you will normally be forgiven for using a type of language which is too formal, whereas careless use of slang or colloquial expressions may offend, particularly in view of the fact that such utterances always sound worse than when used by a native speaker.

The problem is very complex and goes beyond the scope of a book such as this. The following suggestions, however, should prove useful in this matter:

1   You should acquire a good, recently-published dictionary, in which differences in register and style are clearly indicated.

2   You should pay close attention to the *social context* in which a given word (or turn of phrase) occurs, so that you may use it in similar circumstances in the future. As your knowledge increases, you will be able to refine your sense of appropriateness.

The following devices, however, are very often used in familiar French by native speakers and would therefore not raise many eyebrows if you were to adopt them.

(*a*)   Omission of the **ne** element of the **ne . . . pas** (*not*) negation.

Compare:	Il mange **pas**.	*He does not eat.*
and:	Il **ne** mange **pas**.	
or:	Elle est **pas** partie.	*She has not gone.*
and:	Elle **n'**est **pas** partie.	

(b) Systematic use of **on** (*one*) as a replacement for **nous** (*we*).

Compare:	**On** est arrivés à midi.	*We arrived*
and:	**Nous** sommes arrivés à midi.	*at midday.*
or:	**On** ira voir le film.	*We shall go and*
and:	**Nous** irons voir le film.	*see the film.*

(c) Use of **c'est** (*it is*, singular) instead of **ce sont** (*it is*, plural) with a third person plural.

Compare:	**C'est** les voisins qui reviennent.	*It is the neigh-*
and:	**Ce sont** les voisins qui reviennent.	*bours coming back.*
or:	**C'est** eux les coupables.	*It is they*
and:	**Ce sont** eux les coupables.	*who are guilty*

(d) Formulation of questions without using an inversion or a question marker.

Compare:	Vous êtes sûr?	
and:	Êtes-vous sûr? *or* Est-ce que vous êtes sûr?	*Are you sure?*
or:	Tu écoutes?	
and:	Écoutes-tu? *or* Est-ce que tu écoutes?	*Are you listening?*

Note: In such cases, the 'question quality' is given by the intonation (voice pitch) which rises instead of going down as it would in a normal statement.

Whenever you come across a new familiar expression, make a mental note of the context in which it occurred so that you may, in turn, use it in the right way.

Pronunciation

Refinement of one's oral performance can be achieved in several ways, and in particular with the help of phonetics. Phonetics is the study of speech sounds. In modern dictionaries, each word entry is followed by its phonetic transcription composed of symbols from the International Phonetic Alphabet (IPA). This means that if you know the value of the relevant IPA symbols, you will be able to pronounce a given word accurately, even though you may never have seen or heard it before. This is why a section containing the description of the relevant IPA symbols, along with information on stress patterns and syllable structure, has been included as an appendix. Learning those symbols and their values will be a great help in your future language studies.

In addition, your oral performance may be dramatically improved by listening regularly to authentic French language material such as songs, stories or news broadcasts. All you need to do is to record such items and listen repeatedly to their contents to absorb the meaning and the sound of French words, thereby increasing your linguistic competence.

Accents and diacritic signs

Accents have a very important role to play in written French. They can be used to modify the sound of a vowel or to serve as markers to differentiate between certain words which would otherwise look exactly alike:

Compare: **la**   *the*   and: **là**   *there*
or: **ou**   *or*   and: **où**   *where*
or: **a**   *has*   and: **à**   *at, to*

In the above cases, a grave accent is used to distinguish the two forms.

Similarly, diacritics like the apostrophe ('), the diaresis (¨) or the cedilla (̦), signal a change in the syllable or sound structure of a word. An explanation of the role and position of such signs has also been included in the Appendix.

Remember: Accents (and diacritics) cannot be used at random; they must *always* be carefully and properly placed.

Explanations concerning French pronunciation, syllable structure, stress and the role of accents and other signs have been included in the appendices. It is hoped that some readers may find them informative and profitable.

Key points

1   French nouns fall into two categories: masculine and feminine.

2   When learning a new noun, it is advisable to learn it with the relevant definite or indefinite singular article to avoid agreement mistakes later.

3   In French 'vowel-vowel clashes' at word boundaries are avoided by a variety of means: (elision, liaison and even alteration of the form of some words).

4   Certain types of words (determiners and adjectives) carry gender or number information about the noun(s) they are related to; certain other types (prepositions, adverbs) do not.

5   In French there are precise rules concerning the relative position of words in a sentence. These rules may be quite different from those which apply in English.

SECTION I

Some of the Jigsaw Pieces:
The Noun and its Associates

2 The Definite Article

The French definite article is broadly equivalent to the English *the*. It varies in gender (masc/fem) and in number (sing/plur) with the noun which follows.

Form

	Singular	*Plural*
Masculine	le/l'	les
Feminine	la/l'	les

Le mari *The husband* (masc. sing.)
La femme *The wife* (fem. sing.)
Les garçons *The boys* (masc. plur.)
Les filles *The girls* (fem. plur.)

Remember: The **e** of **le** and the **a** of **la** disappear if the next word begins with a vowel or 'mute h', to avoid the vowel-vowel clash (see appendix I).

L'ami *The friend* (masc. sing.)
L'amie *The friend* (fem. sing.)

NB Because of its importance as an 'advance warning system', the non-reduced singular form of the article **le**, **la**, should not be separated from the noun when learning new vocabulary. Consider the two words as a whole **article + noun** and not as separate entities.

Special forms

When linking words (prepositions) like **à** (*at*, *to*, *in*) or **de** (*of*, *from*) are used before the article, they combine with it in the following way:

(*a*) In the case of **à**:

	Singular	*Plural*
Masculine	au/à l'	aux
Feminine	à la/à l'	aux

Il va **au** travail. (and not *Il va à le travail.)   *He is going to work.*
Nous allons **aux** Etats-Unis (and not *Nous allons à les Etats-
Unis.)   *We are going to the United States.*

Note: **à l'** is used when the next word begins with a vowel or a mute
'h' to avoid the vowel-vowel clash.

(*b*)   In the case of **de**:

	Singular	*Plural*
Masculine	du/de l'	des
Feminine	de la/de l'	des

Il vient **du** travail. (and not *Il vient de le travail.)   *He is coming
from work.*

Nous arrivons **des** Etats-Unis. (and not *Nous arrivons de les
Etats-Unis.)   *We have just arrived from the United States.*

Note: **de l'** is used when the next word begins with a vowel or mute
'h' to avoid the vowel-vowel clash.

Important remarks concerning the use of definite articles

The definite article is used far more frequently in French than in
English. Consequently, its meaning may not be exactly the same in
the two languages.

Compare: **Les gens** = 'people' as a category, as opposed to
animals or plants, *but also* 'a specific group
of people'

and: **The people** = people belonging to a specific group: a
nation, an estate, a gathering . . .

Because of this, it is safe to assume as a general rule that, if the definite
article is used in a given context in English, it will be used in the
corresponding French context. (There are very few exceptions.)

the boy   le garçon
the queen   la reine
the guests   les invités
The Alps   Les Alpes

In addition to the above the definite article is used before the noun in
the following cases:

1   With the names of continents, countries, regions, states, lakes,
rivers, mountains.

L'Afrique   *Africa*
La Hollande   *Holland*
Le Yorkshire   *Yorkshire*
La Bretagne   *Brittany*
La Tamise   *The Thames*
Les Pyrénées   *The Pyrenees*

Note: In the case of feminine-singular names of countries and regions **à la** will be replaced by **en** if the meaning is *going to* or *staying in*.

Il va **en** Espagne (and not *Il va à l'Espagne.)   *He is going to Spain.* (fem. sing.)

Ils sont **en** Bretagne (and not *Ils sont à la Bretagne.)   *They are in Brittany.* (fem. sing.)

With the same category of names, if the meaning is *coming from*, **de la** or **de l'** will be replaced by **de** or **d'**.

Il arrive **d'**Allemagne (and not *Il arrive de l'Allemagne.)   *He's just arrived from Germany.* (fem. sing.)

Vous venez **de** France. (and not *Vous venez de la France.)   *You are coming from France.* (fem. sing.)

2   With names of substances, materials and processes.

J'utilise **le** bois, **le** sable, **le** ciment et **la** pierre.   *I use wood, sand, cement and stone.*

Le charbon et **le** pétrole sont rares.   *Coal and oil are rare.*

L' or, **l'**argent et **les** diamants sont chers.   *Gold, silver and diamonds are expensive.*

3   With nouns representing a broad category, group or profession.

Les jeunes protestent.   *Young people are protesting.*

Les riches ont tout.   *Rich people have everything.*

Les politiciens sont ambitieux.   *Politicians are ambitious.*

4   With nouns expressing a general quality, trait or fault.

La paresse est un défaut.   *Laziness is a fault.*

La gourmandise est un péché.   *Greed is a sin.*

Le courage est une qualité assez rare.   *Courage is a fairly rare quality.*

5   With nouns representing an abstract concept.

Le beau, **le** bien, **le** vrai sont là pour nous guider.   *Beauty, goodness, truth are here to guide us.*

La mort me fait peur, **la** vie aussi.   *Death frightens me, so does life.*

6   With names of languages and nationalities

Il apprend l'espagnol.   *He is learning Spanish.*

Les Français sont individualistes.   *French people are individualistic.*

7   With names of seasons, days, parts of days (if speaking in general terms)

> Il fait froid l'hiver, mais **les** étés sont doux.   *It is cold in winter, but summers are mild.*
>
> En automne, **les** soirées sont courtes.   *In autumn, evenings are short.*
>
> **Le** samedi et **le** dimanche nous sortons.   *We go out on Saturdays and Sundays.*

But: If you refer to *last* or *next* Monday, Tuesday, etc. you do *not* use the definite article:

> Samedi soir, je passerai le voir.   *(Next) Saturday evening I shall drop by and see him.*
>
> Ils sont partis lundi.   *They left on Monday.*

The phrase *in the morning* meaning *tomorrow morning* is translated in French by **demain matin**.

In **le lundi**, **le jeudi**, etc., the singular form of the article is sufficient to give the idea of a regular occurrence; the plural is not normally acceptable.

---

8   With nouns indicating title, rank, whether or not they are followed by the name of the bearer.

> **le** président Kennedy   *President Kennedy*
>
> **la** reine Elizabeth   *Queen Elizabeth*
>
> **le** comte Dracula   *Count Dracula*
>
> **le** général de Gaulle   *General de Gaulle*
>
> **le** général et **le** premier ministre arrivent.   *The General and the Prime Minister are arriving.*

Note: If you are talking *directly* to the bearer of the title, you should use Monsieur, Madame, Messieurs—before the title, unless a special form of address is available like **(Votre) Excellence** *your Excellency* etc.

> Madame **la** Comtesse   *Countess/Your ladyship*
>
> Messieurs **les** Députés   *Honourable Gentlemen* (to MPs)
>
> Monsieur **le** Président   *Mr President*

9   With names of academic subjects, crafts, hobbies, sports:

> Je déteste **la** chimie.   *I hate chemistry.*
>
> Il adore **les** langues.   *He adores languages.*
>
> Elle apprend **la** poterie.   *She is learning pottery.*
>
> Vous aimez **le** football?   *Do you like football?*
>
> Elle préfère **la** lecture.   *She prefers reading.*

10 With nouns indicating parts of the body, where in English you would use *a* or a possessive.

> Ce chien a **le** nez froid. *This dog has a cold nose.*
>
> Il met **les** mains dans **les** poches. *He puts his hands in his pockets.*
>
> Il a **le** crâne fracturé. *He has a fractured skull.*
>
> Je me brosse **les** dents. *I am brushing my teeth.*
>
> Vous vous lavez **les** mains. *You are washing your hands.*
>
> Elle a mal à **la** tête. *Her head is hurting.*

But: If the noun indicating a part of the body is qualified by an adjective, **le** is replaced either by the appropriate indefinite article **un**, **une**, **des** (*a; some*):

> Le chien a **un** petit nez froid. *The dog has a small cold nose.*

or by the appropriate possessive adjective: **son**, **sa**, **ses** (*his/her*):

> Il met **ses** grosses mains dans **ses** poches. *He puts/is putting his big hands in his pockets.*

11 In expressions where a price per item or speed per unit of time is given.

> *Ce vin coûte 70F* **la** bouteille! *This wine costs 70F a bottle!*
>
> Il roulait à 140 km à **l'**heure. *He was driving at 140 km an hour.*

12 With the preposition **à**, to describe a peculiarity or a distinguishing feature characterising a person, animal or thing.

> L'homme **à la** jambe de bois *The man with a wooden leg*
>
> La femme **à la** robe rouge *The woman in the red dress*
>
> La maison **aux** volets verts (aux = *à les- masc. plur.) *The house with the green shutters*

Omission of the definite article

In certain circumstances, the definite article can be omitted:

(*a*) in proverbs:

> Pauvreté n'est pas vice. *Poverty is no vice.*
>
> Pierre qui roule n'amasse pas mousse. *A rolling stone gathers no moss.*

(*b*) in set expressions/phrases:

> Travail – Famille – Patrie *Work – Family – Country* (the motto of the Vichy Regime)
>
> Liberté – Egalité – Fraternité *Freedom – Equality – Fraternity* (the motto of the French Republic)

(*c*) in lists of items or people:

Tables, chaises, vaisselle, tout était cassé. *Tables, chairs, crockery, everything was broken.*

Hommes, femmes et enfants ont péri dans les flammes. *Men, women and children perished in the flames.*

(*d*) if, in a sentence, two nouns follow each other and the second is in apposition to the first (that is to say if it gives extra information about the first), the article of the second noun is omitted:

Paris, capitale de la France, est une belle ville. *Paris, the capital of France, is a lovely city.*

(*e*) in expressions of the type: *the more . . . the more, the less . . . the less* (or a combination of the two):

Plus il travaille, plus il devient riche. *The more he works, the richer he becomes.*

Plus je regarde, moins je comprends. *The more I look, the less I understand.*

Note: (d) and (e) above are two of the rare occasions when the English definite article is not translated by its French equivalent.

(*f*) in expressions where two nouns are present and the second noun is used as an adjective:

La Banque d'Angleterre   *The Bank of England*

Le vin de Bourgogne   *Burgundy wine*

Les fromages de France   *French cheeses*

Un tapis de Perse   *A Persian carpet*

Key points

1 The French definite article can be used to indicate either a broad category or concept, or (as the English *the*), a specific and well defined sub-category.

2 The definite article is used far more frequently in French than in English. If it is used in English, it is very likely that it will also appear in French.

3 The definite article (except in its reduced form **l'**) carries advance information about the gender and/or number of the noun that follows.

4 When learning a new noun, you should always try to remember it with its article (singular form).

5 The definite article is required before names of countries, regions, rivers, mountains, seas and lakes, languages or nationalities.

6 The definite article *must* also be used when the noun refers to a broad category or concept, a representative group or profession, a given type of activity (artistic, scientific, scholarly, etc.).

7 With nouns expressing abstract concepts (Good, Evil, Life, etc.) or general qualities or faults (Beauty, Laziness, etc.), the definite article *must* also be used.

8 With nouns referring to parts of the body two possibilities may occur:

(*a*) If 'ownership' is unambiguous, particularly through the use of **avoir** (*to have*) or of a reflexive construction, the definite article will suffice.

(*b*) If 'ownership' may be open to ambiguity or misinterpretation, or if the noun is qualified by an adjective, the definite article must be replaced by a possessive adjective.

9 In expressions where a quantity (distance, money, weight) per unit is stated, the definite article will be used to translate the English *a* or *per*.

10 The definite article may be omitted in proverbs and set expressions as well as in (long) lists of things or beings.

11 The definite article is *not normally* used before a noun placed in apposition to another (i.e. following *and* giving extra information about it), unless an expression individualizing the second noun is also included.

3 The Indefinite and Partitive Articles

The indefinite article

The French indefinite article is, in the singular, the equivalent of the English *a* or *an*. In the plural it has the meaning of *some/several*, *a certain number of* or, in interrogative sentences (questions), the meaning of *any*.

Note: **un** and **une** can also have the meaning of *one*.

Form

	Singular	*Plural*
Masculine	un	des
Feminine	une	des

Note: The indefinite article, like the definite one, varies according to the gender (masculine/feminine) and number (singular/plural) of the noun which follows. Like the definite article, it serves as an 'advance warning system':

Un chien	⟶ **Des** chiens
A dog	*(Some) dogs*
Voici **une** lettre	⟶ Voici **des** lettres
Here is a letter	*Here are (some) letters*
J'ai **un** visiteur	⟶ J'ai **des** visiteurs
I have a visitor	*I have (some) visitors*
Vous avez **une** allumette?	⟶ Vous avez **des** allumettes?
Do you have a match?	*Do you have (any) matches?*

Important remarks concerning the use of indefinite articles

In English, the use of a plural noun without the article (e.g. dogs), could convey two different meanings:

1 the noun could refer to a *general category*:
   Dogs are faithful.

In this case, the French equivalent would be preceded by the definite article (see p. 16 above):

Les chiens sont fidèles.

2   the noun could refer to an *unspecified number of individual things or beings*:

There are dogs in the garden.

In this case, the meaning would be *some, a certain number of* and the French equivalent would be preceded by the indefinite article **des**:

Il y a **des** chiens dans le jardin.

So, it is essential to choose the right type of article if you wish to convey the correct meaning!

Normally, the French indefinite article is used in the same way as its English equivalent (*a*, *an*). There are, however, certain differences in its usage between the two languages, as illustrated below.

Characteristic differences in usage

The indefinite article is *not* used in French in the following cases:

1   Before the words **cent** (*a hundred*) and **mille** (*a thousand*)

Voilà cent francs.   *There's a hundred francs.*

J'ai mille et une choses à faire.   *I have a thousand and one things to do.*

It should be noted that in the above examples *a* really means *one*.

2   After the word **sans** (*without*), *except* if the meaning is *without a single* or *without so much as a . . .*

Il sort sans chapeau.   *He's going out without a hat.*

Le voyageur sans bagages.   *The traveller without luggage.*

But: Il part **sans un** mot, **sans un** regard. *He's leaving without a single word, without a single glance.*

3   Before nouns indicating nationality, occupation, religion, creed, etc:

Je suis Français.   *I am a Frenchman.*

Il est chauffeur de taxi.   *He is a taxi driver.*

Elle est catholique.   *She is a Catholic.*

But not when **c'est** (*it is/he is/she is*) is used:

C'est **un** ingénieur.   *He is an engineer.*

C'est **une** Anglaise.   *She is an Englishwoman.*

4   In exclamative phrases or sentences expressing a strong feeling: surprise, admiration, distaste, loathing, etc. beginning with **quel**, **quelle** (*what a . . . !*)

Quel désastre!   *What a disaster!* (masc. sing.)

Quelle vie!   *What a life!* (fem. sing.)

Quels imbéciles!   *What fools!* (masc. plur.)

5   After **comme** when the meaning is *as* (occupying the post of . . .)
Il travaille ici comme jardinier.   *He works here as a gardener.*
But: if the meaning is *like* (in the same way as), the indefinite article is used:
Compare: Il travaille comme apprenti.   *He's working as an apprentice.*
and: Il travaille comme **un** apprenti.   *He's working like an apprentice.* (i.e. badly)

6   After **ni** in the expression **ni . . . ni** (*neither . . . nor*)
Compare: J'ai **une** écharpe et **des** gants.   *I have a scarf and gloves.*
and: Je n'ai **ni** écharpe **ni** gants.   *I have neither scarf nor gloves.*

Special forms of the indefinite article

1   *All* forms of the indefinite articles (**un**, **une**, **des**), become **de** (or **d'** to avoid the vowel-vowel clash), in the following circumstances:

(*a*)   In negative sentences, with such expressions as **ne . . . pas** (*not any*), **ne . . . plus** (*no longer*), **ne . . . jamais** (*not . . . ever*), **ne . . . guère** (*hardly*).
Compare: Elle a **un** enfant.   and: Elle **n**'a **pas d'**enfant.
She has a child   *She doesn't have a child.*
or: Il y a **une** plage.   and: Il **n'**y a **pas de** plage.
There is a beach.   *There isn't any beach.*
or: Je fume **des** cigares.   and: Je **ne** fume **jamais de** cigares.
I smoke cigars.   *I never smoke cigars.*
or: Vous avez **des** problèmes.   and: Vous **n'**avez **guère de** problèmes.
You have problems.   *You have hardly any problems.*

But remember: Elle n'a pas **un** ami means *She doesn't have one single friend* (see 2 above).

(*b*)   After words and expressions denoting a collection (small or large) of things or beings, such as: **beaucoup** (*many*), **un petit nombre** (*a small number*), **un grand nombre** (*a large number*), **un certain nombre** (*a certain number*), **une foule** (*a crowd*), **une poignée** (*a handful*), etc.
Compare: J'achète **des** cadeaux.   and: J'achète **beaucoup de** cadeaux.
I'm buying gifts.   *I'm buying a great many gifts.*

or: Voici **des** pièces.   and: Voici **une poignée de**
                                                      pièces.
      Here are (some) coins.   *Here is a handful of coins.*
or: Il y a **des** gens.   and: Il y a **une foule de** gens.
      There are people.   *There is a crowd of people.*

2   In addition, the plural form **des** of the indefinite article becomes
de (or **d'** to avoid the vowel-vowel clash), when the noun in its plural
form is preceded by an adjective:

Compare: **Des** enfants   and: **De** petits enfants
              (Some) children   *(Some) small children*
or: **Des** amis   and: **De** bons amis
              (Some) friends   *(Some) good friends*
or: **Des** pommes   and: **D'**énormes pommes
              (Some) apples   *(Some) enormous apples*

But: if the elements **adjective** + **noun** are 'welded together' to form a
set expression, **des** remains intact.

Compare: **De** jeunes filles   and: **Des** jeunes filles
              Girls who happen to   *Girls*
                be young
or: **De** petits pois   and: **Des** petits pois
              Peas which happen to   *Garden peas*
                be small

Note: The above remarks concerning special forms of the Indefinite
article also apply to the partitive article, which is studied below.

The partitive article

The French partitive article is, in its singular form, the equivalent of
some or *a certain amount of* when referring to a noun which cannot
easily be divided into countable units, (e.g. some water, some bread).
The plural form of the partitive article is the same as that of the
indefinite: **des**.

Form

	Singular	*Plural*
Masculine	du/de l'	des
Feminine	de la/de l'	des

The partitive article varies according to the gender and number of the
noun that follows.

In the singular (masc. and fem.), it changes to **de l'** before a vowel or a mute 'h', to avoid the vowel-vowel clash (see appendix I).

Du pain!   *I want some bread!*
Il boit **de la** bière.   *He's drinking beer.*
Voulez-vous **de l'**eau?   *Do you want some water?* (fem. sing.)
Je mange **des** confitures.   *I'm eating jam.* (fem. plur.)
Voilà **de l'**argent.   *There's some money.* (masc. sing.)

Important remarks concerning the use of partitive articles

Normally, the partitive article is used in French when in English *some* or *a certain amount of* (or *any* in a question), followed by a noun in the singular, would be required:

De l'eau minérale   *Some mineral water*
De la viande   *Some meat*
Du café   *Some coffee*

Compare:	**De la** bière	and:	**Une** bière
	Some beer		*A beer*
or:	**De l'**ordre	and:	**Un** ordre
	A certain amount of order		*An order*
or:	**Du** travail	and:	**Un** travail
	Some work		*A job*

In certain circumstances, however, the partitive article has to be modified as indicated below.

Special forms of the partitive article

1   As was the case for the indefinite article, all forms of the partitive article become **de** (or **d'** to avoid the vowel-vowel clash) in the following constructions:

(*a*)   In negative sentences (see 1(*a*) on page 24).
Il n'a **jamais d'**argent.   *He never has any money.*
Pas de chance!   *No luck!*
Vous n'avez **plus de** travail.   *You have no more work.*

(*b*)   After words and expressions denoting a collection of things or beings (see 1(*b*) on page 24).
Ils ont **beaucoup d'**argent.   *They have a great deal of money.*
J'ai **peu de** patience.   *I have little patience.*
Une pincée de sel   *A pinch of salt*

2   In the plural, **des** becomes **de** or **d'** in the circumstances outlined in 2 on page 25.

Des confitures	⟶	**De** bonnes confitures
Jam (fem. plur.)		*Good jam*
Des épinards	⟶	**D'**excellents épinards
Spinach (masc. plur)		*Excellent spinach*

Key points

1   The indefinite article is, in its singular forms **un**, **une**, the equivalent of *a* or *an*; in the plural, it can be translated by *some*, *a certain number of* or simply by the noun without any article.

2   The partitive article is, in its singular form **du**, **de la** (or **de l'** to avoid a vowel-vowel clash), the equivalent of *a certain amount of*. The plural form **des** is *not normally* translated in English.

3   The indefinite and the partitive articles can act as 'advance warning systems' for the noun which follows; because of this, they cannot normally be omitted, except in very precise circumstances.

4   In negative sentences and after phrases referring to a collection of things or beings, *all* forms of the indefinite and partitive articles become **de** (or **d'** to avoid the vowel-vowel clash).

5   The indefinite article is *not* used in French in the following circumstances:
(a)   before **cent** (*a hundred*) and **mille** (*a thousand*);
(b)   before nouns expressing creed, nationality, occupation, religion, *except* when those nouns are introduced by **c'est/ce sont** (*it is*);
(c)   in exclamative sentences, after the appropriate form of **quel . . . !** (*what (a) . . . !*);
(d)   to translate *as* (*in one's capacity as*). *But* if the meaning of *as* is *like*, the article will be required;
(e)   in the negative expression **ni . . . ni** (*neither . . . nor*).

6   If, in the plural form, the indefinite (or partitive) article is followed by an adjective preceding a plural noun, **des** will be reduced to **de** (or **d'** to avoid the vowel-vowel clash), *except* if the group **adjective + noun** forms a recognised set phrase.

7   After expressions indicating a quantity, large or small, the plural form **des** (indefinite or partitive) will be reduced to **de** (or **d'** to avoid the vowel-vowel clash).

8   Negative expressions meaning **not any** are normally translated as **ne . . . pas de/ne . . . pas d'** as applicable. If, however, the meaning is: *not a single . . ./not so much as a . . .* , the expression **ne . . . pas un(e)** should be used.

4 The Demonstrative Adjective

The demonstrative adjective is used in French as in English to 'attract attention' to the noun which follows, to make the thing(s) or being(s) it refers to 'stand out' from others in the same category.

Form

	Singular	*Plural*
Masculine	ce/cet	ces
Feminine	cette	ces

(a) In its above forms, the demonstrative adjective is the equivalent of *both* this/these *and* that/those.

(b) The alternative masc. sing. form **cet** is used when the following word begins with a vowel or mute 'h', to prevent the vowel-vowel clash.

(c) The demonstrative adjective varies according to the gender and/or number of the noun which follows. So, like most other determiners (definite, indefinite and partitive articles) it serves as 'an advance warning system' for that noun.

Ce travail est difficile. *This work is difficult.*

Regardez **cette** chambre. *Look at this room.*

Ces fleurs sont superbes. *Those flowers are superb.* (fem. plur.)

J'adore **ces** enfants. *I adore those children.* (masc. plur.)

But: **Cet** animal est féroce. *This animal is ferocious.*

or: **Cet** hôtel est complet. *This hotel is fully booked.*

Important remarks concerning the use of demonstrative adjectives

In most cases, the French demonstrative adjective is used in the same circumstances as its English equivalents (*this/these* or *that/those*). If, for any reason, it becomes necessary to distinguish between the two meanings, in order to indicate an opposition (either clearly stated or implied) in space or time, all that is needed is to place -ci (*here*) or -là (*there*) after the noun. The words in brackets may be stated or implied.

> **Cette** bière-**ci** est bonne (mais **cette** bière-**là** est mauvaise). *This beer is good (but that beer is bad).*
>
> J'aime **ce** costume-**là** (mais pas **ce** costume-**ci**). *I like that suit (but not this suit).*
>
> **Cette** remarque-**ci** est plus logique (que **cette** remarque-**là**). *This remark is more logical (than that remark).*

In French, the demonstrative adjective, usually followed by -là, can be used to express a strong feeling (distaste or affection).

> Ne parlons pas de **ces** choses (-**là**). *Let's not talk about those things.*
>
> Je déteste **ces** gens (-**là**). *I hate those people.*
>
> Ah **ces** enfants! *Oh, those children!*

Note: In French, the demonstrative adjective is normally repeated after each noun in a series:

Compare: **Ces** hommes, **ces** femmes et **ces** enfants sont perdus!

and: *These/those men, women and children are lost!*

or: Achetez **ces** livres et **ces** magazines.

and: *Buy these/those books and magazines.*

Special uses

Apart from its ordinary usage, the demonstrative adjective can be present in the following circumstances:

(*a*) In certain exclamations with the meaning of *what (a). . . !* or *such (a). . . !*

> Mon Dieu, **ce** travail! *My goodness, what a (= an awful) job!*
>
> **Cette** idée! *What an (= a preposterous) idea!*

(*b*) In commercial correspondence, **ce jour** (lit: *this day*) can be used for *today* and **à ce jour** for *to date*.

> Nous avons reçu **ce jour** votre lettre du . . . *We have received today your letter of . . .*
>
> A **ce jour**, nous n'avons pas reçu votre chèque. *To date, we have not received your cheque.*

(*c*) When the English definite article *the* is used with a strong demonstrative meaning, it is better to translate it with the French demonstrative adjective:

> **Cette** femme est malade. *The (= this) woman is sick.*
>
> **Cet** homme est un fou! *The (= this) man is a lunatic!*

Key points

1   The demonstrative adjective agrees in gender and/or number with the noun which follows.

2   In the masculine singular, **ce** is replaced by **cet** whenever the next word begins with a vowel or a mute 'h' (to avoid the vowel-vowel clash).

3   The French demonstrative adjective can have the meaning *this/these* or *that/those*. If a distinction needs to be drawn, you simply need to add **-ci** (*-here*) or **-là** (*-there*) after the noun.

4   In general, the French demonstrative adjective is used in the same way as its English equivalent. There are, however, a few cases where usage differs.

5   When a list of nouns is involved, the demonstrative adjective (if required) must appear before *each* item.

6   The demonstrative adjective may be used in exclamative sentences with the meaning of *what (a) . . . !/such (a) . . . !*.

7   In commercial correspondence, the expressions *today* and *to date* may be translated in French by **ce jour** and **à ce jour** respectively.

8   The strong demonstrative value of the English definite article *the* makes it necessary, in certain circumstances, to translate it with the appropriate form of the French demonstrative adjective.

5 The Possessive Adjective

Possessive adjectives in French, as in English, are used to indicate ownership or close relationship. There are, however, very important differences in their use between the two languages. In French, the possessive adjective does not agree in gender with the possessor (owner) but gives information on the gender and number of the being(s) or thing(s) owned.

Compare: Voilà **sa** chaise.

and: *Here is his chair*.

In French, the possessive tells us that only one chair is involved (**sa** as opposed to **ses**) and that the word **chaise** is feminine. It also tells us, as does its English equivalent, that one owner is involved.

In English, the possessive tells us that the owner is male (*his* as opposed to *her* or *its*) but gives no information about the thing owned: the clear difference in sound between the singular (*chair*) and the plural (*chairs*) makes it unnecessary for the possessive to carry information about number.

So *remember*:

   in French = **possessive** agrees with '**owned**'

   in English = **possessive** agrees with **owner**

Form

	Person	OWNED			Engl. equivalent
		One		*More than one*	
OWNER		masc.	fem.	masc./fem.	
One	1st	mon	ma	mes	*my*
	2nd	ton	ta	tes	*your* (familiar)
	2nd	votre	votre	vos	*your* (polite)
	3rd	son	sa	ses	*his/her*
					its/one's
More than one	1st	notre	notre	nos	*our*
	2nd	votre	votre	vos	*your*
	3rd	leur	leur	leurs	*their*

Notes: As previously mentioned, the form **vous** (*you*) and its corresponding possessives **votre/vos**, can be used to address *either* one person (it is then a mark of politeness and respect) *or* several people.

> Monsieur Legrand, **votre** femme et **vos** enfants sont ici! *Mr Legrand, your wife and (your) children are here!*

The familiar form **tu** and its corresponding possessives **ton/ta/tes**, are used when talking to relatives, close friends, fellow-members of a close-knit group *or* to express contempt towards a stranger (see Unit 1, pp. 3–4).

Since in French certain nouns are masculine and others feminine and since the singular and plural forms generally sound the same, it is *logical* for the possessive adjective to have separate forms to denote masculine singular, feminine singular and plural.

Compare:　**Mon frère** est parti.　*My brother has gone.*
and:　**Mes frères** sont partis.　*My brothers have gone.*
or:　**Ta soeur** est malade.　*Your sister is ill.*
and:　**Tes soeurs** sont malades.　*Your sisters are ill.*
　The words in bold indicate the agreement relationship.

NB When the word following the possessive adjective is feminine singular and begins with a vowel or a mute 'h', **ma**, **ta**, **sa** are replaced by **mon**, **ton**, **son** to avoid the vowel-vowel clash (see appendix I).

> *****ma hôtesse** becomes: **mon** hôtesse　*my hostess*
> *****ta** énorme **gaffe** becomes: **ton** énorme gaffe　*your enormous blunder*.
> *****sa idée** fixe becomes: **son** idée fixe　*his/her fixed idea*

The use of bold indicates the agreement relationship.

Important remarks concerning the use of possessive adjectives

Although in most cases possessive adjectives are used in a similar way in both languages, there are divergences due to different sentence patterns or grammatical categories. One such case occurs when reflexive verbs are used. A reflexive verb indicates that the action performed by the subject 'falls back' upon the subject, e.g. **je me coupe** *I cut myself*. In such a case, ownership being determined by the verb, there is no need to use a possessive as well. So *****je me coupe ma main** becomes **je me coupe *la* main** *I cut my hand*, or *****il se lave sa figure** becomes **il se lave *la* figure** *he is washing his face*.

Similarly, when ownership is clearly determined by the general meaning of the sentence, the possessive is not used. So *il **marche avec ses mains dans ses poches*** *he is walking with his hands in his pockets* becomes **il marche avec *les* mains dans *les* poches**; *il **met son chapeau sur sa tête** *he is putting his hat on his head* becomes **il met son chapeau sur *la* tête**; *ouvrez **vos yeux et vos oreilles!** *open your eyes and your ears!* becomes **ouvrez *les* yeux et *les* oreilles!**

If, however, the noun 'owned' is qualified by an adjective or adjectival phrase, the possessive will be used:

> ouvrez **vos** jolis yeux et **vos** belles oreilles! *open your pretty eyes and your beautiful ears!*

Normally, a possessive adjective will be used in the singular with *each* being or thing 'owned', because of the gender problem.

Compare: il est venu avec **son** père et **sa** mère

and: *he has come with his father and mother*

but in the plural, one possessive can be used before a list if no special emphasis is required.

> Où sont **vos** frères et soeurs? *Where are your brothers and sisters?*

In some cases, when addressing a superior, particularly in a military context, the possessive is used.

> Pardon, **mon** capitaine! *I beg your pardon Captain!*
>
> Bonjour, **mon** lieutenant! *Good morning Lieutenant!*

Key points

1   In French, the possessive adjective agrees with the thing(s) or being(s) 'owned' and *not* with the owner(s).

2   Since there are 2 genders in French and since the plural form of most nouns sounds identical to their singular form, there are 3 sets of possessive adjectives: masculine singular, feminine singular and plural.

3   The forms **votre** (sing.) and **vos** (plur.) can be used to refer either to *one* owner (polite use) or *several* owners (normal use).

4   When ownership is clearly indicated by the context (use of reflexive verb or general meaning), the possessive adjective is normally replaced by the appropriate definite article.

5   When the noun of the thing(s) or being(s) owned is qualified by an adjective or adjectival phrase the possessive adjective is used *even* if the context clearly indicates ownership.

6   Indefinite, Exclamative and Interrogative Adjectives

Indefinite adjectives

Indefinite adjectives are used in French, as in English, to indicate reference to an undefined quantity or number of things or beings. They cover the whole spectrum of sense from 'none' to all. They agree in gender (masc./fem.) and/or number (sing./plur.) with the noun they refer to; they, too, serve as an 'advance warning system' for that noun, and are therefore generally placed before it.

Note: Because of their sense, it is not normally possible to use adjectives expressing 'none' or 'one' quantities in the plural; nor is it possible to use adjectives meaning 'more than one' or 'all' in the singular. There are, however, some indefinite adjectives which can vary in number as well as in gender. Such adjectives are listed in each of the relevant sense categories of the chart on pp. 36–7.

Important remarks concerning the use of indefinite adjectives

Indefinite adjectives are used when the exact number or quantity of beings or things referred to is not specified (if it were, a numeral would be used). This means that normally, the two categories, indefinite adjective and numeral, are mutually exclusive in a sentence.

However, the following points should be carefully noted:

1   In phrases of the type '**quelque** trente personnes' (*some thirty people*), **quelque** is not an indefinite adjective but an adverb meaning 'approximately' and, as such, does not agree with the noun-phrase 'trente personnes'.

2   If **même** is used with the meaning of *even*, it is not an indefinite adjective but an adverb. As such, it will not be subject to number agreement.

Compare: L'argent, les chèques, les bijoux **même** ont disparu!
The money, the cheques and even the jewels are gone!

and: Les **mêmes** clients reviennent cette année.   *The same customers are coming back this year.*

3   Such expressions as **tout le monde** (*everybody*), **toute la famille** (*the whole family*), **tout le village** (*the whole village*) etc., although

obviously referring to a *group* of things or beings, will be considered as singular for the purpose of agreement.

Tout le monde **est** là. *Everybody is there.*

Toute la famille **est** en vacances. *The whole family is on holiday.*

Tout le stock **est** vendu. *The whole of the stock is sold.*

4 Indefinite adjectives expressing 'zero quantity' are used with the negative **ne** (or **n'** if the next word begins with a vowel — see Appendix I), and the noun they relate to is in the singular:

Aucun voyageur **n'**a été blessé. *Not a single traveller has been wounded.*

Pas une lettre **n'**arrive. *Not a single letter is arriving.*

NB **Aucun/aucune** and **nul/nulle** (*not any/not a single*) are, on very rare occasions, used in the plural (in spite of their meaning), if the noun they refer to does not have a singular form.

Ne payez **aucunes** arrhes, **aucuns** frais. *Do not pay any deposit, any charges.*

Arrhes (f. pl.) *non returnable deposit* and **frais** (m. pl.) *charges/costs* have no singular form with the same meaning.

Exclamative adjectives

They are used in French (as in English) to express a strong feeling — surprise, admiration, indignation, despair, loathing, etc. — about the thing(s) or being(s) to which they refer. The utterance in which they appear always ends with an exclamation mark. They are equivalent to the English *What (a) . . . !*

Form

	Sing.	*Plur.*
Masc.	quel	quels
Fem.	quelle	quelles

The exclamative adjective carries advance information about the gender and number of the noun which follows:

Quel idiot! (m. sing) *What a fool!*

Quelle agréable surprise! (f. sing) *What a pleasant surprise!*

Quels beaux yeux! (m. pl.) *What beautiful eyes!*

Quelles robes magnifiques! (f. pl.) *What magnificent dresses!*

| | VARIATIONS | | | | MEANING | |
| | singular | | plural | | | |
	masc.	fem.	masc.	fem.	sing.	plur.
GROUP I number referred to = none	aucun	aucune	—	—	*not any*	—
	nul	nulle	—	—	*not any*	—
	pas un	pas une	—	—	*(not a single)*	—
	autre	autre	autres	autres	*other*	*others*
	certain	certaine	certains	certaines	*some*	*some*
	chaque	chaque	—	—	*each/every*	—

GROUP II			différents divers	différentes diverses	— —	*different* *various*
number referred to = one or more	maint	mainte	maints	maintes	*many a*	*many*
	même	même	mêmes	mêmes	*same*	*same*
	pareil	pareille	pareils	pareilles	*such (a)*	*such*
	—	—	plusieurs	plusieurs	—	*several*
	quel	quelle	quels	quelles	*what/which*	*what/which*
	quelconque	quelconque	quelconques	quelconques	*any*	*any*
	quelque	quelque	quelques	quelques	*some*	*several*
	tel	telle	tels	telles	*such (a)*	*such*
	tout	toute	tous	toutes	*every*	*all*

NB The dashes signal that certain forms of a given adjective are not available. The correct form of the adjective *must* be chosen to correspond with the gender and number of the noun it qualifies. For example:

Il n'y a **pas une** (seule) place libre. (**place** = fem. sing) *There isn't a (single) seat free.*

Leur retard doit avoir **quelque autre** cause. (**cause** = fem. sing.) *Their lateness must have some other cause.*

Certains jours, il est bizarre. (**jours** = masc. plur.) *Some days, he is peculiar.*

The French exclamative adjective is used in the same circumstances as its English equivalent. The following points should however be noted:

1   In the singular, it cannot be followed by the indefinite article **un** or **une** (*a*).

Quelle superbe bague!   *What a superb ring!*

Quel scandale!   *What a scandal!*

2   The exclamative adjective can sometimes be replaced by the corresponding definite article (**le, la, l'** or **les**) provided the same exclamative intonation is preserved.

Quels imbéciles! = **Les** imbéciles!   *What fools!*

Oh! **quelle** belle robe! = Oh! **la** belle robe!   *Oh what a beautiful dress!*

Interrogative adjectives

Interrogative adjectives are used to express a query about the character or identity of the thing(s) or being(s) referred to. The utterance in which they appear often ends with a question mark. They are translated in English by *which . . . ?* or *what . . . ?* They give advance warning of the gender and number of the noun that follows.

Form

They have the same form as exclamative adjectives:

	Sing.	*Plur.*
Masc.	quel	quels
Fem.	quelle	quelles

Use

Interrogative adjectives are used in a similar way in both languages. The following points should, however, be borne in mind:

1   Sometimes, an exclamative phrase and an interrogative one may have exactly the same components. It is therefore important to be particularly attentive to the intonation (voice-pitch movement) of each of them to differentiate meaning, as you would in English.

Compare: **Quel** courage!   *What courage!*

and: **Quel** courage?   *What courage?*

2   In certain types of sentences, the interrogative adjective is followed by a change in the normal word order (inversion), particularly in 'careful' French. But in 'casual' speech, the inversion is often not made:

Compare: Quelle heure **est-il**? (careful French)

and: Quelle heure **il est**? ('casual' speech)   *What time is it?*

or: Dans quelle chambre **sont-ils**? (careful French)

and: **Ils sont** dans quelle chambre? ('casual' French)   *Which room are they in?*

Key points

1   Indefinite adjectives are used to refer to an undefined quantity or number of things or beings. They cover the whole range of meaning from 'none' to 'all'.

2   Many indefinite adjectives, because of their meaning, cannot vary in number, i.e. they are *either* singular *or* plural. Some, however, can be used in the singular and (with the appropriate agreement) in the plural. Indefinite adjectives vary in gender as required.

3   **Même** and **quelque** can either be indefinite adjectives or adverbs. As indefinite adjectives, they mean *same* and *some* (= *a few*) respectively and agree as appropriate. As adverbs they mean *even* and *approximately* respectively and they are invariable.

4   Indefinite adjectives expressing 'zero quantities' — **aucun, pas un, nul** — are used with the negative adverb **ne** (or **n'** to avoid a vowel-vowel clash). They are normally used with a noun in the singular; if the noun they refer to has no singular form, **aucun** and **nul** can be put in the plural (masculine or feminine).

5   Exclamative adjectives are used in French, as in English, to express a strong feeling — surprise, admiration, indignation, despair, etc. — about the noun they refer to. They carry advance information about the gender and number of that noun.

6   Exclamative adjectives used with a masculine or feminine noun *cannot* be followed, as they can in English by the indefinite article (**un** or **une**).

7   The exclamative adjective is sometimes replaced by the corresponding definite article. The meaning is equivalent so long as the exclamative intonation is retained.

8   Interrogative adjectives are used in French, as in English, to express a query about the character or identity of the thing(s) or being(s) referred to. They have the same form as exclamative adjectives and they, too, carry advance information about the noun's gender and number.

9   In certain types of interrogative sentences, the interrogative adjective is normally followed by an inversion (change in word-order). In 'casual' *spoken French* however, the inversion is often not made.

7 Numerals

In French, as in English, numerals are used with nouns to indicate an exact number of things or beings (cardinal numbers) *or* the rank or position occupied by the thing(s) or being(s) the noun refers to (ordinal numbers).

In each category, there are numerals made up of one word only and numerals made up of several words usually linked together by a hyphen- or **et** (*and*).

1 Cardinal numerals do not agree in gender or number with the noun they refer to except for the following:

(*a*) **un** (*one*) which becomes **une** in the feminine:

    un homme et **une** femme   *one man and one woman*

(*b*) **vingt** (*20*) and **cent** (*100*) which take an **s** if they appear in numbers which are multiples of 20 and 100 *and if*, at the same time, they end the numeral adjective:

    quatre-vingts personnes   *80 people*

but: **quatre-vingt-trois** ans   *83 years*

    deux cents kilomètres   *200 kilometres*

but: **deux cent dix** kilomètres   *210 kilometres*

However, if the last element of the number is either **millier** (*approximately a thousand*), **million** (*million*), **milliard** (*thousand million*) or **billion** (*million million*), **vingt** and **cent** will take an **s** because those elements *are not adjectives* but nouns which are followed by **de** (or **d'** to avoid the vowel-vowel clash).

    quatre-vingts millions de centimes   *80 million centimes*

    neuf **cents** milliards de déficit   *900,000 million deficit*

2 In compounds using numbers between 21 and 71 inclusive, the first unit (= one) of a new decimal set, i.e. 21, 31, 41, 51, 61, 71, will be preceded by the word **et** (*and*); in all other such cases, **et** will *not* be present:

    vingt **et** une cartes postales   *21 postcards*

    soixante **et** onze invités   *71 guests*

but: cent un jours   *101 days*

    six cent un litres   *601 litres*

Form

Cardinal numbers	Corresponding ordinal numbers	Cardinal numbers		Corresponding ordinal numbers
0 zéro		30	trente	trentième
1 un/une	premier/première	40	quarante	quarantième
2 deux	deuxième (second/seconde)	50	cinquante	cinquantième
3 trois	troisième	60	soixante	soixantième
4 quatre	quatrième	70	soixante-dix	soixante-dixième
5 cinq	cinquième	71	soixante et onze	soixante et onzième
6 six	sixième	72	soixante-douze	soixante-douzième
7 sept	septième	80	quatre-vingts	quatre-vingtième
8 huit	huitième	81	quatre-vingt-un(e)	quatre-vingt-unième
9 neuf	neuvième	90	quatre-vingt-dix	quatre-vingt-dixième
10 dix	dixième	91	quatre-vingt-onze	quatre-vingt-onzième
11 onze	onzième	92	quatre-vingt-douze	quatre-vingt-douzième
12 douze	douzième	100	cent	centième
13 treize	treizième	101	cent un(e)	cent unième
14 quatorze	quatorzième	200	deux cents	deux centième
15 quinze	quinzième	201	deux cent un(e)	deux cent unième
16 seize	seizième	1000	mille (mil for dates)	millième
17 dix-sept	dix-septième	1001	mille un(e)	mille unième
18 dix-huit	dix-huitième	2000	deux mille	deux millième
19 dix-neuf	dix-neuvième	1,000,000	un million	millionnième
20 vingt	vingtième	1,000,000,000	un milliard	milliardième
21 vingt et un(e)	vingt et unième	1,000,000,000,000	un billion	billionnième
22 vingt-deux	vingt-deuxième			

3   In compound numbers, the components indicating less than a full hundred are hyphenated *except* when **et** is present (see 2 above):

    quatre-vingt-dix-huit ans   *98 years*

    cent dix-sept mètres   *117 metres*

but: vingt **et** une bougies   *21 candles*

Fractions

Except for $\frac{1}{2}$ (**un demi**), $\frac{1}{3}$ (**un tiers**), $\frac{1}{4}$ (**un quart**), fractions are composed, as in English, of a cardinal over an ordinal:

    trois huitièmes   *three-eighths*

    un sixième   *one-sixth*

    les neuf dixièmes de la population   *nine-tenths of the population*

Important remarks concerning the use of numerals

Broadly speaking, numerals are used in a similar way in French and English. However, the following points should be remembered.

1   When referring to Kings, Queens, Emperors, Popes or other eminent people sharing their name with others, the cardinal number is used, except for the first bearer of the name. In this case *only*, the ordinal is used. In both cases, the number is placed after the name.

    Louis II (Deux)   *Louis the Second*

    Henri IV (Quatre)   *Henry the Fourth*

but: Elizabeth Iere (Première)   *Elizabeth Ist*

    Napoléon Ier (Premier)   *Napoleon I*

2   For the days of the month, cardinal numbers are used *except* for the first day which is indicated by the ordinal number

    le 14 (**quatorze**) juillet et le 15 (**quinze**) août   *the 14th July and the 15th August*

but: le 1er (**premier**) mai   *May 1st*

du 1er (premier) janvier au 31 (trente et un) décembre   *all the year round* (lit: *from January 1st to December 31st*)

3   **Un millier** (*approximately a thousand*), **un million** (*a million*), **un milliard** (*a thousand million*), **un billion** (*a million million*), etc. are *nouns*, not adjectives; they will therefore take an **s** in the plural, and the noun which follows will be preceded by **de** (or **d'** to avoid the vowel-vowel clash):

    un million de francs   *1 million francs*

    quatre milliards d'individus   *4 thousand million individuals*

> With French numbers, a dot is used where a comma would appear in English and vice versa:
>   3.250.000 kilomètres   *3,250,000 kilometres*
>   3,265 mètres *3.265 metres*

4   When a cardinal number is qualified by another adjective like **premier** (*first*), **dernier** (*last*), **suivant/prochain** (*next*), **autre** (*other*), etc. the cardinal number appears *before* the qualifying adjective, and not after as in English:
    les **trois** premiers mois   *the first three months*
    les **deux** dernières années   *the last two years*
    les **dix** autres jours   *the other ten days*

5   Some one-word cardinal adjectives up to and including **cent** (*100*), can be turned into feminine nouns by the addition of the suffix **-aine**. Such nouns generally indicate an approximate number. They are followed by **de** (or **d'** to avoid the vowel-vowel clash).
    une **vingtaine** d'années   *about 20 years*
    une douzaine de jeunes gens   *a dozen (or so) young people*
but: in commercial transactions, **une douzaine** has the meaning of *exactly twelve*.
    une douzaine d'oeufs s'il vous plaît   *a dozen eggs please*

(*a*)   In the case of **dix**, the noun indicating the approximate number becomes **une dizaine** (with a **z** not an **x**).
(*b*)   Such nouns, when used with the definite article **la**, tend to indicate an (approximate) age bracket:
    Elle approche de **la trentaine**.   *She is nearing 30 (years of age)*.
    Il avait atteint **la cinquantaine**.   *He was in his fifties*.

6   For numbers between 1100 and 1999 you can *either* say **mille cent**, **mille deuxcent(s)** etc. (**mil cent, mil deux cent(s)** for a *date*), *or* **onze cent(s), douze cent(s)**, etc.

Nous avons dépensé { **mille cinq cents** francs. / **quinze cents** francs.   *We have spent 1500 francs.*

Kennedy est mort en { **mil neuf cent soixante-trois**. *Kennedy died in 1963.* / **dix-neuf cent soixante-trois**.

Note: In everyday French, it is more common to write dates with figures than with letters.

7   **Mille un(e)** is used for a precise number (*1001*); **mille et un(e)** indicates *a great many*:
    J'ai **mille et une** choses à faire.   *I have a thousand and one (= a lot of) things to do.*

8   In conversation, it is normally accepted when talking about dates of the 20th century, to omit **mil neuf cent** or **dix-neuf cent**:

la guerre de 14–18 (quatorze-dix-huit)   *the 1914–18 war*

le débarquement de juin 44 (quarante-quatre)   *the June 1944 landings*

9   When referring to a specific decade of the 20th century, the relevant number must be preceded by the expression **les années**

les années trente   *the thirties*

les années soixante   *the sixties*

10   For official time-tables and on radio and television, the 24-hour system is used:

Voici les informations de **20 heures**.   *Here is the 8 o'clock (p.m.) news*

départ: **18 heures 12**, quai numéro 6   *departure: 18.12, platform 6*

Cardinal numbers used to indicate particular pages or chapters of a book, acts or scenes of a play, are placed after the noun. When **vingt** and **cent** are used in this way, they do not take an **s** *even* if the conditions of Note 1 (p. 40) are met

Ouvrez le livre à la page **deux cent**.   *Open the book page 200.*

Lisez *l' Avare* de Molière, Acte **II [Deux]** Scène **II [Deux]**   *Read 'l' Avare' by Molière, Act II Scene II.*

Key points

1   Numerals are divided into 2 categories: *cardinals* which indicate a number and *ordinals* which denote a rank or relative position.

2   Cardinal numeral adjectives are invariable except for **un** (*one*; fem.: **une**) and for **vingt** (*20*) and **cent** (*100*) which, in very specific circumstances, take an **s** in the plural.

3   Numerals are made up of either one word only or several words which are, in certain circumstances, linked by **et** (*and*) or a hyphen.

4   The words **millier** (*approximately a thousand*), **million** (*million*), **milliard** (*thousand million*), **billion** (*U.K. billion*) and others denoting still larger numbers, are *nouns* not adjectives; they take an **s** in the plural.

5   Although there is great similarity in the use of numerals in French and English, usage sometimes differs. For Kings, Queens, Popes and for the days of the month, only *the first* is translated by an ordinal number; for all the others the cardinal number is used. When a cardinal number is qualified by another adjective the cardinal number generally comes first.

6   Some cardinal numerals can be transformed into nouns expressing the corresponding approximate number by deletion of the final **e**, if applicable, and addition of the suffix **-aine**.

8 Adjectives

Note: Determiners (possessives, demonstratives, exclamatives) are dealt with in separate chapters.

Adjectives are single or compound words which are used to give certain indications about some of the characteristics, traits, qualities, etc. of the thing(s) or being(s) they refer to. For example:

la **petite** valise **noire**   *the small black case*

ses **grands** yeux **étonnés**   *his/her large wondering eyes*

Although adjectives have the same role in French and English, their position and agreement patterns are totally different in the two languages:

1 In the great majority of cases, adjectives in English are placed before the noun. In French the situation is far more complex and can be influenced by such factors as meaning or length.

Compare:	Il entre dans sa **propre** maison.	change in meaning
	He goes into his own house.	according to position
and:	Il entre dans sa maison **propre**.	
	He goes into his clean house.	

or:	une idée **courageuse**	of the 2 words (adjective
	a courageous idea	and noun), the shorter
and:	une **courageuse** intervention	comes first
	a courageous intervention	

2 In French most adjectives vary in gender and number with the noun(s) they qualify, whereas in English they do not.

Compare: un **bon petit** restaurant pas **cher** (m. sing.)   *a good, small, inexpensive restaurant*

and: une **bonne petite** auberge pas **chère** (f. sing.)   *a good, small, inexpensive inn*

Position of adjectives

The following important points must be remembered about the position of adjectives in French:

1   The majority of adjectives are placed after the noun; if in doubt, it is fairly safe to place the adjective in that position (but see the specific rules stated below).

2   Adjectives denoting colour or shape are placed *after* the noun (except for special stylistic effects).

> Je vois les collines **vertes** et les toits **rouges** du village.   *I see the green hills and the red roofs of the village.*

but: allons dans la *verte* prairie (*poetic effect*)   *let us go into the green meadow*

3   Certain adjectives have different meanings according to their position. They must therefore be placed correctly to convey the right meaning. A list of the most common adjectives belonging to that category is given below.

ancien = *former/ancient*
> un **ancien** cinéma   *a cinema no longer used as such*
> un cinéma **ancien**   *an ancient cinema*

brave = *good/brave*
> une **brave** femme   *a good-hearted woman*
> une femme **brave**   *a brave woman*

certain = *undefined/definite*
> un **certain** changement   *a certain change*
> un changement **certain**   *a definite change*

cher = *close to one's heart/expensive*
> mon très **cher** bijou   *my dearly loved jewel*
> mon bijou très **cher**   *my very expensive jewel*

dernier = *the last of a series/the one before this*
> la **dernière** semaine   *the last week*
> la semaine **dernière**   *last week*

grand = *illustrious (great)/tall*
> un **grand** homme   *a great man*
> un homme **grand**   *a tall man*

mauvais ⎫
méchant ⎬ = *of poor quality/vicious (hurtful)*
> un **mauvais**/**méchant** livre   *a book of no literary value*
> un livre **mauvais**/**méchant**   *a hurtful book*

pauvre = *wretched/penniless, destitute*
> une **pauvre** femme   *a wretched woman*
> une femme **pauvre**   *a penniless woman*

propre = *own/clean*

    sa **propre** voiture   *his/her own car*

    sa voiture **propre**   *his/her clean car*

4 If the noun is qualified by several adjectives, these can *either* retain their normal position, for example:

    une **petite** femme **pauvre**   *a small, destitute woman*

or go after the noun and be 'linked' by a comma or *et* (*and*):

    une femme **petite** et **pauvre**   *a small and destitute woman*

5 Adjectives denoting duration, size or magnitude are generally placed *before* the noun:

    une **énorme** vague   *an enormous wave*

    une **longue** attente   *a long wait*

6 Adjectives indicating permanent or semi-permanent characteristics are generally placed *after* the noun (but see also no. 5 above):

    un homme **chauve**   *a bald man*

    une femme **édentée**   *a toothless woman*

    des enfants **intelligents**   *intelligent children*

7 Adjectives derived from verbs are placed *after* the noun:

    Voici une maison **abandonnée**. (verb = **abandonner**)   *Here is a deserted house.*

    Quelle blancheur **éclatante**! (verb = **éclater**)   *What dazzling white(ness)!*

8 Adjectives which are themselves qualified by another expression are placed *after* the noun even if on their own they normally go before it

compare: une **belle** fille   *a beautiful girl*

and: une fille **belle** comme le jour   *a stunningly beautiful girl* (lit: beautiful as the day)

or: un **grand** jardin   *a big garden*

and: un jardin **grand** comme un mouchoir   *a garden the size of a handkerchief* (= *tiny*)

9 Adjectives denoting origin (geographical, geological, historical, social, religious, ethnic, spatial, etc.), are placed *after* the noun they qualify:

    une chanteuse **américaine**   *an american singer*

    la période **élizabéthaine**   *the Elizabethan period*

    l'église **catholique**   *the Catholic church*

    la classe **ouvrière**   *the working class*

10 Certain adjectives have *no fixed position* and could theoretically be placed either before or after the noun they refer to. In such cases, the *shorter word*, i.e. the one with the smaller number of syllables (on this point see appendix I), will normally come *first*:

Compare: une idée **importante**   *an important idea*
            (2 syl)   (3 syl)
and: une **importante** manifestation   *an important demonstration*
            (3 syl)   (4 syl)

Most of the above rules are often broken to produce special stylistic effects.

Agreement of adjectives

Preliminary remarks

As previously mentioned, most French adjectives agree in gender and number with the noun(s) they refer to. If an adjective is used with several nouns, agreement is made according to sense:

Compare: un homme et un enfant **fatigués**   *a tired man and a tired child*
and: un homme et un enfant **fatigué**   *a man and a tired child*

If there are one or more feminine nouns and one masculine one, the adjective(s) qualifying them will be in the masculine plural.

Des femmes, des fillettes et un petit garçon **fatigués** dormaient.   *Several tired women, girls and a little boy were asleep.*

The basic form of the adjective to which agreement endings will be added, is the masculine singular. That is the form in which the adjective appears in a dictionary.

Most adjectives agree in the normal way indicated below. Some, however, have slightly or markedly modified forms in the feminine singular and/or the masculine plural. Note, though, that however 'irregularly' an adjective may behave, its feminine singular form will only need an **s** to become a feminine plural.

Deux **vieilles** personnes (f. pl.), une **vieille** dame (f. sing.)   et un **vieux** monsieur (m. sing.), attendaient l'autobus.   *Two old people, an old lady and an old gentleman, were waiting for the bus.*

Elle est **heureuse** (f. sing.) et ses filles sont **heureuses** (f. pl.) elles aussi.   *She is happy and her daughters are happy too.*

Adjectives ending in **x** or **s** in the masculine singular do not change in the masculine plural:

un enfant **malheureux**   des enfants **malheureux**
an unhappy child   *unhappy children*
le **gros** colis (m. sing.)   les **gros** colis (m. pl.)
the big parcel   *the big parcels*

Normal agreement of adjectives

In the case of a 'normal' adjective, the following endings are added, as required, to make it agree in gender and number with the noun(s) it qualifies:

	Sing.	*Plur.*
Masc.	—	s
Fem.	e	es

le **petit** hôtel (m. sing.) ⟶ les **petits** hôtels (m. pl.)
the small hotel   *the small hotels*
la **petite** chambre (f. sing.) ⟶ les **petites** chambres (f. pl.)
the small bedroom   *the small bedrooms*

Note: Adjectives ending in **e** (without an accent) in the masculine singular will have the following agreement pattern:

	Sing.	*Plur.*
Masc.	—	s
Fem.	—	s

le feu est **rouge** (m. sing.) ⟶ les feux sont **rouges** (m. pl.)
the light is red   *the lights are red*
la robe est **rouge** (f. sing.) ⟶ les robes sont **rouges** (f. pl.)
the dress is red   *the dresses are red*

Adjectives undergoing slight modifications in the feminine

Certain adjectives undergo a slight change of spelling in their feminine (singular and plural) forms. The most common of those (and, if applicable, the exceptions) are given below.

(*a*) Adjectives ending in **eil**, **el**, **et**, **ien**, **ol**, **on**, in the masculine singular, double their last consonant in the feminine singular (and plural).
Compare: un fauteuil **ancien** *an antique armchair*
and: une chaise **ancienne** *an antique chair*
or: le destin est **cruel** *fate is cruel*
and: la vie est **cruelle** *life is cruel*
Exceptions: The following adjectives, instead of doubling their last consonant, take a grave accent over the **e** preceding that

consonant in the feminine singular (and plural): **complet** *complete*, **concret** *concrete*, **discret** *discreet*, **inquiet** *worried*, **replet** *plump*, **secret** *secret*. For example:

il est **inquiet** (m. sing.) ⟶ elle est **inquiète** (f. sing.)
he is worried   *she is worried*
un voisin **discret** (m. sing.) ⟶ une voisine **discrète** (f. sing.)
a discreet neighbour (man)   *a discreet neighbour (woman)*

The following adjectives have an alternative masculine singular form used to avoid a vowel-vowel clash (see Appendix I) with the next word.

m. sing. normal form	*alternative form*	*m. pl.*	*meaning*
beau	bel	beaux	*beautiful*
nouveau	nouvel	nouveaux	*new*
fou	fol	fous	*mad*
mou	mol	mous	*soft*
vieux	vieil	vieux	*old*

Their feminine singular is formed by doubling the last consonant of that alternative form before adding the usual **e**:

un **beau** jour (m. sing.) ⟶ une **belle** soirée (f. sing.)
a beautiful day   *a beautiful evening*
un désir **fou** (m. sing.) ⟶ une course **folle** (f. sing.)
a mad desire   *a mad race*

(*b*) Adjectives ending in **ieux** or **eux** in the masculine singular will normally end in **ieuse** or **euse** in the feminine singular.

un **curieux** incident   ⟶ une **curieuse** lettre
a curious incident   *a curious letter*
un **heureux** événement   ⟶ une **heureuse** union
a happy event   *a happy union*

Remember: Since those adjectives end in **x** in the masculine singular, they will retain the same form for their masculine plural (see page 48).

(*c*) Adjectives ending in **ot** in the masculine singular will follow the normal pattern of agreement. However there are exceptions to this rule. The following adjectives will double their last consonant before doing so: **boulot** *dumpy*, **palot** *palish*, **sot** *silly*, **vieillot** *old fashioned*.

un garcon **palot**   ⟶ une fillette **palotte**
a rather pale boy   *a rather pale girl*
cet homme est **sot**   ⟶ cette femme est **sotte**
this man is silly   *this woman is silly*

(*d*) Adjectives ending in **in** in the masculine singular follow the normal pattern of agreement, although there are two exceptions: **bénin** *slight = not serious* and **malin** *sly/crafty*.

un rhume **bénin** ⟶ une maladie **bénigne**
a slight cold   *a minor illness*
Il est **malin** mais sa femme est encore plus **maligne**.
He is crafty but his wife is craftier still.

(*e*) Adjectives ending in **al** in the masculine singular follow the normal pattern of agreement except in the masculine plural, where the ending changes to **aux**. Nine adjectives ending in **al**, however, follow the normal agreement exactly; **banal** *banal*, **bancal** *lame*, **fatal** *fatal*, **final** *final*, **glacial** *freezing*, **idéal** *ideal*, **jovial** *jovial*, **natal** *natal*, **naval** *naval*.

un entretien **cordial** ⟶ des entretiens **cordiaux**
a cordial discussion   *cordial talks*
But: un accident **fatal** ⟶ des accidents **fatals**
a fatal accident   *fatal accidents*

(*f*) Adjectives ending in **ais**, **as** or **os** in the masculine singular follow the normal pattern of agreement for the feminine (both singular and plural). Again, though, there are a few exceptions: **bas** *low*, **épais** *thick*, **gras** *fat*, **gros** *big*, **las** *tired*, which double the **s** in the feminine (sing. and plural).

Compare:
le temps est **mauvais** ⟶ la mer est **mauvaise**
the weather is bad   *the sea is rough*
and:
le brouillard est **épais** ⟶ la fumée est **épaisse**
the fog is thick   *the smoke is thick*
The above adjectives do not change in the masculine plural because they already have an **s** in their masculine singular form.

(*g*) Adjectives ending in **gu** in the masculine singular follow the normal agreement pattern except for the fact that in the feminine (singular and plural) the **e** will take a diaresis (¨):
un son **aigu** ⟶ une plainte **aiguë**
a shrill sound ⟶ *a shrill cry*

(*h*) Adjectives ending in **if**, **ef** or **euf** in the masculine singular follow the normal pattern of agreement but change their **f** into a **v** in the feminine (singular and plural):
J'achète un pantalon **neuf** et une chemise **neuve**.
I am buying new trousers and a new shirt.

(*i*) The stem of the following adjectives undergoes a marked change in the feminine (singular and plural), but they nevertheless follow the normal agreement pattern (see, however, page 48).

m. sing. form	*f. sing. form*	*meaning*
blanc	blanche	*white*
franc	franche	*frank*
favori	favorite	*favourite*
frais	fraîche	*fresh/cool*
sec	sèche	*dry*
doux	douce	*soft*
roux	rousse	*reddish*
faux	fausse	*false*
public	publique	*public*

For example:
du pain **blanc**   ⟶ de la poudre **blanche**
white bread   *white powder*

(*j*)   Most adjectives ending in **eur** or **teur** form their feminine singular in **euse** or **teuse** (for the plural, an **s** is added to the relevant form):

un avenir **prometteur**   ⟶ une attitude **prometteuse**
a promising future   *a promising attitude*

However, certain more *unusual* or *learned* adjectives, change **teur** into **trice** in the feminine (for the plural, an **s** is added to the relevant form):

l'argent est **corrupteur**   ⟶ la puissance est **corruptrice**
money is corrupting   *power is corrupting*

(*k*)   Adjectives ending in **g** in the masculine singular add a **u** in the feminine:

un **long** voyage   ⟶ une **longue** marche
a long journey   *a long walk*

Adjectives which break the normal agreement rules

Although some of the adjectives studied hitherto deviate from the normal pattern of agreement, they still vary in gender and number with the noun they refer to. The adjectives listed/indicated below however, are either partially or totally outside the agreement rules as outlined above.

(*a*)   Nouns used as adjectives of colour *do not* vary in gender or number. The most common are: **cerise** *cherry*, **chocolat** *chocolate*, **marron** *chestnut*, **mastic** *putty = grey/beige*, **noisette** *hazel*, **olive** *olive*, **orange** *orange*

la fille aux yeux **noisette**   *the girl with hazel eyes*

Il achète des chaussures **mastic**. *He is buying putty-coloured shoes.*

(*b*) Adjectives of colour made up of more than one word do not vary in gender *or* number:

Compare: Il porte une chemise **bleue**, une veste **verte** et des chaussures **grises**. *He is wearing a blue shirt, a green jacket and grey shoes.*

and: Il porte une chemise **bleu clair**, une veste **vert pomme** et des chaussures **gris foncé**. *He is wearing a light-blue shirt, an apple-green jacket and dark-grey shoes.*

(*c*) Certain adjectives are sometimes used as adverbs to modify the sense of verbs. In such cases the adjective will *not* vary in gender *or* number. The most frequently encountered adjectives of that type are: **bas** *low*, **bon** *good*, **cher** *dear*, **clair** *clear*, **doux** *soft*, **dur** *hard*, **faux** *false*, **ferme** *firm*, **haut** *high*.

Ces fleurs sentent **bon**. *These flowers smell good.*

Elles parlent **bas**. *They speak in a low voice.*

Nous travaillons **dur**. *We are working hard.*

Note: Adjectives used with the verbs **être** (*to be*), **devenir** (*to become*), **sembler** (*to seem*), **paraître** (*to appear*), **rester**/**demeurer** (*to stay/remain*), agree in gender and number with the thing(s) or being(s) they refer to:

Compare: La visite est **chère**. *The visit is dear*

and: La visite coûte **cher**. *The visit cost a lot of money.*

or: La rivière est **basse**. *The river is low.*

and: La rivière descend **bas**. *The river goes down a long way.*

(*d*) The words **demi** *half*, **nu** *bare*, **excepté** *except*, **ci-joint**/**ci-inclus** *herewith*, **compris** *included*, **supposé** *supposed*, **vu** *considering*, when placed *before* the noun, do not agree in gender or number. If placed *after* the noun, they agree as required.

Compare: Il marche **nu**-pieds. *He is walking barefoot.*

and: Il marche pieds **nus**. *He is walking barefoot.*

or: attendez une **demi**-heure *wait for half an hour*

and: attendez une heure et **demie** *wait for an hour and a half*

(*e*) Adjectives following the expression **avoir l'air** (*to seem/have the appearance of being*) can *either* agree normally if a subjective opinion is expressed (**avoir l'air** = *to seem to be*) *or* agree with **l'air** (m. sing.), if an objective assessment is given (**avoir l'air** = *to have the outward appearance of*).

Compare: Cette maison a l'air **vieille** (agreement with **maison**)
This house seems (to be) old. (Subjective opinion)

and: Cette maison a l'air **vieux** (agreement with **l'air**)
This house looks old. (objective assessment)

Note: The difference in meaning is sufficiently slight for you not to worry unduly about it at this stage.

(*f*)   The following adjectives do not vary in gender *or* number: **chic** *chic*, **kaki** *khaki*, **rococo** *rococo*, **snob** *snob*, **sterling** *sterling*.

un uniforme **kaki**   ⟶   des uniformes **kaki**
a khaki uniform   *khaki uniforms*
une livre *sterling*   ⟶   dix livres **sterling**
a pound sterling   *ten pounds sterling*

Note: Usage is not totally consistent and some of the above are sometimes written with **s** in the plural.

(*g*)   The adjective **grand** when used as part of a compound feminine noun singular or plural, does not vary in gender or number. In such cases its meaning is *great/grand/main*.

Compare: ma **grande** tante   *my tall aunt*
and: ma **grand**-tante   *my great-aunt*
or: nos **grandes** mères   *our tall mothers*
and: nos **grand**-mères   *our grandmothers*

Note: In such constructions, **grand** is followed by an apostrophe or a hyphen.

(*h*)   The adjective **possible** (*possible*) follows the normal pattern of agreement *except* if preceded by such expressions as **le plus** *the most*, **le moins**   *the least*, **le mieux** *the best*.

Compare: Il y a deux solutions **possibles**. *There are two possible solutions.*
and: Elles font le moins de fautes **possible**. *They make as few mistakes as possible.*

NB This lesson will seem complex because the behaviour of adjectives in French is dramatically different from that of English adjectives. Return to it as often as needed.

Key points

1 Adjectives are single or compound words used to give certain indications about (some of) the characteristics of the thing(s) or being(s) they refer to.

2 Most adjectives in French agree in gender and number with the thing(s) or being(s) they qualify.

3 Most adjectives have a clearly defined position in the sentence. Some of them change their meaning if their position changes. Since the majority of adjectives are normally placed after the noun, it will be fairly safe to use that position when in doubt.

4 Most adjectives add an **e** to the masculine singular to form the feminine-singular, and an **s** to form the plural for both genders. Certain adjectives, however, do not follow this normal pattern of agreement.

5 Adjectives ending in **x** or **s** in the masculine singular remain the same in the masculine plural.

6 A limited number of adjectives have an alternative masculine singular form used to avoid a vowel-vowel clash with the next word.

7 Nouns used as adjectives of colour do not vary in gender or number with the thing(s) or being(s) they qualify.

8 Compound adjectives of colour do not vary in gender or number.

9 Adjectives used as adverbs do not vary in gender or number.

10 A small number of adjectives remain invariable if placed before the noun they refer to, but agree as required if placed after that noun.

11 The adjective **grand** (*great/grand/main*) when used as part of a compound feminine noun remains invariable and is linked to the following word by an apostrophe or a hyphen. In masculine plural compounds **grand** takes an **s.**

12 The adjective **possible** (*possible*) does not agree in gender or number when used after **le plus** (*the most*), **le moins** (*the least*), **le mieux** (*the best*).

9   The Gender of Nouns

General remarks

Nouns are words (single or compound) used to name beings (human and non-human) and things (substances, processes, feelings, etc.). There are two types of nouns:
- *common nouns* which indicate things or beings belonging to a given class, e.g. **la porte** *the door*, **le travail** *work*, **les enfants** *children*;
- *proper nouns* which identify a specific thing or being, or a specific set of things or beings, e.g. **L'Angleterre** *England*, **Londres** *London*, **le Maroc** *Morocco*, **Churchill** *Churchill*, **les Alpes** *the Alps*. Note that all proper nouns begin with a capital letter.

In French, nouns fall into two gender categories — masculine and feminine. This classification was originally influenced by the Latin system: nouns derived from masculine or neuter Latin names are normally masculine; nouns derived from feminine Latin names are normally feminine. Whether you have studied Latin or not, you may find the following suggestions useful to memorise the gender of French nouns:

1   Always learn the noun *with* its definite *or* indefinite singular article (which give advance warning of the gender). For example, you should learn **le** gouvernement (*government*) and not just gouvernement or **la** chance (*luck*) and not chance.

Remember: Using the wrong gender would, as previously pointed out, result in a cascade of mistakes, since not only most determiners, but also most adjectives, have to agree in *gender* as well as *number* with the noun they refer to.

Compare: un petit village accueillant et reposant   *a small welcoming and restful village*

and: une petite ville accueillante et reposante   *a small welcoming and restful town*

There is no such agreement problem in English.

2   Pay attention to the sense of the noun. Generally, nouns referring to male beings are masculine and nouns indicating female beings are feminine (but see 6 below). For example:

un homme *a man*, **une** fillette *a young girl*, **une** poule *a hen*, **un** étalon *a stallion*

Note:　There are exceptions to this rule, which shall be examined later in this chapter.

3　Look carefully at the endings of nouns. They often give useful guidance about gender.

le développe**ment** (**-ment** = masculine)

la propor**tion** (**-tion** = feminine)

NB:　the formulation of 'theories', as outlined in the introduction, will be of particular use in the discovery of 'rules' concerning gender classification by ending or by meaning.

Since the plural form of most French nouns sounds exactly the same as their singular form, it is vitally important for the speaker to indicate clearly the right gender by using the appropriate form of the determiner and/or adjective.

wrong = *Le vieux dame est mort.

right = **La** vie**ille** dame est mor**te**. *The old lady is dead.*

Before proceeding to a detailed study of the gender of nouns, the following categories should be distinguished:

1　Nouns which refer to things or beings of one gender only; they will vary in number only:

la maison (*the house*)	⟶ les maisons (*houses*)
le mur (*wall*)	⟶ les murs (*walls*)
un arbre (*a tree*)	⟶ des arbres (*trees*)

2　Nouns which, without any alteration in spelling, can refer to a male being in the masculine and to a female being in the feminine. The following are the most commonly encountered.

Masculine	*Feminine*	*Meaning*
un adversaire	une adversaire	*opponent*
un artiste	une artiste	*artist*
le camarade	la camarade	*friend*
le collègue	la collègue	*colleague*
un élève	une élève	*pupil*
un enfant	une enfant	*child*
un esclave	une esclave	*slave*
le locataire	la locataire	*tenant*
le partenaire	la partenaire	*partner*
le secrétaire	la secrétaire	*secretary*
le touriste	la touriste	*tourist*

NB:　In this category, there is no change in the meaning of the word (apart from the gender).

3   Nouns which, with some alteration of their masculine form (ending), can be made to refer to a female being of the same species.

Masculine	Feminine	Meaning
le travailleur un ouvrier	la travailleuse } une ouvrière }	*worker*
le cousin	la cousine	*cousin*
le chien	la chienne	*dog*
le fou	la folle	*mad person*
le Parisien	la Parisienne	*Parisian*
le nouveau	la nouvelle	*newcomer*

4   Nouns which remain exactly the same in spelling when changing from masculine to feminine, but which take on a different meaning in the process. The following are the most common nouns of that type:

Masculine	Feminine
un aide (*male assistant*)	une aide (*help*)
le critique (*critic*)	la critique (*criticism*)
le garde (*guard = person*)	la garde (*guard = action*)
un guide (*guide*)	une guide (*rein*)
le livre (*book*)	la livre (*pound*)
le manche (*handle*)	{ la manche (*sleeve*) { la Manche (*the Channel*)
le moule (*mould*)	la moule (*mussel*)
le manoeuvre (*unskilled worker*)	la manoeuvre (*manoeuvre*)
le page (*page-boy*)	la page (*page = sheet*)
le pendule (*pendulum*)	la pendule (*wall clock*)
le poste (*post*)	la poste (*Post Office*)
le physique (*physique*)	la physique (*physics*)
le radio (*radio operator*)	la radio (*radio*)
le tour (*turn/tour*)	la tour (*tower*)
le vase (*vase*)	la vase (*silt*)
le voile (*veil*)	la voile (*sail*)

5   Nouns which are masculine in the singular and feminine in the plural (sometimes with altered meaning):

Masculine	Feminine
un amour malheureux	des amours malheureus*es*
(*an unfortunate love*)	(*unfortunate loves: poetic*)
un aigle	des aigles
(*an eagle: actual bird*)	(*eagles: emblems on flags/shields*)
le délice	les délices
(*delight*)	(*ecstasies*)
un orgue	des orgues
(*an organ: music*)	(*an organ: music-poetic or pompous*)

6 Nouns of living creatures (singular or plural), which can refer *either* to beings of one sex (as indicated by the noun's gender), *or* to any member of the species *regardless* of sex:

les vaches (fem.)   *cows/cows, oxen and bulls*
les souris (fem.)   *female mice/mice of either sex*
les moutons (masc.)   *rams/sheep of either sex*
les poissons (masc.)   *male fish/fish of either sex*
les mouches (fem.)   *female flies/flies of either sex*
les éléphants (masc.)   *bull elephants/elephants of either sex*
les hommes (masc.)   *men/men and women*

For example:

Les **vaches** sont dans le pré.   *The cows are in the meadow.*

Les **hommes** sont mortels.   *Men are mortal.*

Note: If the ambiguity needs to be removed, this can be done in one of two ways: *either* by using the specific male or female term, if it exists:

Les **vaches** et les **taureaux** sont dans le pré.   *The cows and bulls are in the meadow.*

or by adding the words **mâle** (*male*) or **femelle** (*female*) after the noun as required:

une souris **mâle**   *a male mouse*
un éléphant **femelle**   *a female elephant*

7 Certain nouns referring to human beings which, although of one gender only, can apply to individuals of either sex:

la connaissance   *acquaintance — man or woman*
la personne   *person — man or woman*
la recrue   *recruit — man or woman*
la sentinelle   *sentry — man or woman*
le témoin   *witness — man or woman*
la victime   *victim — man or woman*

8 Certain nouns indicating a profession or status traditionally held

by men have no feminine equivalent. The following are the most frequently-encountered examples:

l'auteur *author*	le journaliste *journalist*
le bourreau *executioner*	le magistrat *magistrate*
le chef *chief*	le ministre *minister*
le diplomate *diplomat*	le peintre *painter*
le docteur *doctor*	le possesseur *owner*
l'écrivain *writer*	le professeur *lecturer*
le guide *guide*	le successeur *successor*
l'ingénieur *engineer*	le tyran *tyrant*

NB   If needed, it is possible to indicate in one of two ways that the noun refers to a woman:

(*a*)   By using the words **femme** (*woman*) or **dame** (*lady*) in connection with that noun, which then takes on the value of an adjective. For example:

J'ai parlé à une **femme docteur**.   *I spoke to a lady doctor.*
Cette **dame** est peintre.   *This lady is a painter.*

(*b*)   By referring to the person as **Madame le . . .** if addressing her directly:

Excusez-moi, **Madame le Ministre**   *Excuse me, Minister*

Hints for the determination of the gender of nouns

The information given below is designed to help you learn and remember the gender of French nouns. For each gender, the information has been subdivided into two sections:

(*a*)   determination of gender by *meaning*; and
(*b*)   determination of gender by *ending*.

Masculine nouns

Determination of the masculine gender by meaning

(*a*)   Nouns referring to beings of the male sex, for example **le fils** *son*, **le cheval** *horse*, **le chien** *dog*.
(*b*)   Nouns identifying the following:
   – *chemical substances and gases*, for example **le carbone** *carbon*, **le sulfate de cuivre** *copper sulphate*, **l'azote** *nitrogen*, **le cyanure** *cyanide*;
   – *colours*, for example **le blanc** *white*, **le jaune** *yellow*, **le rose** *pink*, **le violet** *purple*;
   – *holidays*, such as **le quatorze juillet** *14th July — Bastille Day*,

le quinze août *15th August — Assumption*, but **la Toussaint** *All Saints Day* and **la Noël** *Christmas*. Note, however, that in greetings, or if accompanied by an adjective, **Noël** is masculine. For example:

> (Je vous souhaite **un**) joyeux Noël! *(I wish you a) happy Christmas!*
> Nous avons passé **un** excellent Noël. *We have had an excellent Christmas.*

— *languages*, for example **le chinois** *Chinese*, **le grec** *Greek*, **le russe** *Russian*;

— *metals*, for example **le cuivre** *copper*, **le fer** *iron*, **le plomb** *lead*, **le zinc** *zinc*, but: **la fonte** *cast iron*, **la tôle** *sheet iron*;

— *seasons, months, days of the week*, for example **le printemps** *Spring*, **en décembre dernier** *last December*, **un dimanche** *one Sunday*;

— *trees, shrubs and bushes*, for example **le chêne** *oak tree*, **le peuplier** *poplar*, **le rhododendron** *rhododendron*, **le rosier** *rose-bush*, but: **une aubépine** *a hawthorn*, **la vigne** *vine*, **la ronce** *bramble*;

— *countries not ending in 'e'*, for example **le Portugal** *Portugal*, **le Guatémala** *Guatemala*;

— *flowers not ending in 'e'*, for example **le géranium** *geranium*, **le lilas** *lilac*, **le mimosa** *mimosa*, **l'oeillet** *carnation*;

— *fruit and vegetables not ending in 'e'*, for example **le citron** *lemon*, **le melon** *melon*, **un artichaut** *an artichoke*, **le navet** *turnip*;

— *items of clothing not ending in 'e'*, for example **le blouson** *lumber jacket*, **le pantalon** *trousers*, **le soulier** *shoe*, **le veston** *jacket*;

— *illnesses not ending in 'e'*, for example **le choléra** *cholera*, **les oreillons** *mumps*, **le typhus** *typhus*, but: **la malaria** *malaria*;

— *rivers not ending in 'e'*, for example **le Mississippi** *Mississippi*, **le Nil** *Nile*, but: **la Volga** *Volga*;

— *sciences and scholarly disciplines not ending in 'e'*, for example **le dessin** *drawing*, **le droit** *law*;

— *letters of the alphabet*, for example **un 'a'** *an 'a'*, **un 'c'** *a 'c'*. *Note:* Usage sometimes differs, but the masculine is generally seen as being acceptable in all cases;

— *lorries, ships and aircraft*, for example **le Ford** *Ford Truck*, **le Boeing** *Boeing*, **le Concorde** *Concord*, **le France** *the France* (liner), but: **la Caravelle** (aircraft), **la Marie-Céleste** (ship). *Note*: Usage sometimes differs in the case of ships, but the masculine gender is by far the most widely used;

- *wines, spirits and cheeses named after their region/country of origin*, for example **le bourgogne** *Burgundy wine*, **le cognac** *brandy*, **le roquefort** *Roquefort cheese*, **le hollande** *Dutch cheese*. *Note*: In such cases, the gender is obviously influenced by the fact that the words **vin** (*wine*) and **fromage** (*cheese*) are masculine;
- *nouns borrowed from English*, for example **le parking** *car park*, **le snack-bar** *snack bar*, **le week-end** *week end*, but: **un/une interview** *an interview*, **la star** *top artist*. *Note*: If the borrowed noun refers to a person of the female sex, it will be feminine in French, for example **la Cover-girl** *covergirl*, **la Script-girl** *script girl*.

Determination of masculine gender by ending

Nouns with the following endings are (normally) masculine:

age, for example **le passage** *passage*, **le lavage** *washing*, **le ménage** *housework*, but: **la cage** *cage*, **une image** *an image*, **la nage** *swimming*, **la page** *page*, **la plage** *beach*, **la rage** *rage/rabies*;

ail, for example **l'émail** *enamel*, **le travail** *work*, **le vitrail** *stained glass window*;

al, for example **le carnaval** *carnival*, **le métal** *metal*, **un oral** *an oral examination*;

as, for example **le bas** *lower part/stocking*, **le gras** *fat*, **le tas** *heap*;

eau, for example **le chapeau** *hat*, **le drapeau** *flag*, **le taureau** *bull*, but: **l'eau** *water*, **la peau** *skin*;

eu, for example **le feu** *fire*, **le jeu** *game*, **le pneu** *tyre*;

eur if indicating a person or machine performing a job or task, for example **un aviateur** *an airman*, **le chauffeur** *stoker/driver*, **le mélangeur** *mixer*, **le compresseur** *compressor*;

eux, for example **le creux** *hollow*, **le sérieux** *seriousness*, **le vieux** *old man*;

er/ier if referring to a person performing a job/task, for example **le boucher** *butcher*, **le plâtrier** *plasterer*, **le portier** *doorman*;

in/ain/ein, for example **le lin** *linen*, **le matin** *morning*, **le pain** *bread*, **le sein** *breast*, but: **la fin** *end*, **la main** *hand*;

is, for example **le colis** *parcel*, **le commis** *apprentice*, **le tapis** *carpet*, but: **la vis** *screw*;

ment, for example **le changement** *change*, **le développement** *development*, **un élément** *an element*, but: **la jument** *mare*,

oir, for example **le devoir** *duty*, **le dortoir** *dormitory*, **le pouvoir** *power*, **le savoir** *knowledge*;

ou, for example **le chou** *cabbage*, **le cou** *neck*, **le fou** *madman*, **le trou** *hole*, **le voyou** *thug*, but: **la nounou** *nanny*.

Note: It is possible for you to create many more such categories of nouns, but there may be numerous exceptions to your 'rules'. Nevertheless, it is a worthwhile exercise which will accustom you to look at the language in the right way.

Feminine nouns

Determination of the feminine gender by meaning
(*a*) Nouns referring to beings of the female sex (but see also notes 6, 7 and 8 on pp. 59–60), for example **la fille** *daughter*, **la jument** *mare*, **la chienne** *bitch*.
(*b*) Nouns identifying the following:
  – *countries ending in 'e'*, for example **l'Autriche** *Austria*, **la Belgique** *Belgium*, **la Tunisie** *Tunisia*, but: **le Cambodge** *Cambodia* (now Kampuchea), **le Mexique** *Mexico*, **le Zaïre** *Zaire*;
  – *flowers ending in 'e'*, for example **la rose** *rose*, **la tulipe** *tulip*, **la violette** *violet*, but: **le chèvrefeuille** *honeysuckle*;
  – *fruit and vegetables ending in 'e'*, for example **l'amande** *almond*, **la carotte** *carrot*, **la fraise** *strawberry*, **la pomme de terre** *potato*, **la prune** *plum*, **la tomate** *tomato*, but: **le pamplemousse** *grapefruit*;
  – *garments ending in 'e'*, for example **la chemise** *shirt*, **la cravate** *tie*, **la veste** *jacket*, but: **un imperméable** *a raincoat*, **le passe-montagne** *balaclava*;
  – *illnesses ending in 'e'*, for example **la fièvre** *fever*, **la peste** *plague*, **la rougeole** *measles*, **la tuberculose** *tuberculosis*, but: **le malaise** *feeling of sickness*;
  – *rivers ending in 'e'*, for example **la Loire** *Loire*, **la Seine** *Seine*, **la Tamise** *Thames*, but: **le Danube** *Danube*, **le Rhône** *Rhone*, **le Zambèze** *Zambezi*;
  – *sciences and scholarly disciplines ending in 'e'*, for example **la biologie** *biology*, **la chimie** *chemistry*, **la politique** *politics*;

- *sports, games and leisure pursuits ending in 'e'* (but *not* in **isme**), for example **la marche** *walking*, **la course** *running*, **la danse** *dancing*, **la peinture** *painting*, **la poterie** *pottery*. *Note*: **le culturisme** *body building*, **le cyclisme** *cycling*, etc.
- *vehicles other than lorries, aircraft, boats*, for example **une Austin** *Austin car*, **la Citroën** *Citroen car*, **la Suzuki** *Suzuki motorbike*, **la bicyclette** *push-bike*, **la motocyclette** *motorbike*, but: **le tricycle** *tricycle*.

Determination of feminine gender by ending

Nouns with the following endings are (normally) feminine:

ance/anse/ence/ense, for example **une avance** *advance*, **la chance** *luck*, **la danse** *dance*, **la défense** *defence*, **la prudence** *care = prudence*, **la violence** *violence*, but: **le rance** *rancid taste*, **le silence** *silence*;

ée, for example **l'arrivée** *arrival*, **l'épée** *sword*, **la gelée** *frost/jelly*, **la montée** *climb*, but: **un athée** *atheist*, **le lycée** *Grammar school*, **le mausolée** *mausoleum*, **le musée** *museum*;

esse, for example **la caresse** *caress*, **la finesse** *finesse*, **la messe** *mass*, **la paresse** *laziness*, **la tresse** *plait*;

ette/otte, for example **la chambrette** *small bedroom*, **la botte** *boot*, **la buvette** *refreshment bar*, **la chemisette** *short-sleeved shirt*, **la flotte** *fleet*, **la fourchette** *fork*, **la roulotte** *gipsy caravan*;

eur if expressing an abstract notion, for example **l'ardeur** *passion = fire*, **la chaleur** *heat*, **la hauteur** *height*, **la peur** *fear*, **la valeur** *valour/value*, but: **le bonheur** *happiness*, **le malheur** *unhappiness*. Note that if the noun ending in **eur** refers to a *machine* or *person* doing a specific type of activity, it will be masculine, for example **le brûleur** *burner*, **le contrôleur** *inspector*, **le coureur** *runner/racing driver*. **le mélangeur** *mixer*, **le voleur** *thief*;

rie, for example **la boucherie** *butcher's shop*, **la cavalerie** *cavalry*, **la galerie** *gallery*, **la patrie** *fatherland*;

sie/tie, for example **la bourgeoisie** *middle class*, **la courtoisie** *courtesy*, **la démocratie** *democracy*, **la fantaisie** *whim*, **la partie** *party*, **la sortie** *exit*, but: **le messie** *messiah*, **le sosie** *look-alike*;

sion/tion, for example **la confusion** *confusion*, **la contraction** *contraction*, **l'érosion** *erosion*, **la perfection** *perfection*, **la question** *question*, **la version** *version*, **la vision** *vision*, but: **le bastion** *bastion/stronghold*;

té if expressing an abstract notion, for example **la beauté** *beauty*, l'égalité *equality*, **la fraternité** *fraternity*, **la liberté** *freedom*, but: **le doigté** *touch = knowhow*. *Note*: If the noun ending in **té** refers to a *non-abstract* thing or being, it will be masculine, for example **le comité** *committee*, **le pâté** *pâté*, **le velouté** *velouté = soup/sauce*;

ture, for example **la confiture** *jam*, **la couverture** *blanket*, **la facture** *bill*, **la fracture** *fracture*, **l'ouverture** *opening*, **la structure** *structure*, **la voiture** *car*.

Note: As mentioned above, it is possible for you to create more categories by examining noun endings and formulating your own theories. Doing this will accustom you to look for the underlying 'logic' of the language.

Key points

1   French nouns fall into two distinct gender categories: masculine and feminine.

2   In spite of the apparent arbitrariness of the division, it is possible to organise categories based on meaning which, with some exceptions, will help learners to find out which gender a given noun belongs to.

3   In addition to categories based on meaning, it is also possible to assign many nouns to one or the other of the two gender categories according to ending. *Note*: With practice, learners will develop a 'feel' for the gender of the new nouns they encounter.

4   It must be remembered that the gender of a noun affects the adjectives and other determiners associated with it. All the necessary agreements *must* be made where appropriate.

5   *Generally*, nouns referring to beings of the male sex are masculine and nouns referring to beings of the female sex are feminine.

6   There are, however, cases when a noun of one gender may refer to:

(*a*)   beings of the other sex;

(*b*)   beings of both sexes.

7   There are a number of cases when, for a given noun, a change in gender will determine a change in meaning. Special care should be taken to try and remember such nouns.

8   It is possible for learners to experiment with 'theories' concerning the gender of nouns according to meaning and, to a larger extent, according to endings. It is a worthwhile exercise, which will encourage them to look for the 'underlying unity' of the language.

10   The Plural of Nouns

Simple (one-word) nouns

The majority of French simple nouns form their plural by adding an s
to their masculine or feminine singular form.

Remember: Most adjectives connected with a plural noun will
follow the agreement pattern as appropriate. For example:

La grande porte	⟶ Les grandes portes
The big door	*The big doors*
Le petit garçon	⟶ Les petits garçons
The small boy	*The small boys*

Some categories of nouns, however, do not follow the general rule
outlined above. They are examined below:

1   Nouns ending in **s**, **x** or **z** in the singular do not change in the
plural. For example:

Un **bas** nylon	⟶ Des **bas** nylon
A nylon stocking	*Nylon stockings*
Le petit **vieux**	⟶ Les petits **vieux**
The little old man	*The little old men*
Un joli **nez**	⟶ De jolis **nez**
A pretty nose	*Pretty noses*

2   Nouns ending in **au**, **eau** or **eu** in the singular, add an **x** in the
plural. For example:

Le **noyau**	⟶ Les **noyaux**
The kernel/core	*The kernels/cores*
Le **bateau**	⟶ Les **bateaux**
The boat	*The boats*
Le **feu** rouge	⟶ Les **feux** rouges
The traffic light	*The traffic lights*

Exceptions: The following take an **s** in the plural: **le bleu**
bruise/boiler suit, **le landau** *pram*, **le pneu** *tyre*. For example

Mes quatre **pneus** sont à plat.   *My four tyres are flat.*

3   Nouns ending in **al** in the singular form their plural in **aux**:

Le **cheval** sauvage	⟶ Les **chevaux** sauvages
The wild horse	*The wild horses*
Un **métal** précieux	⟶ Des **métaux** précieux
A precious metal	*Precious metals*

Exceptions: The following six nouns take an **s** in the plural: **le bal** *dance*, **le carnaval** *carnival*, **le chacal** *jackal*, **le festival** *festival*, **le récital** *recital/concert*, **le régal** *delight/feast*.

Note: **Un idéal** (*ideal*) has two plural forms: **des idéals** *or* **des idéaux**
4   The following six nouns ending in **ail** in the singular, form their plural in **aux**: **le bail** *lease*, **le corail** *coral*, **l'émail** *enamel*, **le soupirail** *air vent*, **le travail** *work*, **le vitrail** *stained glass window*. For example
>Les **vitraux** de la cathédrale sont magnifiques.   *The stained glass windows of the cathedral are magnificent.*

5   The following *seven* nouns ending in **ou** in the singular, form their plural in **oux**: **le bijou** *jewel*, **le caillou** *stone*, **le chou** *cabbage*, **le genou** *knee*, **le hibou** *owl*, **le joujou** *toy* (child's word), **le pou** *louse*. For example:
>Ciel, on m'a volé mes **bijoux**!   *Good Heavens, someone has stolen my jewels!*
>L'enfant adorait ses **joujoux**.   *The child adored his toys.*

6   Four nouns have two plural forms (regular and irregular), which may have quite different meanings, as shown in the table below:

Singular	Regular plural	Irregular plural
un aïeul	des aïeuls	des aïeux
a grandfather	*grandfathers*	*forefathers*
l'ail	les ails	les aulx
garlic	*garlic: modern form*	*garlic: obsolete form*
le ciel	les ciels	les cieux
the sky	*skies: in paintings*	*skies/heavens*
un oeil	des oeils	des yeux
an eye	*round windows*	*eyes*

7   Nouns created from invariable words (adverbs, prepositions, conjunctions), remain invariable in the plural, for example:
>Les **si** et les **mais**   *The ifs and buts*
>Les **pourquoi** et les **comment**   *The whys and wherefores*

Compound nouns

Compound nouns can be made up of a combination of the following elements:

(*a*) variable words (adjectives, nouns, past participles), which may take the mark of the plural according to the rules stated below.

(*b*) invariable words (adverbs, conjunctions, prepositions, verbs), which will remain invariable at all times.

Both these elements are illustrated in the examples below:

Le petit-fils	⟶ **Les petits-fils** (adj.+noun)
The grandson	*The grandsons*
Un ouvre-boîte	⟶ **Des ouvre-boîtes** (verb+noun)
A tin-opener	*Tin-openers*
Le haut-parleur	⟶ **Les haut-parleurs** (adv+noun)
The loudspeaker	*The loudspeakers*

The following cases must be distinguished:

1 Some compound nouns are so closely 'welded' together that the identity of the components has been forgotten and they are now treated as one word.

Un portefeuille	⟶ Des portefeuilles
A wallet (lit: *leaf-carrier*)	*Wallets*
Le contrevent	⟶ Les contrevents
The shutter (lit: *wind-shield*)	*The shutters*

Exceptions:

Le bonhomme	⟶ Les bonshommes
The (old) fellow	*The (old) fellows*
Un gentilhomme	⟶ Des gentilshommes
A gentleman	*Gentlemen*

Note the plural of the following forms of *direct* address:

Madame	⟶ **Mes**dames
Madam	*Ladies*
Mademoiselle	⟶ **Mes**demoiselles
Miss	*Young ladies*
Monsieur	⟶ **Messieurs**
Sir	*Gentlemen*

2 *Noun + noun compounds* Normally, both components can be put into the plural when required:

Un chou-fleur	⟶ Des choux-fleurs
A cauliflower	*Cauliflowers*
Une chauve-souris	⟶ Des chauves-souris
A bat	*Bats*

There are, however, some exceptions to this rule.

(*a*) If the nouns are linked by a preposition: **à** *to*/*for*, **de** *of*/*from*, **en** *in*, **pour** *for*, etc., *stated or implied*, the second noun will remain singular. For example:

Un arc-en-**ciel**   ⟶ Des arcs-en-**ciel**
A rainbow   *Rainbows*
Le timbre-**poste**   ⟶ Les timbres-**poste**
   (= pour la poste)
The postage stamp   *The postage stamps*

(*b*) If the second noun represents a 'generic' name (i.e. the name of a whole species, class or group of beings or things), it does not take the plural form.

Le ver à **soie**   ⟶ Les vers à **soie**
The silkworm   *The silkworms*
Un soutien-**gorge**   ⟶ Des soutiens-**gorge**
A bra (lit: *Support-bosom*)   *Bras*
Le moulin à **vent**   ⟶ Les moulins à **vent**
The windmill   *The windmills*

(*c*) A small number of such compounds do not change in the plural.

Un (des) coq-à-l'âne   *Abrupt change(s) of subject*
Un (des) pied-à-terre   *Small occasional lodgings (−)*
Un (des) pot-au-feu   *Stew(s)*
Un (des) tête-à-tête   *Tête-à-tête(s)*

3 *Noun + adjective compounds*   Normally, both elements take the plural form when required.

Un coffre-fort   ⟶ Des coffres-forts
A safe   *Safes*
Un franc-maçon   ⟶ Des francs-maçons
A freemason   *Freemasons*

Note: In *feminine plural compounds*, **grand** (*grand/great*) can either remain invariable or take an **s**. For example:

Une **grand**-mère   ⟶ Des **grand(s)**-mères
A grandmother   *Grandmothers*
La **grand**-tante   ⟶ Les **grand(s)**-tantes
The great-aunt   *The great-aunts*

4 *Adjective + adjective compounds*   Normally, both elements take the plural form when appropriate:

Le dernier-né   ⟶ Les derniers-nés
The last-born child   *The last-born children*
Le sourd-muet   ⟶ Les sourds-muets
The deaf-and-dumb man   *The deaf-and-dumb men*

Note: If one of the adjectives is used in an adverbial sense, it will remain invariable

Un **nouveau**-né   Des **nouveau**-nés
A newly born child   *Newly born children*

5   *Verb + noun compounds*   The verb element remains invariable in the plural. The noun normally agrees in number, *except* if it represents a 'generic' name (i.e. the name of a whole species, group or category).

Le couvre-feu	⟶ Les couvre-feux
The curfew	*The curfews*
Un garde-fou	⟶ Des garde-fous
A hand-rail	*Hand-rails*
But: Un abat-**jour**	⟶ Des abat-**jour**
A lamp-shade	*Lamp-shades*
Le gratte-**ciel**	⟶ Les gratte-**ciel**
The sky-scraper	*The sky-scrapers*
Un coupe-**papier**	⟶ Des coupe-**papier**
A paper-knife	*Paper-knives*
Un brise-**glace**	⟶ Des brise-**glace**
An ice-breaker	*Ice-breakers*

Note: If the word **garde** used as the first element of the compound refers to a *person*, it will take an **s** in the plural. If it refers to an *object*, it will remain invariable:

Compare:	Un **garde**-malade	⟶ Des **gardes**-malades
	A male nurse	*Male nurses*
and:	Une **garde**-robe	⟶ Des **garde**-robes
	A wardrobe	*Wardrobes*

6   *Invariable word + noun compounds*   In such compounds, the noun alone may take the plural form when required.

Un à-coup	⟶ Des à-coups
A jolt/jerk	*Jolts/jerks*
Un non-sens	⟶ Des non-sens
A meaningless phrase	*Meaningless phrases*

Note: If a compound noun is made of two (or more) invariable words, it will of course remain invariable in the plural.

Un (des) on-dit   *Rumour(s)* (lit: *one says*)

Un (des) passe-partout   *Master-key(s)*

Un (des) va-et-vient   *Two way switch(es)*

Foreign nouns

For this category, the rules of plural formation are fairly unstable, but the following guidelines may be helpful:

If the word comes from a language in which plural formation is the same as in French, it will easily be integrated and follow the normal rule. For example:

Un pullover   ⟶ Des pullovers
A jumper   *Jumpers*
Le parking   ⟶ Les parkings
The car-park   *The car-parks*

2   If the word comes from Latin or Italian and is commonly used, it may follow the normal rule.

Un maximum   ⟶ Des maximums (*also* maxima)
A maximum   *Maxima*
Un référendum   ⟶ Des référendums (*also* référenda)
A referendum   *Referendums*

3   If the word *is not* fully assimilated, its plural form may be the one used in the language of origin.

Un graffito   ⟶ Des graffiti
A graffito   *Graffiti*
Un barman   ⟶ Des barmen
A barman   *Barmen*
Un lied   ⟶ Des lieder
A ballad   *Ballads*

Note: There is, as yet, great confusion about the word **media** (= *mass media*):

or   Un medium
       Un media   Des media (*or* des média *or* des médias)

Proper nouns

In this category, several cases must be distinguished:

1   Proper nouns referring to famous royal families take the plural when required:

Les Bourbons   *The Bourbon family*
Les Stuarts   *The Stuarts*

2   Proper nouns referring to families other than those mentioned above, remain invariable:

Les **Dupont** sont invités par les **Lebrun.**   *The Duponts are invited by the Lebruns.*

3   Proper nouns referring to works of art produced by a given artist, take the plural form when required:

Trois **Picassos** ont été volés.   *Three Picasso paintings have been stolen.*

4   Proper nouns used to refer to people of the same artistic or intellectual calibre as the original bearer of the name take the plural form when necessary:

Les **Einsteins** et les **Flemings** sont rares.   *People like Einstein and Fleming are rare.*

Note: Usage often differs in this latter category.

Nouns which can only be used in the plural or in the singular

1   The following are some of the nouns which *cannot* be used in the singular:

les archives   *archives* (fem.), **les arrhes**   *non-returnable deposit* (fem.),

les confins   *confines* (masc.), **les entrailles**   *entrails* (fem.),

les frais   *expenses* (masc.), **les mathématiques**   *mathematics* (fem.),

les menottes   *handcuffs* (fem.), **les pourparlers**   *discussions* (masc.),

les ténèbres   *darkness* (fem.), **les vivres**   *food supplies* (masc.), etc.

2   The following categories of nouns are *not normally* used in the plural:

(*a*)   adjectives used as nouns and expressing broad concepts and 'eternal' values; for example **Le beau** *Beauty*, **le bien** *Good*, **le mal** *Evil*, **le vrai** *Truth*;

(*b*)   Infinitives used as nouns; for example **L'avoir** *financial possessions*, **le devenir** *evolution*, **le savoir** *knowledge*, etc.

(*c*)   generic names of products, materials, substances; for example **le bois** *wood*, **le fer** *iron*, **la laine** *wool*, **le pétrole** *crude oil*, etc.

(*d*)   names of intellectual or artistic disciplines; for example **la biologie** *biology*, **la chimie** *chemistry*, **la musique** *music*, **la sculpture** *sculpture*, etc., but: **les mathématiques** *mathematics*.

Nouns which change their meaning in the plural

A small number of nouns change their meaning when put in the plural:

Singular	Plural
la bonté *goodness*	⟶ les bontés *favours*
la chance *luck*	⟶ les chances *opportunities*
la douceur *softness*	⟶ les douceurs *sweets*
la volonté *willpower*	⟶ les volontés *whims/fancies*
le ciseau *chisel*	⟶ les ciseaux *scissors*
la lunette *spy-glass*	⟶ les lunettes *glasses = spectacles*

Nouns which change their pronunciation in the plural

Three nouns, although they follow the normal rule of plural formation, change their pronunciation in the plural (for an explanation of phonetic symbols see Appendix I):

Un boeuf	[bœf]	⟶ Des boeufs	[bø]
An ox		*Oxen*	
Un oeuf	[œf]	⟶ Des oeufs	[ø]
An egg		*Eggs*	
Un os	[ɔs]	⟶ Des os	[o]
A bone		*Bones*	

Key points

1 *The majority* of French nouns form their plural by adding an **s** to their masculine or feminine singular form. Some, however, do not follow this rule.

2 Nouns ending in **s**, **x** and **z** remain the same in the plural.

3 *Most* nouns ending in **au**, **eau** and **eu** in the singular, take an **x** in the plural.

4 *Most* nouns ending in **al** in the singular, change **al** to **aux** in the plural.

5 *Most* nouns ending in **ail** and **ou** follow the normal rule of plural formation. There are, however, exceptions in both cases.

6 *Four* nouns have two plural forms (regular *and* irregular). The meaning of those two forms is *not* automatically identical.

7 Nouns created from invariable words (adverbs, conjunctions, prepositions, verbs) remain invariable in the plural.

8 Compound nouns may be composed of two types of elements: *invariable ones* (mentioned in 7 above); and *variable ones* (adjectives, nouns, past participles). The first category will *not* take the plural form *in any circumstances*. The second will take the plural as appropriate, unless the general sense of the word makes the agreement illogical (reference to generic categories, broad concepts, etc.).

9 The rules of plural agreement for foreign nouns are not absolute: if the noun is 'well integrated' (i.e. very frequently used) the normal rule will apply (add an **s**). If not, the foreign noun may retain its original plural form.

10 The rules governing the plural of proper names in French are complex and flexible. If the proper name refers to the members of an illustrious family or to the intellectual or artistic production of the rightful bearer of the name, the plural agreement will be made when appropriate. In most other cases the proper name will remain invariable in the plural.

11 Some French nouns have no singular form and *must*, therefore, *always* be used in the plural.

12 A certain number of nouns representing broad concepts, intellectual disciplines or 'generic categories' are not normally used in the plural. If they are, the meaning of the plural form may be quite different from that of the singular form.

11 The Pronoun

Note: for the purpose of exemplification, some pronoun categories are, at times, mentioned out of turn. Please refer to the sections clarifying those categories if in doubt.

Pronouns are words which can replace nouns or nominal expressions. Some pronouns can even replace whole sentences:

> La neige est épaisse. **Cela** m'inquiète. *The snow is deep. That worries me (that = the fact that the snow is deep).*

Pronouns enable us to speak and write in a more concise and elegant way, and to avoid tiresome repetitions.

Compare: La dame regarde ses deux enfants. Ses deux enfants jouent. Ses deux enfants sont heureux. Cet enfant-ci court; cet enfant-là chante. La dame est fière de ses deux enfants.

and: La dame regarde ses deux enfants. **Ils** jouent. **Ils** sont heureux. **Celui-ci** court; **celui-là** chante. **Elle** est fière d'**eux**. *The lady is looking at her two children. They are playing. They are happy. This one is running; that one is singing. She is proud of them.* (In the second version most of the nouns have been replaced by the appropriate pronouns.)

French nouns, as stated on many previous occasions, are not all of the same gender and can generally vary in number. The pronouns which are to replace them must therefore carry as much information as possible about gender and number. Consequently, there will be marked differences between the French and English pronoun systems. For example *I need them* could be translated in French either as: J'ai besoin d'**eux** (if *them* represents a masculine plural) or as: J'ai besoin d'**elles** (if *them* represents a feminine plural). It is therefore wise to assume that not all pronouns will function in the same way in the two languages.

There are six distinct categories of pronouns. Each category has a special role to play and it is crucial, whenever the forms are different, to distinguish clearly between them. The categories are as follows: personal, demonstrative, possessive, relative, interrogative, indefinite. They will be examined in turn.

Personal pronouns

As their name suggests, they 'point out' who is the 'performer' (subject) or the recipient (object) of the action.

Subject pronouns

They indicate the performer(s) of an action.

Number	Person	Pronoun	Meaning
Singular	1st 2nd 2nd 3rd 3rd 3rd	je/j'† tu vous il elle on	*I* *you* (familiar form) *you* (polite form) *he* (also used to replace non-human masculine nouns) *she* (also used to replace non-human feminine nouns) *one* (neutral pronoun to avoid specific reference to persons of one or other gender)
Plural	1st 2nd 3rd 3rd	nous vous ils elles	*we* *you* (normal plural) *they* (masculine only or masculine + feminine) *they* (feminine only)

† When **je** is followed by a vowel or a mute 'h' it loses its **e**.

There are a number of points to bear in mind with the use of subject pronouns:
1 On their own, **je** (*I*) **tu** (*you*—familiar) **on** (*one*) **nous** (*we*) and **vous** (*you*—plural or polite singular) do not carry any gender information. That information will often appear in the ending(s) of the accompanying adjective(s) (if any).

Compare: **Je** suis content. *I am pleased.* (The ending of the adjective **content** reveals that the subject **je** is masculine.)

and: **Je** suis conten**te**. *I am pleased.* (In this case, the ending of the adjective reveals that the subject is feminine.)

or: **Vous** êtes fatigu**é**. *You are tired.* (The ending of the adjective indicates that **vous** refers to a male person — polite singular.)

and: **Vous** êtes fatiguées. *You are tired.* (The ending shows that
                the remark is addressed to several female persons —
                normal plural.)

NB   Using the polite form **vous** to address one person in French is
not a sign of stand-offishness but of respect.
2   **Il**, which normally refers to a masculine being or thing, can also be
used in French as an impersonal pronoun. In such cases, it does not
refer to any specific thing or being and is then the equivalent of the
English impersonal form *it*. For example:

    Il pleut? Non, **il** neige.   *Is it raining? No, it is snowing.*

    Il faut partir!   *It is necessary to go.*

    Il importe d'être calme.   *It is important to be calm.*

3   In good French, **on** (*one*) is always followed by the 3rd person
singular of the verb (even though it may have the meaning of *people*):

    Le soir venu, **on** rentrait fatigué mais ravi.   *When the evening
    came one* (i.e. *people*) *went home tired but delighted.*

NB   For the purpose of agreement, **on** is considered as a masculine
singular pronoun. The endings of the adjectives in the preceding
example make the fact clear.

4   In familiar French, **on** is often used instead of **nous**. In this case
any agreement is made as if **on** was really **nous**:

    On est sort**is** tous les quatre hier soir.   *The four of us went out
    last night.*

5   Sometimes, for the purpose of emphasis, another set of pronouns
is used to 'reinforce' the subject pronouns; in this case such pronouns,
called *disjunctives*, usually appear before the subject ones. They are
listed on pages 81–2.
Compare: J'abandonne.   *I give up.*
and: **Moi**, j'abandonne.   *As for me, I give up.*

6   To translate English constructions where two subject pronouns
are linked by *and* or *or*, two disjunctives will be used in French. For
example:

    Lui et **moi** (and not *****il** et **je**) viendrons vous chercher.   *He and I
    will come and fetch you.*

    Qui va répondre, **toi** ou **moi**? (and not, *****tu** ou **je**).   *Who is going
    to answer, you or I?*

7   When translating expressions of the type *It is (not) I* . . . the
subject pronoun will be replaced by the corresponding disjunctive:

    C'est **moi** (and not *****c'est **je**) qui ai appelé la police.   *It is I who
    called the police.*

    C'est **lui** (and not *****c'est **il**) que je veux voir.   *It is he I want to see.*

Ce n'est pas **toi** (and not *ce n'est pas **tu**) le coupable.   *You are not the culprit.* (lit: *it is not you the culprit*)

8   More generally, the subject pronoun cannot be used without a verb or solely with the auxiliary **être** (*to be*) or **avoir** (*to have*) as it can in English.

Compare: *Who has broken the vase? I have!*

and: Qui a cassé le vase? Moi! (and not *j'ai)

To all intents and purposes, it is as if the expression *It is . . . who . . .* had simply been omitted and rule 8 above does therefore apply.

9   In comparisons, after expressions such as **plus . . . que** (*more than*) **moins . . . que** (*less than*), **aussi . . . que** (*as . . . as*) **comme** (*as*), the subject pronoun is replaced by the corresponding disjunctive pronoun (see pages 81–2):

Elle est plus jeune que **toi**.   *She is younger than you (are).*

Ils gagnent moins que **moi**.   *They earn less than I (do)*

Object pronouns

They are used to refer to the thing(s) or being(s) affected by the action performed by the subject(s). They are sub-divided into two groups: *direct object* (accusative) and *indirect object* (dative). Since the distinction between these two groups seems to create confusion in the mind of some learners, here is a simple (if not foolproof) way of finding out which is which. After the subject and the verb have been stated, ask the question **qui?** (*who?*) or **quoi?** (*what?*). If this question has an answer, you will have to substitute the appropriate direct object pronoun when required:

Tu vois la rivière?   *Do you see the river?*

Oui, je **la** vois. (je vois quoi? = la rivière, fem. sing.)   *Yes, I see it.*

Et votre repas?   *What about your meal?*

Nous **le** mangeons! (nous mangeons quoi? = le repas; masc. sing.)   *We are eating it!*

Note: Be sure that the answer you obtained was to the question **qui?** or **quoi?** *and not* **à qui?** (*to whom?*) or **à quoi?** (*to what?*), otherwise the pronouns you need are the indirect object ones!

Compare: Il regardait le tableau; il **l'**admirait. (il admirait quoi? = le tableau; masc. sing.)   *He looked at the painting; he admired it.*

and: Il regardait le chien; il **lui** parlait. (Il parlait à qui? = au chien; masc. sing.)   *He looked at the dog; he spoke to it.*

Direct object (*accusative*) pronouns

Number	Person	Pronoun	Meaning
Singular	1st 2nd 2nd 3rd 3rd	me/m' (moi) te/t' vous le/l' la/l'	*me* *you* (familiar form) *you* (polite form) *him* (also used to replace non-human masc. nouns) *her* (also used to replace non-human fem. nouns)
Plural	1st 2nd 3rd	nous vous les	*us* *you* (normal plural form) *them* (to replace masculine or feminine human or non- human nouns)

For example:

> Il a perdu sa fille de vue. Est-ce que vous **la** voyez? (vous voyez qui? = sa fille; fem. sing.)   *He has lost sight of his daughter. Do you see her?*

> Tes parents sont là; je **les** ai appelé. (j'ai appelé qui? = tes parents; masc. plur.)   *Your parents are here; I called them.*

Note: When the next word begins with a vowel or mute 'h', **me, te, le** and **la** lose their **e** or **a** to avoid the vowel-vowel clash. For example:

> Cette affiche, nous **l'**avions vue.   *We had seen this poster.* (lit: *this poster, we had seen it.*)

There are a number of points to observe regarding the use of this pronoun:

1   Throughout the system **vous** could refer to a masculine singular, a feminine singular, a masculine plural or a feminine plural. Information about the gender and number of the noun referred to, will be carried by the past participle (if any).

Compare: Je **vous** ai **vu**.   *I have seen you.* (masc. sing.: no **e** and no **s** at the end of **vu**)

and: Je **vous** ai **vue**.   *I have seen you.* (fem. sing.:**e** at the end of **vu**)

and: Je **vous** ai **vus**.   *I have seen you.* (masc. plural: **s** at the end of **vu**)

and: Je **vous** ai **vues**.   *I have seen you.* (fem. plural: **es** at the end of **vu**)

2 The rules concerning gender and number agreement should be respected *every time* the pronoun is used, not only in the case of the past participle, but with any adjective or determiner relating to the pronoun.

Compare: Ils l'ont connu tout petit. *They have known him since he was very small.*

and: Ils l'ont connue toute petite. *They have known her since she was very small.*

Here again, the endings give the clue to the gender and number of the being(s) or thing(s) referred to.

3 A number of English verbs give the impression that they take a direct object complement (accusative) when the recipient is a person. Beware of them: in French they are used with **à** and take an indirect object pronoun. The most frequent of those are:

to allow = permettre (à)	to order = commander (à)/
to ask = demander (à)	ordonner (à)
to forbid = interdire (à)	to permit = permettre (à)
to forgive = pardonner (à)	to sell = vendre (à)
to give = donner (à)	to telephone = téléphoner (à)
to grant = accorder (à)	to write = écrire (à)

With those verbs, the appropriate question to ask would not be **qui/quoi?** (*who/what?*), but **à qui/à quoi?** (*to whom/to what?*), as previously mentioned.

Compare: Tu as vendu la voiture? Oui, je l'ai vendue. (j'ai vendu quoi? = la voiture)
  Have you sold the car? Yes, I have sold it.

and: Tu as vendu la voiture à Robert? Oui, je la **lui** ai vendue. (je l'ai vendue **à qui** =à Robert)
  Have you sold Robert the car?   Yes I have sold it to him.

DO NOT write or say:
  *Je **le** vends la voiture *for*: Je **lui** vends la voiture. *I sell him the car.* (= *to him*)
  or *Elle **le** permet de sortir *for*: Elle **lui** permet de sortir. *She allows him to go out.* (= *to him*).

---

4 There are some verbs in French which admit a direct object (accusative) but which are used in English with a preposition (*for, to, at*). Among those are the following: **attendre** *to wait for*, **demander** *to ask for*, **écouter** *to listen to*, **espérer** *to hope for*, **regarder** *to look at*. For example:

  Nous **les** attendons depuis hier. *We have been waiting for them since yesterday.*

  Voulez-vous **les** écouter? *Do you want to listen to them?*

5   In the positive imperative tense, the pronoun **me** (*me*) is replaced
by **moi**, which is then placed after the verb. For example:

Suivez-**moi**!   *Follow me!*

Ecoutez-**moi**!   *Listen to me!*

but: Ne **me** suivez pas!   *Do not follow me!*

Ne **m**'écoutez pas!   *Do not listen to me*

Indirect object (dative) pronouns

These pronouns are used to replace the noun of the recipient(s) when
the latter is separated from the verb by the preposition **à**.

Number	Person	Pronoun	Meaning
Singular	1st 2nd 2nd 3rd	me/m' (moi) te/t' vous lui	*(to) me* *(to) you* (familiar) *(to) you* (polite form) *(to) him or her* (also used to replace masc. or fem. non-human nouns)
Plural	1st 2nd 3rd	nous vous leur	*(to) us* *(to) you* *(to) them* (used to replace *all* masc. or fem. nouns)

Il faudrait **lui** téléphoner. (téléphoner à qui?)   *We should
telephone him/her.*

J'espère que vous **leur** donnerez le bonjour de ma part. (donner à
qui?)   *I hope that you will give them my regards.* (lit: *that you
will give to them 'good day' from me*)

There are a number of points to observe regarding the use of these
pronouns.

1   Some verbs, although constructed with the preposition **à** (*to*), do
not take the indirect object pronouns but the disjunctive ones when
referring to a *person*. The most common of those verbs are:

aller à		= *to go to*	
courir à		= *to run to*	
penser à	quelqu'un	= *to think of*	somebody
rêver à		= *to dream of*	
venir à		= *to come to*	

For example:

Je pense **à toi**. (and not *je te pense)   *I think of you.*

Elle courut **à moi**. (and not *elle me courut) *She ran towards me.*

2   In the positive imperative, **me** (*to me*) is replaced by **moi**. This, however, *does not* occur in the negative.

Compare: Donnez-**moi** du pain (and not *me donnez du pain) *Give me some bread.*

and: Ne **me** donnez pas de pain. *Do not give me any bread.*

3   Since **lui** can refer to a masculine or to a feminine (human or non-human), this may give rise to some ambiguity. The context should normally clarify the meaning. If, however, you wish to make absolutely clear who or what you are referring to, you may do so by using the appropriate disjunctive pronoun (see below) together with the indirect object pronoun.

Je les ai vus tous les deux; je ne **lui** ai rien dit **à lui,** mais je **lui** ai tout raconté **à elle**.   *I saw them both; I said nothing to him, but I told her everything.*

The pronoun **leur** must not be confused with the possessive adjective **leur/leurs** (*their*). For example:

Je **leur** ai donné leur argent de poche et leurs bonbons.   *I have given them their pocket money and their sweets.*

Disjunctive (or prepositional) pronouns

These pronouns, apart from the specific uses outlined in the above sections — reinforcement of the subject pronoun, replacement of subject pronouns in structures with **et** (*and*) or **ou** (*or*) and in expressions of the type **C'est moi qui . . .** (*it is I who . . .*) or after the positive imperative — *must also be used* whenever the verb and the 'recipient' of the action are linked by a preposition such as **avec** (*with*), **de** (*to/of/about*), **contre** (*against*), **derrière** (*behind*), **devant** (*in front of*), **pour** (*for*), **sous** (*under*), **sur** (*on*), **vers** (*towards*) etc., and in some cases **à** (*of/to*), as previously mentioned.

For example:

Elle a fait une petite promenade à pied avec **eux**.   *She went for a little walk with them.*

Nous ne pouvons rien faire pour **elle**.   *We can do nothing for her.*

Restez derrière **moi**!   *Stay behind me!*

Number	Person	Pronoun	Meaning
Singular	1st	moi	*me/myself*
	2nd	toi	*you/yourself* (familiar form)
	2nd	vous	*you/yourself* (polite form)
	3rd	lui	*him/himself* (also used to replace masc. non-human nouns)
	3rd	elle	*her/herself* (also used to replace fem. non-human nouns)
	3rd	soi	preposition + *one/oneself* (used for human nouns when no specification of the gender is possible or required)
Plural	1st	nous	*us/ourselves*
	2nd	vous	*you/yourselves* (normal plural)
	3rd	eux	*them* (masc. plural)
	3rd	elles	*them* (fem. plural)

There are a number of points to observe regarding the use of these pronouns:

1   It should be remembered that **vous** (*you/yourself/yourselves*) could refer to any of the following:
   (i) a male person;
   (ii) a female person;
   (iii) a group of people (male or male + female);
   (iv) a group of people (female).

Therefore great care should be exercised about possible agreement.

2   **Soi** (*one/oneself*) is, in modern French, only used in connection with the indefinite personal pronoun **on** (*one/somebody*) followed by the 3rd person singular of the appropriate verb. It may, however, refer to an unspecified number of persons. For example:

   On doit toujours porter ses papiers sur **soi**. *One* (= *people*) *must always carry one's* (= *their*) *papers with oneself* (= *them*).

Those two pronouns are used when the speaker or writer does not know (or does not want to specify) the gender of the person or persons concerned.

Very often, French people avoid the use of **on** and **soi** and replace them with **vous** with the appropriate person of the verb. So, the above example often becomes:

> **Vous** devez toujours porter vos papiers sur **vous**. *You must always carry your papers with you.*

3   For the purpose of emphasis or clarification, the word **même(s)** (*self/selves*) is sometimes used after the disjunctive pronoun, particularly to translate the emphatic forms *myself*, *yourself*, etc.

> Elles ont fait tout le travail **elles-mêmes**. *They did all the work themselves.* (fem. plur.)
>
> Je vais vérifier cela **moi-même**. *I am going to check that myself.* (masc./fem. sing.)
>
> On n'est jamais mieux servi que par **soi-même**. (proverb) *Don't count on others* (lit: *one is never better served than by oneself*)

Reflexive pronouns

Such pronouns are used with certain verbs or in certain constructions to indicate that the action stated by the verb 'falls back' on the performer(s). In a reflexive construction, therefore, the reflexive and subject pronouns refer to the same person(s). For example:

> Je **me** prépare à partir. *I am getting ready to go.* (lit: *I am preparing myself to go*)
>
> Nous **nous** arrêtons. *We are stopping.* (lit: *we are stopping ourselves*)

Number	Person	Pronoun	Meaning
Singular	1st 2nd 2nd 3rd	me/m' te/t' vous se/s'	*(to) myself* *(to) yourself* (familiar form) *(to) yourself* (polite form) used for all 3rd persons singular including the impersonal **on**
Plural	1st 2nd 3rd	nous vous se/s'	*(to) ourselves* *(to) yourselves* used for all 3rd persons plural (masc./fem.; sing./plur.; human/non-human)

Note: Although there are in French some verbs which are exclusively reflexive, such as: **s'enfuir** *to flee*, **s'évanouir** *to faint*, etc., there are a great many others which can be used reflexively *or* non-reflexively. It is therefore essential to use the reflexive pronoun wherever the action 'falls back' on to the performer(s), even if in English the reflexive construction (myself, yourself, etc.) is not considered essential or acceptable.

Compare: Il a lavé.   *He has washed (something/someone).*
and: Il s'est lavé.   *He has washed (himself).*
or: Nous regardons les enfants.   *We are looking at the children.*
Nous **nous** regardons.   *We are looking at ourselves.*

For example:
Ce soir, nous **nous** coucherons de bonne heure.   *Tonight we shall go to bed early.* (verb = **se coucher**)
Je **me** suis coupée avec le couteau à pain.   *I cut myself with the bread knife.* (verb = **se couper**)

Notes:
1   The ending of coupée in the previous example indicates that the performer (who is also the recipient) is feminine.
2   **me**, **te** and **se** lose their **e** when the word which follows them begins with a vowel or mute 'h' (to avoid the vowel-vowel clash).

Points to bear in mind regarding the use of these pronouns:
1   From the above examples, it is obvious that the compound tenses of reflexive verbs are always constructed with the auxiliary **être** (and not with **avoir**):
Nous **nous sommes** réveillés à six heures. (and not *nous nous avons réveillés à six heures) *We woke up at six o'clock.* (verb = **se réveiller**)
Je **me suis** trompé (ad not* je m'ai trompé) *I made a mistake* (verb = **se tromper**)
2   It is important, in order to make the past participle agree correctly, to know whether the reflexive verb is constructed with the accusative (direct object) or with the dative (indirect object). The following suggestion may prove useful to distinguish between the two.

(*a*)   reconstruct the sentence *mentally* with the auxiliary **avoir** (*to have*);
(*b*)   then, ask the question **qui?** or **quoi?** after the past participle, as in the case of object pronouns. If the question **qui?** or **quoi?** admits the subject pronoun as an answer, the construction is an

accusative one and the accompanying past participle will agree in gender and number with the subject (i.e. performer). For example:

Elle s'est lav**ée**. (Elle a lavé qui? = elle-même, fem. sing.) *She washed.* (Whom did she wash? =herself)

Ils se sont **vus**. (Ils ont vu qui? = eux-même, masc. plur.) *They saw themselves.* (Whom did they see? = themselves)

But if it is the question **à qui?/à quoi?** which admits the subject pronoun as an answer, this will indicate an indirect object construction and no agreement will be needed. For example:

Elle s' est d**it** que c'était fini. (Elle a dit **à qui** = à elle-même) *She said to herself that it was all over.* (To whom? = to herself)

Ils **se** sont donné deux jours. (Ils ont donné deux jours **à qui?** = à eux-mêmes) *They gave themselves two days.* (They gave to whom? = to themselves)

Compare: Elle s'est donn**ée** à lui. (Elle a donné **qui?** = elle-même) *She gave herself to him.*

and: Elle s'est donn**é** du mal. (Elle a donné du mal **à qui?** = à elle-même) *She went to a lot of trouble.* (lit: *She gave trouble to herself*)

3 Under the heading 'reflexives' are sometimes included verbs which are really 'reciprocal', i.e. denoting that the action of the performer(s) affects the recipient(s) who in turn reciprocate(s). For example:

Robert et Paul **se** sont battus. *Robert and Paul fought (each other),* i.e. *Robert fought Paul and Paul fought Robert.*

Note: It is therefore possible to come across sentences which may be ambiguous. For example **Ils se sont blessés** could mean either *They wounded themselves* (reflexive), or *They wounded each other* (reciprocal).

Usually, the context will clarify the meaning; if the ambiguity needs to be removed, this can be done by selecting the appropriate form from the following: **l'un l'autre, l'une l'autre, les uns les autres, les unes les autres** (*each other/one another*) and placing it after the verb to indicate reciprocity.

Compare: Aidez-**vous**, le ciel vous aidera. (reflexive; proverb) *God helps them that help themselves.* (lit: *help yourself and Heaven will help you*)

and: Aidez-vous **les uns les autres**. *Help one another.* (reciprocal)

4 There is another small group of verbs which also use the reflexive pronouns in their construction. Unlike the previous categories, they

cannot be used without those pronouns. The most common are:
s'écrouler *to collapse*, **s'emparer de** *to seize*, **s'enfuir** *to flee*, **s'évanouir** *to faint*, **se repentir** *to repent*. Here the pronouns have no reflexive value. For example:

La jeune femme **s'**est évanoui**e**. *The young woman fainted.*

Les soldats **se** sont emparés des armes. *The soldiers seized the weapons.*

NB The agreement is made as in the case of direct object reflexives.

Notes:

1 The reason why the above three categories are often treated as one is obviously because they all use the same pronouns (**me, te, se, nous, vous, se**).

2 Normally 'reciprocal' verbs should not be used in the singular (since they need two performers). In practice, however, it is possible with the help of a preposition such as **avec** (*with*), to retain the reciprocal meaning with a singular.

Il **se** bat avec son frère. *He and his brother fight.* (= with each other)

Elle **s'**est disputée avec son mari. *She and her husband had a row.* (= with each other)

5 A reflexive construction is sometimes used idiomatically in French to replace a passive one. For example:

Les oeufs **se vendent** à la douzaine. *Eggs are sold* (lit: *sell themselves*) *by the dozen.*

Un grand bruit **s'**est fait entendre. *A loud noise was* (lit: *made itself*) *heard.*

Cette maison **se** construit vite. *This house is being built* (lit: *building itself*) *quickly.*

The pronouns *en* and *y*

They are often called pronominal adverbs because they can be used both as adverbs and as pronouns.

1 *As adverbs* they are used to indicate the place where (for **y**) and whence (for **en**) the action takes the performer(s). For example:

Il y a le feu à l'usine. J'**y** vais. *There is a fire at the mill. I am going (there).*

Ne parlez pas de la guerre, il **en** vient. *Do not talk about the war, he has just come back (from it).*

2 *As pronouns* they are normally used to replace nouns (or equivalents) referring to things or non-human beings, in sentences where the verb is constructed with the following prepositions:

de *of/with* in the case of **en**

à *to/about* in the case of **y**

before a noun or nominal expression. For example:

> Tu penses à l'accident? Oui j'**y** pense. *Are you thinking about the accident? Yes I'm thinking about it.*
>
> Tu parles du film? Oui j'**en** parle. *Are you talking about the film? Yes I'm talking about it.*

Notes:

1 It is possible to find **en** and **y** used in constructions referring to humans:

> Vous avez parlé de lui? Oui j'**en** ai parlé. *Did you talk about him? Yes I talked about him.*
>
> Pensez-vous à moi? Oui j'**y** pense. *Do you think of me? Yes I do.*

2 **En** can have a partitive meaning (= *some of it/them*):

> Vous avez de la viande? J'**en** veux! *Do you have any meat? I want some!*

3 **Y** is omitted before the future and conditional forms of aller:

> Vous irez la voir? Oui j'irai. (and not *j'y irai) *Will you go and see her? Yes I will (go).*

The position of object pronouns

A close look at the examples given so far in this chapter, reveals that the position of direct object pronouns follows a certain pattern in relation to the verb.

Two cases must be distinguished:

(*a*) constructions where the imperative affirmative is used;

(*b*) all other constructions (including the imperative negative).

We shall examine each case in turn.

Constructions with the verb in the imperative affirmative
The pattern is as follows:

	Number	*Persons*	*1*		*2*	*3*	*4*
			A	**B**			
	Singular	1st 2nd 2nd 3rd	moi (me) toi (te) vous	le, la/l'	moi/m' toi/t' vous lui	Y	en
Verb +	Plural	1st 2nd 3rd	nous vous	les	nous vous leur		

Notes:

1   The combination of pronouns, when permissible, will occur in the order shown (1 to 4).

2   The pronouns of column 1 A and B are direct object pronouns (answers to **qui?/quoi?**).

3   In column 1 A the direct object pronouns **me** and **te**, unacceptable in this context, are replaced by **moi** and **toi** respectively.

4   The pronouns of column 2 are indirect object pronouns (answers to **à qui?/à quoi?**).

5   Some of the pronouns of columns 1 B and 2 lose their vowel when the next word itself begins with a vowel or mute 'h'.

Main combinations and restrictions

1   Only one of the two groups (A *or* B) of column 1 can be used with a given verb.

2   Group B of column 1 can be used before the pronouns of column 2:

> Vendez-**le-moi**.   *Sell it* (masc. sing.) *to me*.
>
> Rends-**la-leur**.   *Give it* (fem. sing.) *back to them*.

3   The pronouns of column 2 should *not* be used with the pronoun of column 3.

4   The pronouns of column 2 can be used with the pronoun of column 4:

> Prêtez-**m'en** deux.   *Lend me* (= *to me*) *two of them*.
>
> Donne-**nous-en** un morceau.   *Give us* (= *to us*) *a piece of it*.

The verb in any other tense (including the imperative negative)

In this case the object pronouns are placed, in the order shown, before the verb (in a simple tense construction) or before the auxiliary (in a compound tense construction).

Number	Person	1 A	1 B	2	3	4	5	
Singular	1st 2nd 2nd 3rd	se/s'	me/m' te/t' vous	le, la/l'	lui	y	en	} + Verb aux
Plural	1st 2nd 3rd	se/s'	nous vous	les	leur			

Notes:

1   The combination of these pronouns, when permissible, will occur in the order shown (1 to 5).

2   Some of the pronouns of columns 1 and 2 lose their vowel when the next word itself begins with a vowel or mute 'h'.

3   The pronouns of column 1 B represent the following three categories: *direct object* (accusative), *indirect object* (dative) and *reflexive*; since they have the same form and are mutually exclusive, little harm is done by having one column instead of three.

4   The pronouns of column 2 are direct object pronouns (answers to **qui?/quoi?**).

5   The pronouns of column 3 are indirect object pronouns (answers to **à qui?/à quoi?**).

Main combinations and restrictions

1   Only one of the two groups (A *or* B) of column 1 can be used in 'good' French with a given verb.

2   The pronouns of column 1 B can *only* be used in connection with those of column 2 *if* they are indirect object (dative), or reflexive

> Je **vous le** donne.   *I am giving it* (masc. sing.) *to you.*
>
> Est-ce que vous **nous les** avez rendus?   *Have you given them back to us?*

Note: The ending of **rendus** indicates that **les** refers to a masculine plural noun.

3   The direct object pronouns of column 2 can be used with the indirect pronouns of column 3:

> Vous allez **la lui** présenter.   *You are going to introduce her to him* (or *her*).
>
> Nous regrettons de ne pas **la leur** avoir donnée.   *We regret not having given it* (fem. sing.) *to them.*

Note: The object pronouns are placed before the verb which they relate to *even* if it is in the infinitive mood.

4   The direct object pronouns of column 2 can be used with either that of column 4 *or* 5:

> Elle **l'y** a poussé.   *She pushed him to it.*
>
> Je **l'en** avais averti.   *I had warned him of it.*

5   The pronouns of column 1 can be used before the one in column 4:

> Vous **m'y** faites penser.   *You make me think of it.*

6   The pronouns of column 4 and 5 can usually be used together:

> Nous **y en** avons discuté.   *We discussed about it there.*

Demonstrative pronouns

Demonstrative pronouns are used to 'single out' the noun they replace. They can be divided into two groups with unequal demonstrative power. Except in the case of neutral pronouns (see below) they vary according to the gender and number of the noun they represent. For example:

> Je vais prendre **celui-ci** et **celle-là**.   *I shall take this one* (masc. sing.) *and that one.* (fem. sing.).

The two groups are as follows:

Simple (one-word) demonstrative pronouns

As their demonstrative power is weak, extra information is needed to clarify the identity of the noun they represent. That is why they have to be accompanied by a relative clause (giving additional information about the noun they refer to, with or without a preposition (**à** *to*, **de** *of/from*, **avec** *with*, **contre** *against*, **pour** *for*, **sans** *without*, etc.

	Singular		Plural
Masc.	celui	neutral form = ce	ceux
Fem.	celle		celles

Points to bear in mind regarding the use of these pronouns:

1   The neutral form **ce**, which is still considered as a masculine singular for agreement purposes, is used when the speaker is unable (or unwilling) to ascribe a specific gender or number to the noun which the pronoun replaces.

Compare: Voici des fruits; prenez **celui** que vous voulez.   *Here is some fruit; take the one you wish.* (**fruit** = masc.)

and: Voici des fruits; prenez **ce** que vous voulez.   *Here is some fruit; take what (whatever) you wish.*

or: Il y a trois menus. Choisissez **celui** qui vous plaît.   *There are three menus. Choose the one you like.* (**menu** = masc.)

and: Voilà la carte. Choisissez **ce** qui vous plaît.   *Here is the list of dishes. Choose what you like.*

In the first instance the pronoun refers to a specific noun, so a gender can easily be ascribed to it, whereas in the second, the thing referred to is vague, unspecified.

2   Be sure not to forget to make the necessary gender and number agreements if there are adjectives or past participles involved:

Cette cliente est **celle** qui est venu**e** ce matin. (**cliente** = fem. sing.)   *This customer is the one who came this morning.*

Ces clefs sont **celles** que j'avais laiss**ées** sur la table. (**clés** = fem. plur.)   *These keys are the ones I had left on the table.*

3   There are a few cases when the neutral form **ce** can be used without an accompanying clause. It can be explained by the fact that, in such constructions, **ce** is really a modification of **cela**, which belongs to the second category of demonstrative pronouns. For example:

Ce disant, (= en disant cela) il ouvrit le coffre-fort. *As he was saying that, he opened the safe.*

4 **Celui** and **ceux** can often be used to refer to a person or persons of either sex.

Celui qui sortira le dernier fermera la porte. *The person who comes out last will close the door.*

Que **ceux** qui ne sont pas contents le disent. *Let those who are not happy say so.* (*those* = *the people*)

Compound (two-word) demonstrative pronouns

They are formed by combining the above pronouns with **-ci** (*here*) or **-là** (*there*) to distinguish between things or beings relatively closer or further away, in space or time, from the speaker. They have a very strong demonstrative value and are used to replace a noun preceded by a demonstrative adjective. Unlike the first category, they can function on their own (i.e. without additional information). Their form varies according to the gender and number of the noun they replace.

Note: **ceci**, **cela** and **ça** can be seen as contractions of **ce . . . ici** and **ce . . . là** and therefore deserve the denomination 'compound demonstrative pronouns'.

	Singular		*Plural*
Masc.	celui-ci celui-là	*neutral sense:* ceci cela/ça	ceux-ci ceux-là
Fem.	celle-ci celle-là		celles-ci celles-là

Points to bear in mind regarding the use of these pronouns:

1 Although in theory **-ci** is supposed to refer to someone or something relatively closer in space or time, and **-là** to someone or something relatively further away, pronouns formed with **là** are preferred in everyday French, except in cases where some misunderstanding is likely to occur. For example:

Quel costume prenez-vous, **celui-ci** ou **celui-là**? (costume = masc. sing.) *Which suit are you taking, this one or that one?*

Ouvrez cette fenêtre-ci; **celle-là** est bloquée (fenêtre = fem. sing.) *Open this window; that one won't open.* (lit: *is blocked*)

But: J'ai besoin d'un cendrier; passez-moi **celui-là**.   *I need an ash-tray; pass me this (or that) one.*
2   The neutral forms **ceci** and **cela/ça** (without an accent!), whilst being considered masculine-singular for the purpose of agreement, are used when the subject is unable (or unwilling) to ascribe a specific gender or number to the noun they replace. For example:

Il est toujours en retard; **cela** est irritant.   *He is always late; that is irritating.* (that = the fact that he is always late)
Faites ce que vous voulez, **ça** m'est égal.   *Do what you want, it's all the same to me.* (it = whatever you want to do)

3   **Ça** is used in familiar French to replace **cela** which seems to be considered as elevated in style. In this case, the pronoun often retains its vowel *even* when the next word begins with a vowel:

Ça a marché! (fam.)   *It worked!*

4   A distinction between what has been said and what is going to be said can be made by using a pronoun with **-là** (in the first case) and **-ci** (in the second).

Compare: Ecoutez-bien **ceci**: Je veux que vous partiez à l'instant.   *Listen carefully to this: I want you to go this minute.*
and: J'exige la vérité, rappelez-vous **cela**.   *I demand the truth, remember that.*

Possessive pronouns

Possessive pronouns are used to replace a 'noun phrase' containing a possessive adjective or, more generally, whenever ownership needs to be indicated.

They are equivalent to **mine**, **yours**, **his/hers**, etc. in English:

C'est le sac de ta soeur? Oui c'est **le sien**.   *Is it your sister's bag? Yes it's hers.*

> It is crucial to remember that, in French, the possessive pronoun agrees with the being or thing owned and not with the owner.

Since possessive pronouns replace nouns which can vary in gender *and* number, they have different forms to indicate those variations.

Compare: J'ai trouvé un sac. C'est **le mien**! (sac = masc. sing.)   *I have found a bag. It is mine!*
and: J'ai trouvé une montre. C'est **la mienne**! (montre = fem. sing.)   *I have found a watch. It is mine!*

Owner	person	Owned				Meaning
		one		*more than one*		
		masculine	feminine	masculine	feminine	
one	1st	le mien	la mienne	les miens	les miennes	*mine*
	2nd	le tien	la tienne	les tiens	les tiennes	*yours* (familiar)
	2nd	le vôtre	la vôtre	les vôtres	les vôtres	*yours* (polite form)
	3rd	le sien	la sienne	les siens	les siennes	*his/hers/its*
more than one	1st	le nôtre	la nôtre	les nôtres	les nôtres	*ours*
	2nd	le vôtre	la vôtre	les vôtres	les vôtres	*yours* (normal plur.)
	3rd	le leur	la leur	les leurs	les leurs	*theirs*

For example:

> Pouvez-vous me prêter une carte? J'ai perdu **la mienne**. *Can you lend me a map? I have lost mine.* (**carte** = fem. sing.)

> Ne touchez pas à ces livres; ce sont **les miens**. (**livres** = masc. plur.) *Do not touch those books; they are mine.*

There are a number of points to bear in mind regarding the use of these pronouns:

1 Since those pronouns include a definite article, **le, la, les**, that article will combine in the normal way with **à** (*at/to*) and **de** (*of/from*) when those prepositions precede the pronoun. For example:

> Quand je parle de problèmes, je ne pense pas **aux vôtres** mais **aux miens**. (**problèmes** = masc. plur.) *When I am talking about problems, I am not thinking of yours but of mine.*

2 In some idiomatic expressions it has become difficult, if not impossible, to find out what noun the possessive pronoun stands for. Such expressions have to be remembered and used *as they are*:

> A **la vôtre**! *or* A **la** bonne **vôtre**! *Your health!* or *Your very good health!*

> Il y met **du sien**. *He is pulling his weight.*

> Elle a encore fait **des siennes**. *She has been up to her old tricks again.*

3 Unlike the possessive adjectives, which they resemble, **nôtre** and **vôtre** as pronouns take a circumflex accent in all cases:

> Ce n'est pas votre tour, c'est **le nôtre**. *It is not your* (adj.) *turn it's ours.* (pron.)

4 The masculine plural possessives -**les miens, les tiens**, etc. — can be used to refer to parents or relatives. For example:

> Je vous déteste, vous et **les vôtres**! *I hate you and your family!*

5 The 3rd person singular possessive pronouns -**le sien, la sienne**, etc. — can be used with the indefinite subject pronoun **on** (*one/*

somebody) or any other singular indefinite adjective or pronoun with the meaning of *one's own*:

> J'ai apporté les cadeaux: chacun aura **le sien**.   *I have brought the presents: everyone will have his own.*
>
> Voulez-vous ma voiture? Non, tout le monde a **la sienne**. *Do you want my car? No, they all have their own.*

Relative pronouns

Relative pronouns are words used to connect a noun or phrase they represent (called the antecedent), with a sense-group which follows (called a relative clause) and which contains useful additional information about the antecedent. They correspond to the English pronouns *what, which, who, whom, that*. For example:

> Voici l'*homme* **qui** vous a insulté.   *Here is the man who insulted you.*
>
> Voilà l'*endroit* **où** j'ai vu l'animal.   *There is the spot where I saw the animal.*

(The word in bold is the pronoun; the one in bold italic the antecedent.)

Relative pronouns can be divided into the following two categories:

Simple (one-word) relative pronouns

They do not vary according to the gender or number of the antecedent.

For example:

> C'est lui **qui** est parti le premier.   *It is he who went first.*
>
> Le travail **que** vous faites est excellent.   *The work you are doing is excellent.*
>
> Connaissez-vous la ville **où** je suis né?   *Do you know the town where I was born?*
>
> C'est un film **dont** on parle beaucoup.   *It is a film which people talk a great deal about.*

Note: **que** will lose its **e** when the next word begins with a vowel or a mute 'h' to avoid the vowel-vowel clash:

> J'aime le disque **qu'**il a acheté.   *I like the record he bought:*

Form	Usage	Meaning
qui	It is used to refer to the subject (performer) of the action, whether thing or being. It can be used on its own or with prepositions.	*who/which/whom* (subject)
que	It is used to refer to the object (recipient) of the action, whether thing or being. It *cannot* be used with a preposition.	*that/which/whom* (direct object)
quoi	It is used to refer to things only and is *always* preceded by a preposition.	(*with, on, above*, etc.) *which*
dont	It is used to replace constructions in which the noun was preceded by the preposition **de** (*of/from*). It can refer to things *or* beings.	*of which/of whom/where*
où	It is used to indicate position or destination in space or time. It can be used with certain prepositions: **de**, **par**, **vers**, etc.	*where (when)*

Points to bear in mind when using these pronouns:
1   All the above pronouns, with the exception of **quoi**, can refer to things or beings:
>   Regardez les rochers **qui** sont tombés.   *Look at the rocks which have fallen.*
2   **Quoi**, which refers to things only and must be preceded by a preposition, is very often used in neutral constructions with **ce**, when the gender or number of the thing(s) referred to is not known, or not clearly defined:
>   Vous savez **ce** à **quoi** je fais allusion.   *You know what I am alluding to.* (lit: *that to which I am alluding*)
3   In sentences where the antecedent of the relative pronoun **que** is not clearly stated, the neutral demonstrative **ce** will automatically be used as antecedent. This is *not* the case in English:
Compare: Je ne comprends pas **ce** qu'il veut.
and: *I don't understand what* (lit: *that which*) *he wants.*
or: Faites **ce que** vous pouvez.
and: *Do what* (lit: *that which*) *you can.*
4   Whereas in English it is sometimes acceptable to omit certain relative pronouns, it is not possible to do so in French:

Compare: C'est cette plage **que** je préfère.

and: *It is this beach (that) I prefer.*

or: Le vendeur à **qui** j'ai parlé est malade.

and: *The salesman (whom) I talked to is ill.*

5   Although **qui** and **quoi** can be used immediately after the preposition **de** (*of/from*) to introduce a relative clause, a construction with **dont** will normally be preferred:

Possible: La victime **de qui** j'ai entendu les cris . . .

Preferred: La victime **dont** j'ai entendu les cris . . .

           The victim whose screams I heard . . .

Possible: La chose **de quoi** vous parlez est scandaleuse.

Preferred: La chose **dont** vous parlez est scandaleuse.

           The thing you are talking about is scandalous.

6   Relative pronouns are regularly used after the simple demonstrative pronouns **celui, celle, ceux, celles** (*the one(s)*). For example:

    Prenez **celui que** vous préferez.   *Take the one* (masc. sing.) *you prefer.*

Note: **Ce** will be used in such a construction when the speaker does not know, or does not wish to state, what the gender or number of the antecedent is:

    Dites-moi **ce qui** vous inquiète.   *Tell me what (the thing which) worries you.*

7   Compound demonstrative pronouns — **celui-ci, celle-là**, etc. — can also be used before single relative pronouns when a very strong demonstrative meaning is required:

    Je vais prendre **celui-ci, qui** a l'air plus tendre.   *I shall take this one* (masc. sing.), *which seems more tender.*

Note: In such cases, the demonstrative and the relative pronouns are normally separated by a comma.

8   **Qui** is sometimes used in idiomatic phrases to refer to any individual, male *or* female, with the meaning of *whoever* or *he/she who*:

    Qui va à la chasse perd sa place. (*saying*)   *He who leaves the queue loses his place.* (lit: *He who goes hunting . . .*)

    Qui dort dîne. (*saying*)   *He who goes to sleep will not feel hunger pangs.* (lit: *He who sleeps dines*)

9   **Que** is sometimes used in proverbs and sayings as a subject pronoun instead of **qui**:

    Advienne **que** pourra. (**que** = **ce qui**)   *Come what may.*

10   Certain relative clauses introduced by **qui** can be replaced by a present participle, providing the verb they contain describes an action in progress at the time.

Compare: Je vis mon père **qui** lisait son journal.

and: Je vis mon père **lisant** son journal. *I saw my father (who was) reading his paper.*

In such cases the present participle remains **invariable**.

11 Although the pronoun **où** is generally used to give spatial information, it can also be used in French with expressions of time. Its English equivalent is then *when*:

Compare: C'était l'époque **où** j'étais heureux.

and: *It was the time when I was happy.*

or: Le jour **où** tout ira bien . . . *The day when everything will be fine . . .*

Compound (two-word) relative pronouns

These pronouns are formed by the relevant combination of the definite article *and* the pronoun **quel** (*which*) 'welded' together. They vary according to the gender and number of their antecedent. They are normally used in constructions involving a preposition — **à** (*at/to*), **pour** (*for*), **sans** (*without*), etc. — as are their English equivalents *which/whom*.

	Sing.	*Plur.*
Masc.	lequel	lesquels
Fem.	laquelle	lesquelles

For example:

L' idéal pour **lequel** nous luttons. (**idéal** = masc. sing.) *The ideal which we are fighting for.*

C'est l'homme avec **lequel** je travaille. (**homme** = masc. sing.) *It is the man whom I work with.*

Note: Since those pronouns include the definite article **le, la, les**, it is logical to expect that, when they occur immediately after the prepositions **à** and **de**, they will combine with them in the following way:

with **à**: auquel, à laquelle, auxquels, auxquelles

with **de**: duquel, de laquelle, desquels, desquelles

Ces vacances **auxquelles** je pense sans arrêt. (**vacances** = fem. plur.) *Those holidays which I think about all the time.*

Je ne connais pas l'incident **auquel** vous faites allusion. (**incident** = masc. sing.) *I do not know the incident you are alluding to.*

Points to bear in mind regarding the use of these pronouns:

1　In French, the preposition which is used with the pronoun *must* be placed immediately before it. In English, it is normal to place the preposition at the end of the clause.

Compare:　Le stylo **avec lequel** il écrivait.　*The pen (which) he was writing with.*

> The French relative pronoun *cannot* be omitted in any circumstances.

2　In constructions where the compound relative is to appear immediately after the preposition **de**, the use of **dont** is normally preferred. This makes for a shorter, more elegant sentence.

Compare:　C'est la vie **de laquelle** il rêve.

and:　C'est la vie **dont** il rêve.　*That is the life he is dreaming of.*

or:　Les monuments **desquels** vous parlez.

and:　Les monuments **dont** vous parlez.　*The monuments you are talking about.*

But:　If the antecedent is separated from the relative by a prepositional phrase, **dont** cannot be used:

　La dame **dans l'auto** de laquelle j'ai laissé mon sac.　*The lady in whose car I left my bag.*

　Le bâtiment **à l'entrée** duquel il se tenait.　*The building at the entrance of which he stood.*

3　**Lequel, laquelle, lesquels, lesquelles** are sometimes used to replace the subject pronoun **qui** to give a feeling of emphasis or to avoid ambiguity.

　Il téléphona à sa soeur, **laquelle** lui annonça la nouvelle.　*He telephoned his sister, (and it was she) who told him the news.*

　Le fils du boulanger, **lequel** était fort riche, acheta la ferme.　*The son of the baker who* (the son) *was very rich, bought the farm.*

Note concerning relative clauses introduced by single or compound pronouns:　The learner must bear in mind that agreement rules, whenever applicable, must be respected across clause boundaries.

　Les photos que nous avons prises et qui sont prêtes, sont excellentes.　*The photos that we took and which are ready are excellent.*

The participle and adjectives agree with **photos** = fem. plur.

Interrogative pronouns

Interrogative pronouns are used to formulate direct or indirect questions (see below) about the thing(s) or being(s) they relate to.

With the exception of **dont**, they are identical with the relative pronouns presented in the preceding section. They are the equivalents of the English interrogatives *who, whom, what, where*, etc. They can, with the exception of **que** (*what*), be used with a preposition which will be placed immediately before them. For example:

Pour qui travaillez-vous? *Who do you work for?*

Avec quoi écrivez-vous? *What are you writing with?*

As in the case of the relatives, we shall divide them into two categories:

Simple (one-word) interrogative pronouns

Form	Usage	Meaning
Qui . . . ?	It is used to refer to persons only. It can be used alone or with a preposition.	*Who? Whom?*
Que . . . ?	It is used to refer to things or non-human beings only. It cannot be used with a preposition.	*What?*
Quoi . . . ?	It is used to formulate a question about things when a preposition is present. (it can also be used on its own in a small number of cases.)	(*With, For, on . . .) What?*
Où . . . ?	It is used to ask information about the position or destination of a thing or being. It can be used with *or* without a preposition	*Where?*

For example:

Qui est là? *Who is there?*

Que décidons-nous? *What are we deciding?*

Par quoi allez-vous commencer? *What are you going to begin with?*

Où veux-tu aller? *Where do you want to go?*

Note: When followed by a word beginning with a vowel, or a mute 'h', **que** becomes **qu'** to avoid the vowel-vowel clash:

Qu' avez-vous dit? *What did you say?*

Qu' est-ce qu'il y a? *What is the matter?*

Compound (two-word) interrogative pronouns

Their two constitutive elements (matching definite article and pronoun) are 'welded' together. They vary according to the gender and number of the thing(s) or being(s) they refer to and their use suggests the formulation of a choice. They correspond to the English pronoun *Which one(s)?*

	Sing.	*Plur.*
Masc.	lequel	lesquels
Fem.	laquelle	lesquelles

Notes:

1   The above pronouns combine with the prepositions **à** and **de** in precisely the same way as the similar relative pronouns:

> **Auquel** de ces deux livres tenez-vous le plus? (**livre** = masc.)
> *Which one of those books do you value most?*
>
> J'ai deux frères. **Duquel** parlez-vous? (**frère** = masc.)   *I have two brothers. Which one are you talking about?*

2   Compound interrogative pronouns can be used on their own or with a preposition:

> J'ai vu un des dossier. Ah oui? **Lequel?**   *I saw one of the files. Oh yes? Which one?*
>
> Ils ont deux filles. **Avec laquelle** sortez-vous?   *They have two daughters. Which one are you going out with?*

Points to bear in mind regarding the use of simple and compound interrogative pronouns:

1   Simple (one-word) pronouns do *not* carry any gender or number information. They can therefore refer to any number of things or beings of either gender:

> **Qui** est venu à la réunion?   *Who came to the meeting?*
>
> **Où** irez-vous? En France, en Espagne et au Portugal!   *Where will you go? To France, Spain and Portugal!*
>
> **Que** plantez-vous? Des légumes!   *What are you planting? Vegetables!*

2   **Qui**, **quoi** and **où** can be used on their own or with a preposition:

> **Qui** viendra me chercher?   *Who will come and fetch me?*
>
> **Avec qui** partez-vous?   *Who are you going with?*
>
> **Où** se cachent-ils?   *Where are they hiding?*
>
> **Par où** sont-ils descendus?   *Which way did they go down?*

3   All interrogative pronouns can be used in elliptical (i.e. shortened) constructions with an infinitive. In such cases, the performer of the action is not stated but the context should make

things clear. In the following examples *one* is arbitrarily used as the subject.

Qui croire? *Who is one to believe?*

Que faire? *What should one do?*

Où aller? *Where should one go?*

or: **Lequel** choisir? *Which (one) should one choose?*

4 Questions are classified into two distinct categories:

(a) Those asked *directly* to someone, as in a face to face dialogue. In this case, the question stands on its own as an independent clause (this is the case in all the above examples), and ends with a question mark.

(b) Those asked *indirectly*. In this case, it is as if the speaker were asking the question to himself. Indirect questions normally follow a main clause in which verbs like **se demander** (*to wonder*), **ne pas savoir** (*not to know*), **n'être pas sûr** (*not to be sure*) etc. are used.

Compare: **Avec qui** déjeunez-vous? (direct)

Who are you having lunch with?

and: Je ne sais pas **avec qui** vous déjeunez. (indirect)

I do not know who you are having lunch with.

The distinction between direct and indirect questions is important because the word order used in the formulation of the question may differ:

In direct questions there is (normally) an inversion: the verb is followed by the pronoun. For example:

Où sont-ils? *Where are they?*

Avec quoi écrirez-vous? *What will you write with?*

In indirect questions there is no inversion: the normal word order is preserved. For example:

Je ne sais pas **où** ils sont. *I do not know where they are.*

Je me demande **avec quoi** vous écrirez. *I wonder what you will write with.*

Note: Question marks are *not* used at the end of indirect questions.

5 In ordinary French (written and spoken) it is possible to formulate questions about people in the following ways. Instead of just beginning a question with **qui** we can say **Qui est-ce qui** . . . (subject) or **Qui est-ce que** . . . (object). For example:

Qui est-ce qui parle? = **Qui** parle? *Who is speaking?*

Qui est-ce que vous invitez? = **Qui** invitez-vous? *Who are you inviting?*

6   It is also possible to formulate questions about things or non-human beings in a similar way. Instead of beginning a question with **que** we can say **Qu'est-ce qui** . . . (subject-with impersonal verbs) or **Qu'est-ce que** . . . (object). For example:

> **Qu'est-ce qui** se passe? = **Que** se passe t-il? *What is happening?*
>
> **Qu'est-ce que** tu fais? = **Que** fais-tu? *What are you doing?*

7   It is possible to use similar structures with **où** (or **quoi** if preceded by a preposition). For example:

> **Où est-ce qu'**ils habitent? = **Où** habitent ils? *Where do they live?*

Note: The above alternative structures can be used with a preposition, *except* when they replace que, as in 6 above:

> **Avec qui est-ce que** tu sors? *Who are you going out with?*
>
> **D'où est-ce que** tu viens? *Where are you coming from?*

The less elevated but nevertheless correct ways of formulating a question outlined in 5, 6 and 7 above, eliminate the need for a change in word order, often perceived as highbrow by ordinary speakers. This perception explains why, in 'spoken' French, the inversion is often not made, *even* in the absence of the alternatives mentioned above.

Compare: **Où** vas-tu? ('good' French)

> **Où est-ce que** tu vas? ('ordinary' French)
>
> **Où** tu vas? ('spoken' French) *Where are you going?*

or: **A qui** téléphonez-vous? ('good' French)

> **A qui est-ce que** vous téléphonez? ('ordinary' French)
>
> **A qui** vous téléphonez? ('spoken' French)
>
> *Who are you telephoning?*

> **De quoi** parliez-vous? ('good' French)
>
> **De quoi est-ce que** vous parliez? ('ordinary' French)
>
> **De quoi** vous parliez? ('spoken' French)
>
> *What were you talking about?*

Indefinite pronouns

Indefinite pronouns are used when no precise indications are given about the identity — or number — of things or beings referred to. They correspond to the English pronouns *everybody*, *nobody*, *people*, *someone/somebody* etc.

Note: If an indefinite pronoun does not have a plural form, it cannot be used in a plural construction; conversely, if a pronoun has no singular form, it cannot be used in a singular construction.

So, you must

say or write: **Quelqu'un a** frappé. *Someone knocked.*

and not: ***Quelqu'un ont** frappé.

or: **Plusieurs ont** péri. *Several perished.*

and not: *** Plusieurs a** péri.

or: **Tout le monde est** malade. *Everyone is ill.*

and not: *** Tout le monde sont** malades.

It is very important to remember those constraints to avoid making strings of agreement mistakes. For example:

Chacun est content. *Everyone* (masc. sing.) *is happy.*

Chacune est contente. *Everyone* (fem. sing.) *is happy.*

Certains sont descendus. *Some* (masc. plur.) *went down.*

Certaines sont descendues. *Some* (fem. plur.) *went down.*

On s'était perdu dans le noir. *One* (masc. sing. i.e. *people*) *had got lost in the dark.*

Points to bear in mind regarding the use of these pronouns:

1 The pronouns of Group I (meaning = 'none') are normally used with the negative particle **ne**. For example:

Personne n'a voulu attendre. *Nobody wanted to wait.*

Rien n'a changé. *Nothing has changed.*

Aucun ne bougea. *No-one* (masc. sing.) *moved.*

In such sentences, the **verb** is in the **singular** and the negative particle **pas** must *not* be used.

2 Very rarely, the expression **d'aucuns** (*some people*) can be encountered in sentences of the type:

D'aucuns disent que . . . *Some people say that . . .*

3 **Autrui** is used as a masculine singular, usually with a preposition:

Soyez bon **envers autrui**. *Be kind to your fellow-beings.*

4 **Certains, certaines** (*some*), are only used in the plural:

Certains disent qu'il a quitté sa femme. *Some say he has left his wife.*

5 The pronouns **l'un, l'autre**, etc. are often used in the same sentence to distinguish between two individual things or beings or two groups:

La vieille avait deux fils; **l'un** était médecin, **l'autre** journaliste. *The old woman had two sons; one was a doctor, the other (was) a journalist.*

6 There is often hesitation as to whether agreement with **plus d'un** should be in the singular or the plural. Both are usually accepted and you could say or write

either: **Plus d'un a** refusé.

or: **Plus d'un ont** refusé.

More than one refused.

| | VARIATIONS | | | | MEANING | |
| | Singular | | Plural | | | |
	masc.	fem.	masc.	fem.	sing.	plur.
GROUP I number referred	aucun	aucune	—	—	no-one	—
	nul	(nulle)	—	—	none	—
	pas un	pas une	—	—	*not a single one*	—
to = none	personne	—	—	—	nobody	—
	rien	—	—	—	nothing	—
GROUP II	—	—	d'aucuns	d'aucunes	—	some (people)
	autrui	—	—	—	*every fellow human*	—
number	—	—	certains	certaines	—	some
	chacun	chacune	—	—	each one	—
	le même	la même	les mêmes	les mêmes	the same	the same ones
referred to = one or more	l'un	l'une	les uns	les unes	one	some
	l'autre	l'autre	les autres	les autres	the other	(the) others

n'importe qui	—	—	—	{anyone {whatever	—
n'importe quoi	—	—	—	{anything {whatever	—
plus d'un	plus d'une	plus d'un	plus d'une	more than one	more than one
quelqu'un	quelqu'une	quelques-uns	quelques-unes	someone	some (people)
qui que				whoever	—
quiconque				whosoever	—
quoi que				whatever	—
tel	telle	tels	telles	such (a)	such
tout	toute	tous	toutes	{everything {everyone {everybody	all
tout le monde	—	—	—		—

NB The dashes signal that certain forms of a given pronoun are not available; any necessary agreement (of verbs, adjectives, past participles) should be made accordingly.

7   **Qui que** (*whoever*) and **quoi que** (*whatever*) are both used as masculine singulars and *must* be followed by a verb in the subjunctive mood:

> **Quoi que** vous fassiez, vous ne gagnerez pas.   *Whatever you do, you shall not win.*

8   **On** (*one*) is used in singular constructions as a subject pronoun:

> **On** mange pour vivre.   *One eats (in order) to survive.*

In addition, **on** may sometimes be used to replace any one of the subject pronouns in familiar French:

> **On** sort ce soir?   *Are we going out tonight?*
>
> Ah je vois, **on** se repose!   *Oh I see, you are having a rest!*
>
> **On** travaille dur au Japon.   *They work hard in Japan.*

9   **Quiconque** (*whoever*) is always used as a masculine singular and any agreement should be made accordingly:

> **Quiconque** a accepté ne le regrettera pas!   *Whoever agreed shall not regret it!*

10   Although **tout** is generally used with the meaning of *everything*, it can also mean *everyone*. In both cases, agreement is made in the singular.

Compare: **Tout** est en ordre.   *Everything is in order.*

and: **Tout** dormait dans la ville.   *Everyone was asleep in the town.*

Key points

1   Pronouns are grammatical words used to replace noun-phrases, thereby avoiding tiresome repetitions. They can, in certain circumstances, even replace whole sentences.

2   There are six distinct categories of pronouns: personal, demonstrative, possessive, relative, interrogative and indefinite. Each of these has a specific grammatical role.

3   Personal pronouns serve to indicate the performer(s) or recipient(s) of an action. *Note*: It should be remembered that the French system makes it *imperative* that *all* suitable agreements (masculine/feminine, singular/plural) of adjectives, past participles, etc. be made as appropriate.

4   The indefinite pronoun **on** can only be used as a subject pronoun and *must*, in 'good' French, be followed by the 3rd person singular of the relevant verb.

5   Direct object (accusative) pronouns must *not* be confused with indirect object (dative) pronouns. The former replace the direct object complement (answer to **qui?/quoi?**). The latter replace the indirect object complement (answer to **à qui?/à quoi?**).

6   There are very clear rules for the agreement of the past participle in transitive and intransitive constructions. Those rules should be followed faithfully.

7   Certain verbs function differently in the two languages; their construction (accusative, dative, etc.) should be carefully checked, since the choice of the suitable pronoun is dictated by the type of construction involved.

8   Disjunctive pronouns must be used after prepositions (**à, de, pour, sans,** etc.). In addition, they may appear in certain circumstances to replace *or* reinforce subject pronouns.

9   Reflexive pronouns serve to indicate constructions in which the action performed by the subject 'falls back' upon him/her (reflexive) or affects someone else, who in turn reciprocates (reciprocal).

10   Although a small number of verbs *cannot* be used in non-reflexive (or more accurately non-pronominal) constructions, e.g. **s'enfuir** (*to escape*), **s'évanouir** (*to faint*), etc., many others can be constructed non-reflexively as well as reflexively.

11   The prescribed rules of gender and number agreement apply in reflexive constructions whenever appropriate.

12   The relative position of the above pronouns in a sentence is fixed and the rules governing it must be adhered to. It should be noted, however, that a special set of rules applies if the verb is in the Imperative *positive* Tense.

13   Demonstrative pronouns are used to 'single out' the noun they replace. If, for any reason, special emphasis is required, simple (one word) pronouns may be reinforced with the use of the appropriate particle **-ci** (*here*) or **-là** (*there*).

14   The neutral form **ce** (*this/that*) is used whenever it is not possible — or desirable — to ascribe a definite gender or number to the thing(s) referred to.

15   Possessive pronouns agree in gender *and* number with the noun of the thing(s) or being(s) 'owned' and not, as in English, with that of the 'owner'.

16   Relative pronouns are used to introduce subordinate (relative) clauses. Those pronouns *represent* the noun-phrase expressed in the (preceding) main clause.

17   In French, it is *not possible* to omit relative pronouns.

18   Relative pronouns preceded by **de** are normally replaced by **dont** (*whose/of which*).

19   Interrogative pronouns are used to formulate direct or indirect questions. With the exceptions of **dont**, they are identical with the relative pronouns. It must be remembered that the word order in *direct* questions is often not the same as in *indirect* ones.

20   Indefinite pronouns are used when no precise indications are available about the gender or number of things or beings referred to.

21   Indefinite pronouns can be divided into two groups:

(*a*)   those referring to 'zero things or beings'. They are used in *negative* constructions with **ne** (but *not* with **pas**) and the verb of the sentence *must* be in the singular;

(*b*)   those referring to 'one or more things or beings'. With those, the correct gender *and* number agreements *must* be made as appropriate.

22   Some indefinite pronouns have no singular form. Others have no plural. Any necessary agreement (of verb, adjective(s), etc.) must be made accordingly.

SECTION II

*Some More Jigsaw Pieces:
The Verb and Its Associates*

12 Tenses, Moods, Voices; Types of Verbs

Note: This is an important chapter which you are advised to read carefully before proceeding to the study of verbs.

General introduction to Tenses

Language learners are sometimes disconcerted by the large number of tenses which are used in French, as in other languages, to situate events in time. Yet those tenses are necessary to give our speech the shades of meaning needed for efficient and unambiguous communication.

Different languages have different ways of indicating whether something happens regularly, is happening now, happened in the past, will happen in the future, would happen (or have happened) if . . . , etc. Such information is usually conveyed by one of several tenses.

In French, tenses can be divided into 2 categories:

1   Tenses where the verbal group is made up of one word only; they are called *simple tenses*. The verb is made up of two distinct sections 'welded' together: a stem and an ending. Whereas the stem will remain reasonably stable, the ending will vary according *to the person performing* the action and also *according to the tense required*: In the following examples the stem is marked in bold, the ending is italic:

   Nous **regard***ons*   *We are looking* (Present)

   Je **parl***ais*   *I was talking* (Imperfect)

   Elle **arriver***a*   *She will arrive* (Future)

2   Tenses where the verbal group is made up of several words (usually two): the auxiliary and the main verb; such tenses are called *compound tenses*. In this category, the main verb will remain reasonably stable; it is the auxiliary which has the task of indicating the performer(s) of the action *and* the tense used. A closer look at the auxiliary will reveal that it is itself made up of a stem and an ending. In the following examples the stem of the auxiliary is marked in bold, the ending in bold italic, and the main verb in italic:

Nous **avons** *regardé   We have looked* (Perfect)
J'**avais** *parlé   I had talked* (Pluperfect)
Elle **sera** *arrivée   She will have arrived* (Future Perfect)
Note: There are sometimes slight variations in the way a verb is divided into a stem and ending. This will be clarified at a later stage.
3   Two auxiliaries are used in French for the formation of compound tenses: **avoir** (*to have*) and **être** (*to be*). They cannot be used at random: certain categories of verbs take **avoir**, others take **être**. This will also be clarified in the next chapter.

The Six Moods and their Tenses

Tenses are grouped into broader categories called Moods. Each Mood is used to convey specific shades of meaning and includes both simple and compound tenses. There are six distinct Moods in French: four Personal Moods (so called because they make it possible, through the person of the verb used, to determine the 'identity' of the performer(s) of the action), and two Impersonal Moods, (so labelled because they give no indication at all about the performer(s) of the action).

Each of those Moods, along with the currently used tenses within it, is presented below.

The Indicative Mood

It is used to indicate the straightforward occurrence of an action along the time-axis. Its tenses are as follows:

The Present
Formation: Stem + endings of the relevant group.
Usage: The present is used to indicate:
1   That an action is occurring at this precise moment:
      Il **mange.** *He is eating.*
2   That an action has been occurring for a while and is likely to continue for some time to come:
      Il **mange** trop. *He eats too much.*
Note: If a distinction between the two is required, it is possible to use an expression which will indicate the fact that the action is in progress: that expression is **être en train de** (*to be in the process of*). For example:
      Il **est en train de manger**. *He is eating (at this very moment).*
3   an 'eternal' truth valid for all times:
      Le crime ne **paie** pas. *Crime does not pay.*

4   eagerness or anticipation:
     Nous **partons** en vacances demain.   *We are going on holiday tomorrow.*
5   a veiled order:
     Tu **prends** le train de huit heures!   *You are taking the eight o'clock train!*
6   the dramatic importance of an action which would normally be expressed in the Perfect Tense:
     Il s'est arrêté au coin de la rue. Soudain il **se retourne. . .**   *He stopped at the street-corner. Suddenly he turned* (lit: *turns*) *round . . .*

The Immediate Future

Formation: Present of **aller** (*to go*) + Infinitive of main verb.
Usage: This tense is used to state that an action is going to happen soon:
     Nous **allons acheter** une voiture.   *We are going to buy a car.*
Note: In spoken French, this tense is often used instead of a Future.

The Immediate Past

Formation: Present of **venir** (*to come*) + **de** + Infinitive of main verb.
Usage: This tense is used to indicate that an action has just taken place:
     Ils **viennent de sortir**.   *They have just gone out.*

The Past Historic

Formation: Stem + endings of the relevant group.
Usage: It is used to indicate that an isolated, finite event took place at a given time in the past:
     Elle le **vit** et **courut** vers lui.   *She saw him and ran towards him.*
It is crucial to remember that the Past Historic can be used to indicate actions which may have lasted a long time, but that the duration (or even repetition) of those actions is seen as *non-important*. The occurrence of the action is the key-point. That is why the Past Historic is the ideal tense for biographies and reports of past events.

      A   B

Il **naquit** à Paris en 1923. Il **fit** ses études au Lycée Montaigne,
         C   D

puis il **alla** à la Sorbonne où il **passa** trois ans . . .
He was born in Paris in 1923. He studied at the Lycée Montaigne, then went to the Sorbonne where he spent three years . . .

In the above example, the periods of study obviously lasted several years and the person attended regularly; but the tense *merely* records the events as having happened separately along the time-axis:

Past   Present   Future

Note: Nowadays, the Past Historic is often avoided, particularly in spoken French, because it is seen as 'affected', and replaced by the Perfect (see below). But in good written style, its use is still recommended.

The Perfect
Formation: Present of **avoir/être** + Past Participle of main verb.
Usage: The Perfect is now used in *everyday speech* to replace the Past Historic:

Il **est descendu** à huit heures et **a commandé** son petit-déjeuner.   *He came down at eight o'clock and ordered his breakfast.*

Note: The above example could be formulated in the Past Historic with the same meaning:

Il **descendit** à huit heures et **commanda** son petit-déjeuner.

The Perfect (as the Past Historic which it often replaces), is used to indicate the *occurrence* in the past of isolated, finite actions along the time-axis, *without placing any emphasis* on their duration.

Note: The combination Perfect + Present is sometimes used in spoken French as an alternative to the more formal Future Perfect + Future.

So you may say: Quand tu **as fini**, tu **viens** me voir.
                                  Perfect   Present

as well as: Quand tu **auras fini**, tu **viendras** me voir.
                          Fut. Perfect   Future

When you have finished you will come and see me.

The Imperfect
Formation: Stem + Imperfect endings (identical for all groups).
Usage: This tense is used to emphasise the duration, repetition or habitual occurrence of an action in the past. In English, the Imperfect is marked by structures like *was . . . ing, used to . . . , was in the habit of . . .* or sometimes *would* (i.e. *used to*). A list of the most common shades of meaning this tense conveys is given below:

1   It is used to indicate that an action *was in progress* when another isolated action occurred:

Les enfants **dormaient** quand nous sommes rentrés. *The children were asleep (i.e. sleeping) when we came home.*

2   It serves to indicate that an action *used to happen* regularly in the past. Here again, it is the *duration or repetitive aspect* which is emphasised, as opposed to the mere 'recording' of the event.

Compare: Il **allait** au restaurant tous les jours. (Imperfect)
                       He used to go to the restaurant every day.
and: Il **alla** au restaurant tous les jours. (Past Historic)
                       He went to the restaurant every day.

In the second example, all the visits to the restaurant are seen as *one global event.*

3   It is used to indicate that an action, through its lasting or recurring quality, used to be *characteristic of a given period* in the past:

Quand j'**étais** jeune, je **sortais** souvent.
                Imperf.   Imperf.
When I was young, I used to go out often.

4   It is sometimes used instead of the Perfect (or Past Historic) to dramatise an event, to give it special prominence.

Les Alliés **ont débarqué** le six juin. Quelques semaines plus
                              Perf.
tard, ils **libéraient** Paris.
             Imperf.
The Allies landed on 6th June. A few weeks later, they liberated Paris.

In this latter sense, the Imperfect should be used seldom and with great care by learners.

---

5   It is used *in conjunction with the Present Conditional* in sentences with **si** (*if*) expressing a condition:

Si j'**avais** le temps je leur **écrirais**
    Imperf.   Pres. Cond.
If I had time I would write to them.

Note: Structures similar to those of the Immediate Future and Immediate Past presented earlier, but using the Imperfect of **aller** (*to go*), or **venir** (*to come*), make it possible to express such shades of meaning as *was/were about to . . .* or *had just . . .* respectively:

J'**allais partir** quand il a appelé.   *I was about to leave when he rang.*

Vous **veniez de partir** quand il est arrivé.   *You had just left when he arrived.*

Both constructions are normally used in conjunction with a Perfect (or Past Historic).

The Pluperfect
Formation: Imperfect of **avoir**/**être** + Past Participle of main verb.
Usage: The Pluperfect is used:
1   To indicate that a past action was totally completed at the time another action occurred. The importance placed on the completed aspect of the action rather than on its simple occurrence, makes it an ideal partner for the Imperfect when it is necessary to highlight the repetition of certain events in the past. For example:

Quand il **avait bu** il nous **racontait** sa vie.
        Pluperf.   Imperf.
When he was drunk (had been drinking) he used to tell us his life-story.

Lorsqu'elle **avait fini** le ménage, elle **lisait** un roman.
        Pluperf.   Imperf.
When(ever) she had finished the housework she used to read a novel.

2   To present a request in a very polite almost apologetic way:

J'**avais pensé** que vous **apprécieriez** . . .
   Pluperf.   Prest. Cond.
I had thought you would appreciate . . .

3   In conjunction with the Conditional Perfect, in sentences with **si** (*if*) expressing a condition:

Si **j'avais su**, je ne **serais pas venu**
      Pluperf.   Cond. Perf.
Had I known (lit. *if I had known*), *I would not have come.*

Note: In such a sentence, the condition is purely academic because it is too late to alter the course of events.

4   In indirect speech, to indicate that the action it describes came before another action expressed in the Perfect (or Past Historic).

Il **a dit** qu'il **avait oublié**. (indirect speech)
   Perf.   Pluperf.
He said that he had forgotten.

which corresponds to: Il a dit: "J'ai oublié". (direct speech)
                He said: "I have forgotten".

The Past Anterior
Formation: Past Historic of **avoir**/**être** + Past Participle of main verb.
Usage: This tense is used to indicate the occurrence of an isolated event in the past, *before* another isolated event took place. This makes

it the ideal partner of the Past Historic (or Perfect) to indicate a close correlation between two actions, *without any reference* to duration or repetition. For example:

Dès qu'il **eut terminé**, tout le monde **applaudit**.
    Past Ant.   Past Hist.
As soon as he had finished, everybody clapped.
Quand elle **fut partie** il **se leva**.
    Past. Ant. Past. Hist.
When she had gone, he got up.

Note: The use of such expressions as: **après que** (*after*), **aussitôt que**/**dès que** (*as soon as*), **lorsque**/**quand** (*when*), emphasises the logical link which exists between the two actions expressed in that type of sentence.

NB: In short, the Past Anterior is to the Past Historic what the Pluperfect is to the Imperfect (or what the Future Perfect is to the Future).

Double Compound Tense (*Passé surcomposé*)

Because of the loss of popularity of the Past Historic in spoken French, an alternative tense had to be introduced to replace the Past Anterior which was also perceived as 'affected'. That alternative tense is constructed as follows:

Present of **avoir** + Past Participle of the relevant Auxiliary + Past Participle of main verb.

Thus: Quand elle **fut partie,** il **se leva**.
        Past. Ant.   Past. Hist.
becomes: Quand elle **a éte partie**, il **s'est levé**.
                Passé surcomp.   Perfect
and: Dès qu'il **eut terminé**, tout le monde **applaudit**.
                    Past Ant.   Past Hist.
becomes: Dès qu'il **a eu terminé**, tout le monde **a applaudi**.
            Passé surcomp.   Perfect

Note: Other **Temps surcomposés** may be constructed on the same pattern, as spoken alternatives to less frequent compound tenses.

Future

Formation: Stem + endings (identical for all verbs).
Usage: The Future is used:
1 To indicate *objectively* that an event will take place at some time in the future:

Nous **reviendrons** demain. *We shall come back tomorrow.*
Vous **finirez** cette lettre tout à l'heure. *You will finish this letter in a while.*

Note: A subjective overtone may be introduced if the future is replaced by an Immediate Future or a Present.

Compare: Nous **partirons** ce soir. (Future = objective statement)
            We shall leave this evening.

and: Nous **allons partir** ce soir. (Immed. Fut. = eagerness)
            We are going to leave this evening.

or: Nous **partons** ce soir. (Present = eagerness/veiled order)
            We are leaving this evening.

2   A moral obligation, an order, a request:

   Tu ne **tueras** point.   *Thou shalt not kill.*

   Je vous **demanderai** de garder cela pour vous.   *I would like you to keep that to yourself.*

Future Perfect

Formation: Future of **avoir/être** + Past Participle of main verb.

Usage: This tense is normally used in conjunction with the Future, to indicate that the completion of an action will precede, and to some extent determine, the occurrence of another action:

   Quand tu **auras fini** le travail je te **paierai**.
              Fut. Perf.   Fut.
   When you have finished the work I shall pay you.

Note the difference in timing between:

   Vous sortirez quand la cloche **sonnera**.

   You will go out when the bell rings.

and: Vous sortirez quand la cloche **aura sonné**.

   You will go out when the bell has rung (has stopped ringing).

The Future Perfect is also used to indicate:

1   That an action will soon be over:

   J'**aurai fini** la réparation à midi.   *I will have finished the repairs by lunchtime.*

2   That an action is very likely to have happened:

   Ils **se seront perdus** dans les bois.   *They will have got lost in the woods* (they most probably have).

   Tu **auras** mal **compris**.   *You must have misunderstood.*

The Conditional Mood

This Mood is normally used to indicate the possible occurrence of an action if certain conditions were (or had been) met. In addition, it can convey other shades of meaning (polite request, guarded statement etc.) which will be examined in turn.

The two most commonly used tenses in this mood are the Present and the Perfect.

The Present
Formation: Stem + endings (identical for all groups).
Important: The *stem* used to form this tense is *exactly the same* as the one used for the Future. In addition, the *endings are the same* as those of the Imperfect.
Usage: The Present Conditional is used:

1 To express the idea that an action would occur, *in the present or the future*, if certain conditions were met:

    Si j'**avais** de l'argent j'**achèterais** un bateau.
      Imperf.   Pres. Cond.
    If I had money I would buy a boat.

Note: In this type of structure, the Conditional can *only* be used in conjunction with an Imperfect. So you must say:

    Si nous **étions** riches, nous **serions** heureux.
        Imperf.   Pres. Cond
    If we were rich we would be happy.

(and not *Si nous **serions** riches nous **serions** heureux).

2 To soften a command into a polite request:
    Nous **voudrions** une chambre pour deux personnes.   *We would like a double room.*

3 To express longings, vague desires or wishes
    J'**aimerais** voyager.   *I would like to travel.*

4 To announce the occurrence of a present or future event which has not yet been *officially* confirmed:

    Le Président **arriverait** demain à Paris.   (*According to rumours) the President will arrive in Paris tomorrow.*

    Selon la radio française, la Reine **serait** souffrante.   *According to French radio, the Queen is unwell.*

Note: This use of the Conditional is very frequent in Radio and Television broadcasts.

5 To express a strong feeling about a present or future action (disbelief, anger, scorn):

    Il me **donnerait** des conseils!   *He has the audacity to give me advice!*

The Perfect
Formation: Present Conditional of **avoir**/**être** + Past Participle of main verb.

Usage: This tense is used:

1   To express the idea that an action *might have occurred* if certain conditions had been met:

> Si j'**avais su**, je ne **serais pas venu**.
> Pluperf.   Cond. Perf.
> *If I had known, I would not have come.*

Note: In this type of structure, it can *only* be used in conjunction with the Pluperfect.

You must say: Si nous **avions été** riches, nous **aurions été** heureux.
> *If we had been rich, we would have been happy.*

and not: *si nous **aurions été** riches nous **aurions été** heureux.

2   To express regrets for lost opportunities:

> J'**aurais aimé** la revoir.   *I would have liked to have seen her again.*

3   To announce the *unconfirmed* occurrence of a recent event:

> Selon lui, trois personnes **auraient été** blessées.   *According to him three people have been wounded.*

The Imperative Mood

This Mood is used for the formulation of commands, request, directives or advice.

Note that the tenses which compose it have only three persons each — 2nd person singular, 1st person plural, 2nd person plural — and that no subject pronoun is used. The Tenses are as follows:

The Present

Formation: Stem + endings of the relevant group.

Usage: The Present Imperative is used:

1   To formulate a command or a warning:

> **Mange** ta soupe! (2nd pers. sing.)   *Eat your soup!*
> Ne **regardez** pas! (2nd pers. plur.)   *Don't look!*

2   To express a request, suggestion, or advice:

> **Essayons** encore! (1st pers. plur.)   *Let's try again!*
> **Prenez** votre temps. (2nd pers. plur.)   *Take your time.*

3   To give instructions:

> **Prenez** la deuxième route à gauche, et **continuez** tout droit. *Take the second road on your left and carry straight on.*

Notes:

1   In order to soften the strong command value of this tense, it is possible, in the second person plural, to use **veuillez** (*would you please*) followed by an Infinitive:

Veuillez me suivre. *Would you please follow me.*

Veuillez accepter l'assurance de mes meilleurs sentiments. (polite formula to end a letter) *Yours faithfully* (lit: *please accept the assurance of my best feelings*)

2   The Present Imperative can be used as an alternative to the **si** clause of a sentence expressing a condition, *provided* the verb of the main clause is in the Present or the Future Indicative.

Compare: **Ayez** bon coeur, on vous exploite.

and: Si vous avez bon coeur, on vous exploite.

         If you are kind-hearted, people exploit you.

or: **Soyez** sévère, on vous craindra.

and: Si vous êtes sévère, on vous craindra.

         If you are strict, people will fear you.

The Perfect

Formation: Present Imperative of **avoir/être** + Past Participle of main verb.

Usage: This tense is used to indicate that an order, a request, a directive, etc. will have to have been carried out by a certain time given as a deadline.

Soyez parti à mon retour. *I want you gone when I return.*

Ayez fait vos valises quand je monterai. *Have your cases packed when I come up.*

Note: Since the Imperative has only 3 persons, it often borrows from the subjunctive the 3rd persons singular and plural to complement its range.

Qu'il **entre**. *Let him come in.*

Qu'ils **mangent** de la brioche! *Let them eat cake!*

The Subjunctive Mood

This Mood is generally used to indicate that an action is envisaged as a vague possibility, a thought, a hypothetical event *and not* as a reality or a certainty.

That is why the Subjunctive is found, in subordinate clauses, after a verb or phrase expressing command, desire, doubt, fear, urgent request, etc. In addition (see Unit 16, pages 203–4 on conjunctions), certain expressions used to introduce a subordinate clause *must be* followed by a Subjunctive. Although this Mood is essentially the Mood of subordinate clauses, it may also be found in main or independent clauses (an independent clause is a clause which is not followed by a subordinate one), to express a strong feeling (enthusiasm, anger), a desire or a wish:

Vive la République!   *Long live the Republic!*

Que dieu vous **garde**!   *May God be with you!*

Important: Using the subjunctive is *not* a matter of choice. Because of its overtones, that Mood must only be used in the appropriate context.

The Tenses which are relevant to our study are presented below.

The Present

Formation: Stem + endings (identical for nearly all verbs).

The two auxiliaries **avoir** (*to have*) and **être** (*to be*) do not follow the pattern exactly (see detailed conjugation charts in the next chapter).

Usage: the Present Subjunctive is used to express the hypothetical or possible occurrence of an action *in the present or the future*:

Je ne crois pas qu'il **parle**.   *I do not believe he will talk (now or later)*.

The present Subjunctive must be used after main clauses containing the following:

1 (*a*) Verbs expressing an order, a request (positive = do or negative = do not), a wish:

commander (*to command*), **demander** (*to ask*), **exiger** (*to demand*), **ordonner** (*to order*), **préférer** (*to prefer*), **souhaiter** (*to wish*), **vouloir**, (*to want*), etc.

(*b*) Expressions also indicating those shades of meaning:

il faut (or **il faudrait**) **que**/**il est nécessaire que** (*it is necessary that*), **il est recommandé que** (*it is recommended that*), **il est souhaitable que** (*it is desirable that*), **il serait bon que** (*it would be advisable that*), etc.

Nous voulons que vous **restiez**.   *We want you to stay.*

Il faut que vous **achetiez** le disque.   *You must buy the record.*

Note: The impersonal structure: **il est** + adjective + **que** *must be* followed by the subjunctive, *except* if the adjective expresses an obvious, inescapable fact (in which case the Indicative will be used):

Compare: Il est important que vous **répondiez**. (Subj.)

It is important that you answer.

and: Il est clair que vous **répondrez**. (Indic.)

It is clear that you will answer.

or: Il est souhaitable qu'il **réussisse**. (Subj.)

It is desirable that he should succeed.

and: Il est certain qu'il **réussira**. (Indic.)

It is certain that he will succeed.

2 (a) Verbs expressing doubt, fear, longing, regret: **avoir peur que**
(*to be afraid that*), **craindre que** (*to fear that*), **douter que** (*to doubt that*), **regretter que** (*to regret that*), etc.

(b) Expressions also indicating those shades of meaning: **il est douteux que** (*it is doubtful that*), **il est peu probable** que (*it is improbable that*), **il est regrettable que** (*it is regrettable that*), **il est triste que** (*it is sad that*), **il n'est pas sûr que** (*it is not sure that*), **il ne semble pas que** (*it does not seem that*), etc.

Il craint que vous ne **disiez** non.   *He fears that you may say no.*

Il n'est pas sûr que je vous **croie.**   *It is not sure that I will believe you.*

3   Interrogative and negative phrases introducing such overtones as doubt, disbelief, reluctance, etc.

Compare: Je suis certain qu'elle **est** malade. (Indic.)
I am certain she is ill.

and: Je ne suis pas certain qu'elle **soit** malade. (Subj.)
I am not certain she is ill.

or: Elle est sûre que nous **sommes** contents. (Indic.)
She is sure we are pleased.

and: Est-elle sûre que nous **soyons** contents? (Subj.)
Is she sure we are pleased?

4   A Superlative:

le mieux (*the best*), **le moins** (*the least*), **le pire** (*the worst*),   **le plus** (*the most*);

C'est le garçon le plus doué que je **connaisse.**   *He is the most gifted boy I know.*

C'est le meilleur repas que j'**aie** jamais mangé.   *It is the best meal I have ever eaten.*

In addition to the above-mentioned cases, the subjunctive *must* be used in a subordinate clause if the latter is introduced by certain 'prescribed' conjunctions, some of which are presented below (for a fuller list, please consult the chapter on conjunctions): **A condition que** (*provided that*), **à moins que** (*unless*), **afin que** (*so that*), **avant que** (*before*), **de crainte que/de peur que** (*for fear that*), **jusqu'à ce que** (*until*), **sans que** (*without*), etc.

The Perfect
Formation: Present Subjunctive of **avoir/être** + Past Participle of main verb.

Usage: This tense is used in the same environment as the Present Subjunctive (i.e. after expressions of command, desire, doubt, regret; after certain 'prescribed' conjunctions, etc.), but it expresses the possibility of the hypothetical action *having already taken place* at the time of the utterance:

Je crains qu'il n'**ait abandonné**.   *I fear he may have given up.*

Croyez-vous qu'il **ait eu** peur?   *Do you think he was frightened?*

Compare: Je ne pense pas qu'ils nous **voient**. (Pres. Subj.)

I do not think they will see us (now or later).

and: Je ne pense pas qu'ils nous **aient vus**. (Subj. Perfect)

I do not think they have seen us (already).

Note: It is possible to use the Subjunctive Perfect to indicate the completed aspect of a projected action by a certain deadline. For example:

Je veux que vous **soyez parti** demain.   *I want you gone by tomorrow.*

Points to bear in mind regarding the use of the subjunctive:

1   Many learners are unduly worried by this seemingly daunting Mood. Just remember that it must be used in very precise and clearly prescribed circumstances. Whenever those circumstances arise, you will know that the Subjunctive is needed.

2   Although the conjunction **que** is almost always present before a subjunctive, it does *not* follow that every time **que** is used, it must have a subjunctive after it!

3   The Subjunctive is generally considered as stylistically 'heavy' (some of its tenses are already fading into oblivion). For that reason, it is often avoided, if at all possible, in spoken French. The main methods used are:

(*a*)   replacement of *the whole* subordinate clause by an Infinitive, whenever the main and subordinate clauses share the same subject.

thus: *Je* ne crois pas que *je* **puisse** rester.

becomes: Je ne crois pas pouvoir rester.

I do not think I can stay.

(*b*)   replacement of *the whole* subordinate clause after certain impersonal constructions (so long as no ambiguities in meaning are created by the substitution).

thus: Il faut que nous **partions**.

becomes: Il nous faut partir.

We must go.

(*c*)   replacement of *the whole* subordinate clause by a noun.

thus: Je doute qu'il **soit** honnête.

I doubt whether he is honest.

becomes: Je doute de son honnêteté.

I doubt his honesty.

All the Moods examined so far were Personal Moods, with the subject(s) performing the action clearly indicated. The following Moods are called Impersonal Moods. They offer no information about the identity of the performer(s) of the action (the context will normally supply that information).

The Infinitive Mood

This Mood merely expresses the abstract idea of the action stated by the verb, without any indication about the performer or of any further shade of meaning. It is considered as the *nominal* (noun-like) form of the verb.

The Tenses it contains are as follows:

The Present

Formation: Stem + **er/ir/re** (according to the group).
Usage: This form is used to situate the action referred to in the present or the future. For example:

Il veut **partir**. *He wants to go (now or later)*.

This is the form in which the verb is found in the dictionary. The ending will tell you which group (1st, 2nd or 3rd) the verb belongs to (see next chapter). This information is useful because, within a given group, verbs tend to behave fairly consistently as far as tense-formation is concerned. Thus, knowing one verb will normally help you to recognise (and form the tenses of) *most* of the other verbs in the same group.

Specific uses of the Present Infinitive

1 It can sometimes be used to replace a whole subordinate clause (s.c.):

Je l'ai vu **partir** = Je l'ai vu **qui partait**.

s.c.

I saw him go.
Il me faut **refaire** le travail = il faut **que je refasse le travail**.

s.c.

I must redo the work.
Note: This is particularly useful to eliminate a 'ponderous' subjunctive.

2 It can be used to shorten an interrogative clause:

Que **faire**? = Qu'est-ce qu'il faut faire?
What is one to do?
Où **aller**? = Où doit-on aller?
Where is one to go?

3   It can replace a noun (and its article):

Mieux vaut **mourir** = Mieux vaut la mort.

It is better to die.

J'adore **marcher** = J'adore la marche.   *I love walking.*

4   It is used with the meaning of an Imperative in *written* notices, instructions for use, recipes, etc.

Ouvrir avec soin = Ouvrez avec soin.

Open with care.

Cuire à feu doux = Cuisez à feu doux.

Cook on a low heat.

Note: When the Infinitive is used to formulate a strong request or an order on written notices, it is often preceded by **Prière de** (*Please. .*) to soften its meaning:

Prière de **fermer** la porte = Fermez la porte s'il vous plaît.
    Please close the door.

Prière de ne pas **fumer** = Ne fumez pas s'il vous plaît.   *Please refrain from smoking.*

5   It can, in a limited number of cases, be used as a noun (with an article or other determiner):

Le **pouvoir** corrompt.   *Power corrupts.*

Il fait son **devoir**.   *He is doing his duty.*

The Perfect

Formation: Present Infinitive of **avoir/être** + Past Participle of main verb.

Usage: This form normally indicates that, at a given time, an action is/was considered as completed.

Je crois vous **avoir dit** d'attendre.   *I think I told you (earlier) to wait.*

Compare: Je vous remercie d'**être venu**. (Inf. Perf.)
    Thank you for being with us.(lit: *having come*).

and: Je vous remercie **de venir** (Pres. Inf.)
    Thank you for coming (now or later).

or: Ils croient **comprendre**.
    They believe they understand (now).

and: Ils croient **avoir compris**.
    They believe they have understood (already).

Specific uses: Like the present infinitive, it can:

1   replace certain subordinate clauses (s.c.):

Il pense **avoir gagné** = Il pense **qu'il a gagné**.
                                                    s.c.

He thinks he has won.

If faut **avoir vu** ce film = Il faut **que l'on ait vu ce film**.
                                                    s.c. (Subj.)

This film must be seen. (i.e. *is a 'must.*)

2   take on the value of a noun:

Merci de m'**avoir aidé** = Merci de votre aide.

Thank you for your help. (lit: *for having helped me*)

3   replace parts of an interrogative sentence beginning with **pourquoi** (*why*):

Pourquoi **être monté**? = Pourquoi êtes-vous monté?

Why did you come up?

Pourquoi **avoir cédé**? = Pourquoi ai-je cédé?

Why did I give in?

Because of the absence of indication about the performer, such constructions could refer to *any* person.

4   Indicate that an action must be completed by a given deadline set in the future. In this case, it follows a verb expressing an order or a request:

Nous devons **avoir quitté** l'hôtel à midi.   *We must be out of the hotel by twelve (noon).*

Il faut **être revenus** ce soir.   *We must be back by tonight.*

Points to bear in mind regarding the use of infinitives:

1   When two verbs follow each other, the second one must be in the infinitive *except* when the first is one of the two auxiliaries **avoir** (*to have*) or **être** (*to be*):

Il doit **répondre**.   *He must answer.*

Nous aimons **voyager**.   *We like travelling.*

Note: In French, the use of a present participle (i.e. *ing* form) in this context is unacceptable.

You must say: Ils aiment **marcher**. (and not *Ils aiment marchant)

They like walking.

2   If a verb follows the prepositions **à** (*to*), **de** (*from*), **pour** (*in order to*), **sans** (*without*), it must be in the infinitive (and *not* in the present participle as is often the case in English):

Il commence à **pleuvoir**.   *It is beginning to rain.*

Vous avez la chance de **gagner**. (and not *. . . de gagnant)   *You have the chance of winning.*

Ils sont partis sans **payer**. (and not *. . . sans payant)   *They left without paying.*

The preposition **par** (*by*) is only used with a verb (in the infinitive) in two expressions: **commencer par** (*to begin by* + verb) and **finir par** (*to end up by* + verb):

Ils ont commencé **par crier** mais ils ont fini **par accepter**

They began by shouting but they ended up by accepting.

3   If an Infinitive follows a verb expressing desire, dislike, longing, preference, it will not be preceded by a preposition.

Vous désirez **parler** au patron?   *Do you wish to talk to the manager?*

Il déteste **attendre**.   *He hates waiting.*

4   If an Infinitive follows a verb expressing a claim, a statement or an assertion, it will not be preceded by a preposition:

Il prétend **avoir été** invité.   *He claims to have been invited.*

Elle dit **être** sa fille.   *She says she is his daughter.*

If **après** (*after*) is followed by a verb, that verb *must* be in the Infinitive Perfect (and not in the Present Infinitive or the Present Participle!)

You must say: Après **avoir parlé** il m'a regardé.

After he had spoken, he looked at me.

and not: *Après parlant (or parler), il m'a regardé.

The Participle

This Mood represents the adjectival form of the verb. The Participle can therefore have two distinct roles: that of a verb (in which case it will be invariable), and that of an adjective (in which case it will agree as required). In this Mood, the following Tenses are found.

The Present Participle

Formation: Stem + { **ant** in 1st and 3rd group verbs / **issant** in 2nd group verbs

NB   For an explanation of the grouping of verbs see next chapter.

Usage: As previously mentioned, this tense has two distinct roles:

1   As a verbal form it can indicate that the action it represents coincides (at any point in time) with another action. In this role, it is used to replace whole relative clauses beginning with **qui** (*who/which*), particularly after verbs of perception.

J'ai vu le vieux **comptant** son argent = qui comptait son argent.   *I saw the old man counting his money.*

Nous les entendons **criant** à tue-tête = qui crient à tue-tête.   *We hear them shouting their heads off.*

Note: In that role, the Present Participle is invariable

2   As an adjective, it indicates a distinctive quality:
   Ils lisent une histoire **intéressante**.   *They are reading an interest-
      ing story.*
   Nous ferons des choses **étonnantes**.   *We will do astonishing
      things.*

Note: In that role, the Present Participle behaves like an adjective
and agrees as appropriate.
Compare: J'entends des cris **déchirants**. (quality)
            I hear heart-breaking cries.
and: J'entends des cris **déchirant** le silence. (action)
            I hear cries breaking the silence.
In this latter case, the Present Participle indicates an action (**qui
déchirent . . .**) and is therefore invariable.

The Gerund

The Gerund is the adverbial form of the verb. It is identical in shape
with the Present Participle, but is preceded by the preposition **en**
(*by/through/whilst*). Since it has the value and role of an adverb, it is
invariable. It is used to modify the meaning of a verbal phrase. The
shades of meaning it can convey (at any point in time) are as follows:
1   It can indicate the co-occurrence of two actions:
   Elle entra **en chantant**.   *She came in singing.*
   Il sortit **en riant.**   *He went out laughing.*
2   It outlines the means by which a result is achieved (*through, by
dint of . . .*):
   C'est **en travaillant** dur que tu réussiras.   *It is by working hard
      that you will succeed.*
   On apprend beaucoup **en regardant** les gens.   *One learns a lot
      through looking at people.*
3   It can express hypothetical situations:
   En acceptant, je perds ma place.   *If I accept I lose my job.*
Be sure to distinguish between:
   J'ai vu l'homme **parlant** à un ami (qui parlait . . .).   *I saw the
      man talking to a friend.*
and: J'ai vu l'homme **en parlant** à un ami (pendant que je
parlais . . .).   *I saw the man while I was talking to a friend.*

The Past Participle

Formation: Stem + **é/i/u** (according to the group).
Some verbs do not conform to this regular pattern (see next chapter).
Usage: The Past Participle has two distinct functions:

1   As a verb, it is used in all compound tenses and serves to emphasise *the completed aspect* of an action:

   J'**ai ramassé** le sac.   *I picked up the bag.*
   Il se sera **endormi**.   *He will have fallen asleep.*

2   As an adjective, it expresses a state:

   Jette ces fleurs **fanées**!   *Throw those wilted flowers out!*
   Le soleil entre par la fenêtre **ouverte**.   *The sun is coming in through the open window.*

Note: A small number of past participles can be used as nouns:

   Donnez moi mon **dû** et je signe un **reçu**.   *Give me what is owed to me and I will sign a receipt.*

Past Participle agreements

See also chapters 11 (Reflexive Pronouns) and 20 (Past Participle agreement with **avoir/être**).

   As outlined earlier, the Past Participle can have several functions:

1   When used as an adjective, it will normally agree in gender and number with the noun or pronoun it relates to:

   Elle regarde la robe **déchirée**.   *She is looking at the torn dress.*
   Laissez la fenêtre **ouverte**.   *Leave the window open.*

Note: Certain Past Participles used as adjectives in set expressions *do not* agree with the noun *when placed before it*, but behave normally when placed after; the most common are: **excepté** (*except*), **passé** (*past/after*), **supposé** (*assumed*), **ci-joint/ci-inclus** (*enclosed*), **étant donné** (*given*), **non-compris** (*not included*), **y compris** (*included*).

Compare: Ouvert tous les jours, **excepté** dimanches et fêtes.
and: Ouvert tous les jours, dimanches et fêtes **exceptés**.
   Open every day, Sundays and public holidays excepted.
or: Veuillez trouver **ci-joint** une photo.
and: Veuillez trouver une photo **ci-jointe**.
   Please find enclosed a photograph.

2   When used as a noun, the past participle agrees as required:

   Signez ces **reçus** s'il vous plaît.   *Please sign these receipts.*
   Debout les **morts**!   *Everybody up!* (humorous)

3   When used with the auxiliary **être** in non-pronominal constructions (i.e. *without* one of the reflexive pronouns: **me, te, se, nous, vous, se**), the past participle agrees as appropriate.

Note: This includes the compound tenses of the 'famous 14': **aller, venir, descendre, monter, entrer, sortir, naître, mourir, partir, arriver, passer, retourner, rester, tomber**, as well as all passive constructions:

   Ils sont **restés** à la maison.   *They stayed at home.*
   Elle a été **mordue** par un chien.   *She has been bitten by a dog.*
   (passive construction)

4   When the past participle is used pronominally (i.e. with a reflexive pronoun) two possibilities arise:

If the verb concerned admits an accusative construction (a direct object), the past participle will agree as required. A practical way of finding out whether the verb is in the accusative is to rephrase the sentence in your mind using **avoir** as the auxiliary and to ask the question **qui?** or **quoi?** after the past participle. If the answer to that question is the reflexive pronoun (representing the subject), the agreement is required. *Otherwise*, no agreement must be made.

Compare: Elle s'est **levée**. (elle a levé qui?: **s'** = elle)   *She got up.*
The construction is an accusative one, hence the agreement.

and: Elle s'est **dit**: "tant pis!" (elle a dit à qui? à **s'** = à elle) *She said to herself: "too bad!"*.
The construction is a dative one, hence no agreement.

Note: Beware of such sentences as:

Elle s'est **coupé** la main. (= elle a coupé la main **à** qui?: à **s'** = à elle — dative, no agreement) *She cut her hand.*

and: Elle s'est **coupée** à la main (elle a coupé qui?: **se** = elle — accusative, agreement)

She cut herself on the hand.

5   When the past participle is used with **avoir**, several possibilities must be envisaged:

(*a*)   If the construction is not an accusative one (i.e. if the verb has no direct object or, practically, if the question **qui?** or **quoi?** asked after the past participle has no answer), there will be no agreement.

Ils ont **entendu** (ils ont entendu quoi? = no answer — no agreement) *They heard.*

Elle a **mangé** (elle a mangé quoi? = no answer — no agreement) *She has eaten.*

(*b*)   If the construction is an accusative one but if the direct object is placed after the past participle, there is no agreement.

Elles ont **mangé les bonbons** (elles ont mangé quoi? = les
                                      Dir. obj.

bonbons   *They ate the sweets.*

Elle a **vu la pièce** (elle a vu quoi? = la pièce).   *She saw the
                                      Dir. obj.*

play.

(*c*)   If the construction is an accusative one *and* if the direct object is placed before the past participle, the agreement will be made as applicable.

Ils nous **ont vu(e)s** (ils ont vu qui? = nous (masc. or fem. plur). *They saw us.*

Remember, for agreement purposes, that the direct object pronouns: **me**, **te**, **le**, **la**, can represent a masculine *or* a feminine singular, and that **nous**, **vous**, **les**, refer to a masculine *or* feminine plural. In addition, **vous** could refer to one person only (polite singular). You could therefore have the following agreements.

$$\left.\begin{array}{l} \text{vu (to a man)} \\ \text{vue (to a woman)} \\ \text{vus (to several people)} \\ \text{vues (to several women)} \end{array}\right.$$

Je vous ai
I saw you

When a sentence contains the relative pronoun **que** (*that*), check the gender and number of its antecedent (i.e. the noun or pronoun it replaces) and, if the clause contains a past participle, make the agreement as required:

C'est la montre que j'avais **perdue** (j'avais perdu quoi?: **que** = la montre — fem. sing. agreement).   *This is the watch I had lost.*

If the past participle occurs in an impersonal construction (i.e. with **il fait, il y a . . .**), it will remain invariable:

Vous savez la crise qu'il y a **eu** (and not *eue)   *You know the crisis there was.*

If the past participle of **coûter** (*to cost*), **peser** (*to weigh*), or **valoir** (*to be worth*) is used in a 'concrete' sense, it will remain invariable; if used figuratively, it will agree as appropriate.

Compare: Je regrette les 300 Francs que cette robe a **coûté**.
            I begrudge the 300F which this dress has cost.
and: Je plains les efforts que ce travail a **coûtés**.
            I begrudge the efforts this job has cost.

Active and passive voice

It is often useful for the listener or reader to know whether the subject of a sentence is performing an action (*active voice*) or is merely subjected to the action (*passive voice*).

Note: the auxiliary **être** (*to be*) is used to turn an active sentence into a passive one.

Compare: Le touriste **achète** une carte postale.
            The tourist is buying a postcard. (active)
and: La carte postale **est achetée** par le touriste.
            The postcard is bought by the tourist. (passive)
or: Le docteur **a examiné** le malade.
            The doctor examined the sick man. (active)
and: Le malade **a été examiné** par le docteur.
            The sick man was examined by the doctor. (passive)

Notes:

1   *Not all* sentences can be turned into the passive voice.
    Il pleut. *It is raining.*

2   The presence of the auxiliary **être** does *not* automatically mean that a sentence is in the passive voice.
    Elle **est arrivée** ce matin. *She arrived this morning.*

Types of verbs

Verbs can also be classified according to the relationship they create between the being(s) or thing(s) performing the action and the object(s) or recipient(s) of that action. On that basis, the following categories are distinguished:

Intransitive verbs

No indication is given as to the object or recipient of the action.
    Il marche. *He is walking.*
    Elles dorment. *They are sleeping.*

Transitive verbs

They give an indication of the object or recipient of the action:
    Vous **donnez** votre passeport.
    You are giving (what?=) *your passport.*
    Il **adore** les enfants.
    He adores (who(m)?) *children.*

    Elle **parle à** sa voisine.
    She is speaking (to whom?=) *to her neighbour.*
    Nous **pensons à** vous.
    We are thinking (of whom?=) *of you.*
In the four sentences given above the first two are examples of 'transitive direct' verbs and the last two of 'transitive indirect' verbs. In the latter, the verb is followed by a preposition: **à** (*to*), **de** (*of*).

Pronominal verbs

They are preceded by one of the appropriate pronouns: **me** (*myself*), **te** (*yourself* — fam.), **se** (*himself, herself, itself, oneself, themselves*), **nous** (*ourselves*), **vous** (*yourself, yourselves*). They indicate:

(*a*) *either* that the action of the performer(s) affects only the performer(s) (reflexive verbs):
    Nous **nous levons** tôt. *We get (ourselves) up early.*
    Ils **se sont coupés**. *They cut themselves.*

(*b*)   *or* that the performer(s) and the recipient(s) perform the same action and that *both* are affected by it (reciprocal verbs).

Nous **nous sommes battus**.   *We fought (each other)*.

Elles **se sont insultées**.   *They insulted each other*.

Although there are verbs in French which only belong to one of the above three categories, many verbs can move from one category to another depending on the pattern of the sentence they are used in. For example:

Je regarde.   *I am looking/watching*. (intransitive)

Je regarde la mer.   *I am looking at the sea*. (trans. direct)

Je regarde à la dépense.   *I am careful about expenses*. (trans. indirect)

Je me regarde.   *I am looking at myself*. (reflexive)

Nous nous regardons.   *We are looking at each other*. (reciprocal)

Impersonal verbs

There is a small group of verbs which are only used in the 3rd person singular (masculine). In that case, the pronoun **il** (*it*) does not refer to any thing or being. Those verbs are called impersonal verbs.

Il pleut et **il fait** du vent.   *It is raining and windy*.

Il faut partir.   *It is necessary to go*.

Key points

1   In order to express accurately the occurrence of an action, there are in French a selection of tenses which make it possible to situate that action in time.

2   Tenses can be made up of one word (*simple tenses*) or several words — usually two — one of which is the auxiliary and the other the main verb (*compound tenses*).

3   The verb (in simple tenses) or the auxiliary (in compound tenses) is made up of a stem and an ending which serves to indicate the performer(s) *and* the position of the action on the time axis.

4   Tenses are grouped into broader categories called Moods which are used to express definite shades of meaning: actual occurrence of an action, possibility, conjecture, command, doubt, regret, etc.

5   The Indicative Mood is used to situate the occurrence of an action on the time axis in relation to other actions or to the present.

6   The Conditional Mood expresses the fact that an action could occur in the present or the future (or could have occurred in the past) if certain conditions were (or had been) met. It is also used to soften commands into polite requests and to express indignation or guarded statements.

7   The Imperative Mood is used to express an order or a request, to give a set of instructions or directions. It has three persons only (2nd singular, 1st plural, 2nd plural) and *no* subject pronouns. It can be supplemented by the 3rd person (singular and plural) of the Subjunctive if required.

8   The Subjunctive Mood is normally used in subordinate clauses to indicate that an action is considered *not* as a reality but as a possible, hypothetical or doubtful event in the past, the present or the future. Because of the shades of meaning it conveys, it *must not* be used at random, but in very precise circumstances (after certain verbs or expressions of command, doubt, fear, longing, etc., or after certain 'prescribed' conjunctions). It can (infrequently) be found in main or independent clauses where it usually expresses such feelings as enthusiasm, indignation or disgust.

9   The Infinitive Mood is an impersonal mood. The Infinitive can have the value of a verb or a noun. As a verb, it will remain invariable; as a noun, it will agree if required. Infinitives may be used in certain circumstances to replace other grammatical elements such as subordinate clauses or nouns.

10   The Participle is also an Impersonal Mood. It can be used as a verb or as an adjective:

(*a*)   As a verb it expresses an action coinciding with that of the main verb. It may be used to replace relative clauses beginning with **qui** (*who*) and remains invariable.

(*b*)   As an adjective, it serves to indicate an 'active' quality (Present Participle) or a state (Past Participle) and, with a few restrictions, agrees like a normal adjective.

The Gerund, which is identical to the Present Participle but is preceded by **en**, is the adverbial form of the latter. It is used to modify the verb-phrase which it accompanies and may express simultaneity, 'means to an end', or hypothetical situations.

11   The Past Participle is used in conjunction with the auxiliaries **avoir** and **être** to form all compound tenses in French conjugation.

12   In compound tenses, the Past Participle follows rigid rules of agreement:

(*a*)   If the Past Participle is used with **être** in non-pronominal verb constructions, it will agree in gender and number like a normal adjective

(*b*)   If it is used pronominally (i.e. essentially with reflexive or reciprocal verbs) in *dative constructions* (when the verb accepts an Indirect Object complement), it will remain unchanged.

(*c*)   If it is used with **avoir**, it will agree as appropriate provided:

(i)   The construction is an accusative one (i.e. the verb accepts a Direct Object complement); *and*

(ii)   That Direct Object complement is placed *before* the Past Participle. The whole problem of agreement therefore hinges on the presence and position of the Direct Object Complement.

13   The actions indicated by most verbs can be expressed in the active voice (i.e. subject(s) performing the action) or in the passive voice (i.e. subject(s) undergoing the action).

13   The Verb

The verb is said to be the most important word in a sentence. It enables the speaker(s) to express actions, feelings, states of mind or body, etc. In order to situate those actions along the time axis (past-present-future) or relatively to each other, verbs are organised into Tenses. Tenses in their turn are grouped into Moods. Each Mood gives extra information (overtones) about the action: actuality, doubt, possibility, regret, wish, etc.

Introductory remarks

Although the general principles involved in the conjugation of verbs are similar in French and English, there are, between the two languages important differences which must be borne in mind:

In English, for a given tense (Present, Past Historic, etc.), the task of distinguishing between persons falls almost entirely on the Subject Pronoun (*I, you, he/she/it, we, you, they*). In French, on the other hand, that task is shared between the Subject Pronouns which are — and generally sound — different *and* the tense ending for each person. A comparative look at the behaviour of a given verb (e.g. **aller** *to go*) in the two languages will clarify that point. The tense shown is the Past Historic.

Persons		*to go*	*aller*
1st 2nd 3rd	sing	*I went* *You went* *He/she/it went*	J'allai Tu allas (fam. sing.) Il/elle alla
1st 2nd 3rd	plural	*We went* *You went* *They went*	Nous allâmes Vous allâtes (polite sing./normal plur.) Ils/elles allèrent

In English the form *went* is the same for all 6 persons; distinction in meaning is made by the pronoun alone. In French the endings **ai, as, a**, etc. change with each person which means that two clues are available (pronoun + ending) instead of one in English (pronoun), to help you recognise the person in question. It is therefore essential to match, for each tense, the correct ending with the correct person; a fairly demanding (but by no means impossible) task, which will be greatly aided by careful scrutiny of the examples given and some of the 'detective work' outlined in the introduction.

Verb groups

Broadly speaking, French verbs fall into a small number of categories organised into three groups. With some notable exceptions presented in the Irregular charts on pages 161–73, verbs in a given category tend to 'behave' in a consistent way for the purpose of stem-determination and tense-formation. Two forms are used to determine which group a given verb belongs to: its *Infinitive* and its *Present Participle*:

(i) the Infinitive is, as we know, the nominal form of the verb, the one which will appear in dictionaries. In English, the Infinitive is signalled by the presence of *to*. In French, the Infinitive is made up of a *stem + an ending*: **er**, **ir** or **re**;

(ii) the Present Participle is the adjectival form of the verb. In English the *ing* ending signals the Present Participle. In French the Present Participle is made up of a *stem + an ending*: **ant** for 1st and 3rd group verbs and **issant** for 2nd group ones.

French verb categories and groups are presented below.

Categories		*Examples*	*Meaning*
a	Infinitive ending = **er**	aim**er**	*to love*
	Pres. Part. ending = **ant**	aim**ant**	*loving*
b	Infinitive ending = **ir**	fin**ir**	*to finish*
	Pres. Part. ending = **issant**	fin**issant**	*finishing*
c	Infinitive ending = **ir**	part**ir**	*to leave*
	Pres. Part. ending = **ant**	part**ant**	*leaving*
d	Infinitive ending = **re**	vend**re**	*to sell*
	Pres. Part. ending = **ant**	vend**ant**	*selling*
e	Infinitive ending = **oir**	recev**oir**	*to receive*
	Pres. Part. ending = **ant**	recev**ant**	*receiving*

Category a represents group I, in which there are roughly 4,000 verbs. It is the largest and the most dynamic group: most of the new verbs created in the language are **er** verbs: **bétoniser** (*to 'pollute' with concrete and buildings*), **réclamiser** (*to advertise*), **robotiser** (*to robotise*), **informatiser** (*to computerise*) are some recently-created examples.

With the notable exception of **aller**, which will be presented in the Irregular Verbs chart, this group is fairly trouble-free.

Category b   represents group II which is approximately 350 strong. It has a very limited number of new additions, e.g. **alunir** (*to land on the moon*). In terms of endings and tense-formation, it is the easiest group to learn.

Categories c, d and e   represent group III which is the most inconsistent, not so much in terms of endings, as in terms of changes to the *stem* (to which the endings will be added). It is approximately 100 strong and several of its members are either very rarely used today (i.e. obsolete), or not used throughout their conjugation (i.e. defective). Unfortunately, some of the most commonly used verbs in the language also belong to that group!

Tense formation

French tenses are formed in one of two ways, as outlined in Unit 12.
Simple Tenses = Stem of main verb + endings.
Compound Tenses = Auxiliary + Past Participle of main verb.
The determination of the correct endings for a given tense is *not* a difficult matter, given a few models and some reflection. The difficulty is to determine how to 'discover' the stem. Here again, some of the detective work outlined in the introduction will be invaluable. Here are some hints which may also prove useful.

(*a*)   Once you have heard or seen one person of the Future or Present Conditional of a verb, you will know the stem used for the whole of those two tenses, however irregular the verb. Let us take two examples:

Aller *to go*
Future   = **j'irai**   ⟶ stem = **ir** + ending = **ai**
                    I shall go
Pres. Cond.   = **Tu irais**   ⟶ stem = **ir** + ending = **ais**
                    You would go
Prendre *to take*
Future   = **elle prendra** ⟶ stem = **prendr** + ending = **a**
                    she will take
Pres. Cond.   = **nous prendrions** ⟶ stem = **prendr** + ending = **ions**
                    we would take

Having learnt the appropriate endings (which, incidentally, are *the same for all verbs*) for each of those two tenses, you will find it extremely easy to make up the rest of the tense yourself.

(*b*)   For the formation of the Future (*and* of the Present

Conditional), the stem will *normally* be either the *full* Infinitive, in the case of **er** and most **ir** verbs, or the Infinitive minus **e**, in the case of **re** verbs. For example:

chercher *to search*
Future: **Ils chercheront** ⟶ stem = **chercher** + ending = **ont**
       They will search

attendre *to wait*
Pres. Cond.: **Vous attendriez** ⟶ stem =
              attendr + ending = **iez** *You would wait*

(c) For all verbs, the endings of the Present Conditional are the same as the *endings* of the Imperfect Indicative. For example:
   pouvoir   *to be able to*
   Imperfect: **Je pouvais** ⟶ stem = **pouv** + ending **ais**
   Pres. Cond.: **Je pourrais** ⟶ stem = **pourr** + ending **ais**

(d) The endings of the Present Indicative of **avoir** (minus the stem **av**), are *also* the endings of the Future Tense for all verbs.

Compare:	J'**ai**	and:	Je ser**ai**
	I have		*I shall be*
or:	Tu **as**	and:	Tu fer**as**
	You have		*You will do*
or:	Nous av**ons**	and:	Nous parler**ons**
	We have		*We shall talk*

(e) In the case of many irregular verbs, the Present Indicative exhibits two stem formations: *one* for the first three persons singular and the third person plural, *and another* for the 2nd and 3rd persons plural. For example:
   boire   *to drink*
   Compare: Je bois, tu bois, il boit, ils boivent ⟶ stem = **boi(v)**
   and: nous buvons, vous buvez ⟶ stem = **buv**

   pouvoir   *to be able to*
   Compare: Je peux, tu peux, il peut, ils peuvent ⟶ stem = **peu**
   and: nous pouvons, vous pouvez ⟶ stem = **pouv**

Note: Despite the fact that the above 'rule' has numerous exceptions, it has the advantage of showing that there is some underlying 'logic' in the language. Careful study of grammatical data will enable you to uncover further 'logical' information by yourself.

Auxiliaries

Auxiliaries are verbs which assist in the formation of Compound Tenses. The two main auxiliaries used for that purpose in French are **avoir** (*to have*) and **être** (*to be*), as previously indicated.

Être

Verbs which take **être** as an auxiliary are:

1   All those constructed pronominally (e.g. reflexive or reciprocal verbs). The pronominal construction is indicated by the presence of one of the following reflexive pronouns: **me**, **te**, **se**, **nous**, **vous**, **se**, (see Unit 11 on-reflexive pronouns), between the subject and the Verb. For example:

Se couper	⟶	Tu **te** coupes (reflexive)
To cut oneself		*You cut yourself*
Se battre	⟶	Nous **nous** battons (reciprocal)
To fight (one another)		*We fight (each other)*
S'enfuir	⟶	Je **m'**enfuis (pronominal)
To run away		*I run away*

2   The following 14 verbs (the 'famous 14'):

Aller	*to go*	Venir	*to come*
Arriver	*to arrive*	Partir	*to leave/go*
Descendre	*to go down*	Monter	*to go up*
Entrer	*to go in*	Sortir	*to go out*
Naître	*to be born*	Mourir	*to die*
Passer	*to go by*	Retourner	*to return/go back*
Rester	*to stay*	Tomber	*to fall*

Notes:

(i)   Most of the above verbs, when constructed with a prefix (usually **re** indicating repetition) — **re**descendre (*to go down again*), **re**partir (*to go again*), etc. — also take **être** as their auxiliary. For example:

Il est **revenu** à trois heures et il est **reparti** à sept heures.
He came back at three and went back at seven.

(ii)   Some of the 'famous 14' can also be used in transitive constructions (i.e. followed by a Direct Object Complement). In such cases, they will take the auxiliary **avoir**.

Compare: Ils **sont** descendus.
            They went down.
and: Ils **ont descendu** la valise.
            They took the case down.
or: Ils **sont** retournés au bureau.
            They went back to the office.
and: Ils **ont retourné** le livre.
            They returned the book.

Avoir

All other verbs take **avoir** as their auxiliary, including **avoir** and être themselves. For example:

Il **a achevé** son travail. *He finished his work.*

Elle **avait rêvé**. *She had been dreaming.*

Ils **ont été invités**. *They were invited.*

Nous **avons eu** des problèmes. *We have had problems.*

In addition to the two auxiliaries examined above, other verbs may be used in a similar capacity. Two categories may be distinguished:

1 *Semi-auxiliaries*: **aller** (*to go*) and **venir** (*to come*). Both may be constructed with an Infinitive to indicate the imminent occurrence of an action (**aller**), or the recent completion of an action (**venir**) and both may be used in the Present *or* the Imperfect Indicative.

Compare: Nous **allons** fermer le magasin.

We are going to close the shop.

and: Nous **allions** fermer le magasin.

We were about to close the shop.

or: Il **vient de** perdre son portefeuille.

He has just lost his wallet.

and: Il **venait de** perdre son portefeuille.

He had just lost his wallet.

Note: In this type of construction **de** or **d'** as applicable is inserted between **venir** and the following infinitive.

2 *Modal auxiliaries*: **devoir** (*to have to*), **faire** (*to have .... done*), **falloir** (*to be necessary*), **pouvoir** (*to be able to*), **savoir** (*to know how to*), **vouloir** (*to want*). They may be used with an infinitive to express certain overtones (desire, moral obligation, order) reminiscent of those expressed by the various Moods (Conditional, Imperative, Subjunctive) previously examined. For example:

Vous **devez** partir = Il faut que vous partiez. *You must go.*

Je **peux** gagner = Il est possible que je gagne. *I can win.*

Model charts

The Conjugation charts of five regular verbs will now be presented in full. Please study these charts carefully, since they contain most of the clues to the secrets of correct French Conjugation. In addition, Irregular Verb charts will also be given at the end of the chapter.

Notes:

1 In order to simplify the verb charts presented below, only one form (**il** for the singular and **ils** for the plural) will be given for the 3rd person. But it is understood that **il** (*he*) also stands for **elle** (*she*) and **on** (*one*), and that **ils** (*they* masc. plur.) also stands for **elles** (*they* fem. plur.).

2 In a further attempt to simplify the model charts, the polite

singular form **vous** will not be entered separately as it was in the pronouns chapter.

Remember that, in compound tenses, the rules of agreement of the past participle will have to be adhered to whenever appropriate. Compare:

vous êtes tombé masc. sing. polite form
vous êtes tombée fem. sing. polite form
vous êtes tombés masc. plur. normal form   *You have fallen*
vous êtes tombées fem. plur. normal form

3 Within the Past Historic, the Imperfect, the Future and the Conditional of a given verb, the *stem*, once determined, *remains constant* and the endings follow a regular pattern.

Auxiliaries: AVOIR

Simple Tenses	*Compound Tenses*
Indicative	
Present	*Perfect*
J'ai	J'ai eu
Tu as	Tu as eu
Il a	Il a eu
Nous avons	Nous avons eu
Vous avez	Vous avez eu
Ils ont	Ils ont eu
Past Historic	*Past Anterior*
J'eus	J'eus eu
Tu eus	Tu eus eu
Il eut	Il eut eu
Nous eûmes	Nous eûmes eu
Vous eûtes	Vous eûtes eu
Ils eurent	Ils eurent eu
Imperfect	*Pluperfect*
J' avais	J'avais eu
Tu avais	Tu avais eu
Il avait	Il avait eu
Nous avions	Nous avions eu
Vous aviez	Vous aviez eu
Ils avaient	Ils avaient eu

Avoir-*cont.*

Simple Tenses	*Compound Tenses*
Future	*Future Perfect*
J'aur**ai**	J'aurai eu
Tu aur**as**	Tu auras eu
Il aur**a**	Il aura eu
Nous aur**ons**	Nous aurons eu
Vous aur**ez**	Vous aurez eu
Ils aur**ont**	Ils auront eu

Conditional

Present	*Perfect*
J'aur**ais**	J'aurais eu
Tu aur**ais**	Tu aurais eu
Il aur**ait**	Il aurait eu
Nous aur**ions**	Nous aurions eu
Vous aur**iez**	Vous auriez eu
Ils aur**aient**	Ils auraient eu

Imperative

Present	*Perfect* (Rare)
2nd pers. sing. Aie	2nd pers. sing. Aie eu
1st pers. plur. Ayons	1st pers. plur. Ayons eu
2nd pers. plur. Ayez	2nd pers. plur. Ayez eu

Subjunctive

Present	*Perfect*
Que j'aie	Que j'aie eu
Que tu aies	Que tu aies eu
Qu'il ait	Qu'il ait eu
Que nous ayons	Que nous ayons eu
Que vous ayez	Que vous ayez eu
Qu'ils aient	Qu'ils aient eu

Infinitive

Present	*Perfect*
Avoir	Avoir eu

Participle

Present	*Past*
Ay**ant**	(Ayant) eu

Auxiliaries: ÊTRE

Simple Tenses	*Compound Tenses*

Indicative

Present	*Perfect*
Je suis	J'ai été
Tu es	Tu as été
Il est	Il a été
Nous sommes	Nous avons été
Vous êtes	Vous avez été
Ils sont	Ils ont été

Past Historic	*Past Anterior*
Je fus	J'eus été
Tu fus	Tu eus été
Il fut	Il eut été
Nous fûmes	Nous eûmes été
Vous fûtes	Vous eûtes été
Ils furent	Ils eurent été

Imperfect	*Pluperfect*
J'étais	J'avais été
Tu étais	Tu avais été
Il était	Il avait été
Nous étions	Nous avions été
Vous étiez	Vous aviez été
Ils étaient	Ils avaient été

Future	*Future Perfect*
Je serai	J'aurai été
Tu seras	Tu auras été
Il sera	Il aura été
Nous serons	Nous aurons été
Vous serez	Vous aurez été
Ils seront	Ils auront été

Conditional

Present	*Perfect*
Je serais	J'aurais été
Tu serais	Tu aurais été
Il serait	Il aurait été
Nous serions	Nous aurions été
Vous seriez	Vous auriez été
Ils seraient	Ils auraient été

Être-*cont.*

Simple Tenses		Compound Tenses
	Imperative	
Present		*Perfect* (Rare)
2nd pers. sing. Sois		2nd pers. sing. Aie été
1st pers. plur. Soyons		1st pers. plur. Ayons été
2nd pers. plur. Soyez		2nd pers. plur. Ayez été
	Subjunctive	
Present		*Perfect*
Que je sois		Que j'aie été
Que tu sois		Que tu aies été
Qu'il soit		Qu'il ait été
Que nous soyons		Que nous ayons été
Que vous soyez		Que vous ayez été
Qu'ils soient		Qu'ils aient été
	Infinitive	
Present		*Perfect*
Être		Avoir été
	Participle	
Present		*Past*
Etant		(Ayant) été

Points to bear in mind regarding the use of **avoir** (*to have*) and **être** (*to be*):

1   As well as being verbs in their own right, **avoir** and **être** are used as auxiliaries to form all the compound tenses in French. To do so, the Past Participle of the main verb is added to the required tense of the *appropriate* auxiliary.

Note: Because of the French system of gender and number agreement, you must *always* check, when using a Past Participle, whether its role or position in the sentence require it to agree with the Subject or the Object. The rules of Past Participle agreement are presented in Chapter 12.

2   The auxiliary **être** is used to form the Passive Voice (Subject undergoing an action). It should be noted, however, that the compound tenses of a passive construction use **avoir** as their auxiliary.

Compare: Il **est** blessé.   and   Il **a été** blessé.
                      (Present)   (Perfect)
                      He is wounded.   *He has been wounded.*

or: Il **était** blessé.   and: Il **avait été** blesse.́
             (Imperfect)   (Pluperfect)
             He was wounded.   *He had been wounded.*

Note: Some transitive verbs (i.e. admitting a Direct Object complement) can, in English, be constructed using the 'passive technique'. For example

    (*a*) *He was given a watch.*
    (*b*) *They were shown the door.*
    (*c*) *I was told a story.*

This is *impossible* in French. Such sentences must be put in the active voice.

    (*a*) On lui a donné une montre.
    (*b*) On leur a montré la porte.
    (*c*) On m'a raconté une histoire.

3   It is possible to create a whole new category of tenses called double-compound tenses (**temps surcomposés**) which are mainly used in spoken French and are formed as follows:

  (i)   *For verbs using the auxiliary* **avoir**: Suitable Compound Tense of **avoir** + Past Participle of main verb. For example:
     Quand il **a eu fini** son travail, il **est parti**.   *When he had finished his work, he went.*

 (ii)   *For verbs using the auxiliary* **etre**: Suitable Compound Tense of **avoir** + **été** + Past Participle of main verb. For example:
     Quand il **a eu été parti** je **suis rentré**.   *When he was gone I returned home.*

Such tenses are used to emphasise the *completed aspect* of a past action in constructions where traditional compound tenses may sound affected or highbrow. The double-compound Perfect is very often used as a partner for the Perfect because the Past Anterior (which was the partner of the Past Historic) sounds over-refined.

Compare: Quand elle **eut mangé**, elle **se leva**. (Past Ant. + Past Hist.)

and: Quand elle **a eu mangé**, elle **s'est levée**. (Pass. Surcomp. + Perfect)   *When she had finished eating, she got up.*

or: Lorsqu'il **fut sorti**, il **refusa** de parler. (Past Ant. + Past Hist.)

and: Lorsqu'il **a eu été sorti**, il **a refusé** de parler (Pass. Surcomp. + Perf.)   *Once he had gone out, he refused to talk.*

Note: All ordinary compound tenses could, if desired, be replaced using the above technique.

Important: In *all* circumstances, the Past Participle of **être** remains invariable.

1ST GROUP VERBS — **aimer** *to love*

Indicative

Simple Tenses	*Compound Tenses*
Present	*Perfect*
J'aime	J'ai aimé
Tu aimes	Tu as aimé
Il aime	Il a aimé
Nous aimons	Nous avons aimé
Vous aimez	Vous avez aimé
Ils aiment	Ils ont aimé
Past Historic	*Past Anterior*
J'aimai	J'eus aimé
Tu aimas	Tu eus aimé
Il aima	Il eut aimé
Nous aimâmes	Nous eûmes aimé
Vous aimâtes	Vous eûtes aimé
Ils aimèrent	Ils eurent aimé
Imperfect	*Pluperfect*
J'aimais	J'avais aimé
Tu aimais	Tu avais aimé
Il aimait	Il avait aimé
Nous aimions	Nous avions aimé
Vous aimiez	Vous aviez aimé
Ils aimaient	Ils avaient aimé
Future	*Future Perfect*
J'aimerai	J'aurai aimé
Tu aimeras	Tu auras aimé
Il aimera	Il aura aimé
Nous aimerons	Nous aurons aimé
Vous aimerez	Vous aurez aimé
Ils aimeront	Ils auront aimé

Conditional

Present	*Perfect*
J'aimerais	J'aurais aimé
Tu aimerais	Tu aurais aimé
Il aimerait	Il aurait aimé
Nous aimerions	Nous aurions aimé
Vous aimeriez	Vous auriez aimé
Ils aimeraient	Ils auraient aimé

aimer *cont.*

Simple Tenses		*Compound Tenses*
	Imperative	
Present		*Perfect* (Rare)
2nd pers. sing. Aim**e**		2nd pers. sing. Aie aimé
1st pers. plur. Aim**ons**		1st pers. plur. Ayons aimé
2nd pers. plur. Aim**ez**		2nd pers. plur. Ayez aimé
	Subjunctive	
Present		*Perfect*
Que j'aim**e**		Que j'aie aimé
Que tu aim**es**		Que tu aies aimé
Qu'il aim**e**		Qu'il ait aimé
Que nous aim**ions**		Que nous ayons aimé
Que vous aim**iez**		Que vous ayez aimé
Qu'ils aim**ent**		Qu'ils aient aimé
	Infinitive	
Present		*Past*
Aim**er**		(Avoir) aim**é**
	Participle	
Present		*Perfect*
Aim**ant**		(Ayant) aim**é**

Note: There are two distinct stems — **aim** and **aimer** — which are used to form the simple Tenses.

Points regarding the use of 1st group (**er**) verbs:
1   **Aller** (*to go*), which is one of the most frequently used verbs in the language, does not follow the normal pattern of tense-formation. Its conjugation is presented in the Irregular Verbs Chart on page 161.
2   Some verbs in this group undergo small changes in order to preserve their phonetic (i.e. sound) pattern. The following examples will help clarify that statement:
   (i)   Because of the sound change of **c** from [s] to [k] when that letter is followed by **a**, **o** or **u**, **c** is replaced by **ç** = [s] whenever, in the course of conjugation, an ending beginning with one of those three vowels is expected immediately after the **c**.

Compare:	Il place	*or*	Il placera
	He is placing		*He will place*
and:	Il plaçait	*or*	Nous plaçons
	He was placing		*We are placing*

In the last two examples, if the **c** were not replaced by **ç** before the **a** or the **o**, it would be pronounced [k]. (See Appendix I.)

(ii) Because of the sound change of **g** from [ʒ] to [g] when that letter is followed by **a**, **o** or **u**, an **e** must be introduced after the **g** whenever, in the course of the conjugation, an ending beginning with **a** or **o** is expected immediately after it.

Compare:	Je mange	or:	Nous mangions
	I am eating		*We were eating*
and:	Je mangeai	or:	Nous mangeons
	I ate		*We are eating*

In the last two examples, if the **g** were not followed by **e** before **a** or **o**, it would be pronounced [g] (see Appendix I).

Note: A look at the endings for each tense will *immediately* reveal where those modifications are needed to preserve the correct sound-pattern of the verb.

3 Verbs in **ayer**, **oyer** and **uyer**: In their modern French version, those verbs change **y** to **i** whenever, in the course of the conjugation, **y** is due to be followed by a mute **e** (**e** without an accent = [ə]).

Compare:	Nous essayons	or:	Nous nettoyons
	We are trying		*We are cleaning*
and:	J'essaie	or:	Je nettoie
	I am trying		*I am cleaning*
But:	J'ai essayé		Il a nettoyé
	I tried		*He cleaned*

Note: The endings **er** and **ez** are pronounced as **é** (= [e]); the **y** will therefore remain before them:

Essay**er**	or: Nettoy**ez**!
To try	*Clean!*

4 Verbs in **eler** and **eter**. Their pattern of behaviour is as follows:

(i) The majority double their **l** or **t** if the letter which follows is a mute **e** (**e** without an accent = [ə]):

Compare:	Nous jetons	or:	Nous appelons
	We are throwing		*We are calling*
and:	Il jet**te**	or:	Il appel**le**
	He is throwing		*He is calling*
But:	J'ai jeté		J'ai appelé
	I threw		*I called*

Note: The 3rd person plural ending **ent** is *always* pronounced like a mute **e** [ə]. The doubling of the consonant will therefore occur:

Ils je**ttent**	or:	Ils appe**llent**
They are throwing		*They are calling*

(ii)   The remainder of **eler** and **eter** verbs (see list below) *do not* double their consonant, but when the environment where they should do so occurs (see (i) above), they change the **e** preceding the consonant into **è** (= [ɛ]).

Compare:	Nous gelons	or:	Nous pelons
	We are freezing		*We are peeling*
and:	Nous gèlerons	or:	Nous pèlerons
	We shall freeze		*We shall peel*
But:	Je suis gelé		Il a pelé
	I am frozen		*He has peeled*
or:	Geler		Pelez!
	To freeze		*Peel!*

The most commonly used verbs in that category are: **acheter** (*to buy*), **démanteler** (*to dismantle*), **étiqueter** (*to label*), **geler** (*to freeze*) and its compounds: **dégeler** (*to defrost*), **congeler/surgeler** (*to deep-freeze*), **harceler** (*to badger*), **marteler** (*to hammer*), **modeler** (*to model*).

Note: The following verbs: **mener** (*to lead*), **semer** (*to sow*), **soulever** (*to lift*), change their **e** to **è** in the same phonetic environment as the above-mentioned category.

5   Verbs ending in **éder**, **éger**, **éler** or **éter** change their **é** to **è** when the syllable they are in is followed by a *final* mute **e** (pronounced [ə]).

> If another syllable follows the mute **e**, the **é** remains unchanged!

Compare:	Céder	or:	Protéger
	To give in		*To protect*
and	Je cède!	or:	Ils protègent
	I give in!		*They protect*
But:	Tu céderas	or:	Elle protégerait
	You will give in		*She would protect*

Note: the previously-mentioned comments concerning **ent**, **er** and **ez** verb endings also apply here.

6   The verbs **envoyer** (*to send*) and **renvoyer** (*to send back*) do not totally conform to the normal rule of tense-formation. In the Future and Present Conditional, their stem is **enverr** and **renverr** respectively. For example:

Nous **enverr**ons	or:	Ils **renverr**aient
We shall send		*They would send back*

2ND GROUP VERBS — **finir** *to finish*

Simple Tenses	*Compound Tenses*
	Indicative
Present	*Perfect*
Je fin**is**	J'ai fini
Tu fin**is**	Tu as fini
Il fin**it**	Il a fini
Nous fin**issons**	Nous avons fini
Vous fin**issez**	Vous avez fini
Ils fin**issent**	Ils ont fini
Past Historic	*Past Anterior*
Je fin**is**	J'eus fini
Tu fin**is**	Tu eus fini
Il fin**it**	Il eut fini
Nous fin**îmes**	Nous eûmes fini
Vous fin**îtes**	Vous eûtes fini
Ils fin**irent**	Ils eurent fini
Imperfect	*Pluperfect*
Je finiss**ais**	J'avais fini
Tu finiss**ais**	Tu avais fini
Il finiss**ait**	Il avait fini
Nous finiss**ions**	Nous avions fini
Vous finiss**iez**	Vous aviez fini
Ils finiss**aient**	Ils avaient fini
Future	*Future Perfect*
Je finir**ai**	J'aurai fini
Tu finir**as**	Tu auras fini
Il finir**a**	Il aura fini
Nous finir**ons**	Nous aurons fini
Vous finir**ez**	Vous aurez fini
Ils finir**ont**	Ils auront fini
	Conditional
Present	*Perfect*
Je finir**ais**	J'aurais fini
Tu finir**ais**	Tu aurais fini
Il finir**ait**	Il aurait fini
Nous finir**ions**	Nous aurions fini
Vous finir**iez**	Vous auriez fini
Ils finir**aient**	Ils auraient fini

Simple Tenses		Compound Tenses
	Imperative	
Present		*Perfect* (Rare)
2nd pers. sing. fin**is**		2nd pers. sing. Aie fini
1st pers. plur. Fin**issons**		1st pers. plur. Ayons fini
2nd pers. plur. Fin**issez**		2nd pers. plur. Ayez fini
	Subjunctive	
Present		*Perfect*
Que je finiss**e**		Que j'aie fini
Que tu finiss**es**		Que tu aies fini
Qu'il finiss**e**		Qu'il ait fini
Que nous finiss**ions**		Que nous ayons fini
Que vous finiss**iez**		Que vous ayez fini
Qu'ils finiss**ent**		Qu'ils aient fini
	Infinitive	
Present		*Perfect*
Fin**ir**		Avoir fini
	Participle	
Present		*Past*
Finiss**ant**		(Ayant) fini

Note: the three stems — **fin**, **finir** and **finiss** — and the Tenses each one occurs in.

Points regarding the use of 2nd group verbs:

NB   There are two conditions that a verb must fulfill in order to belong to this group: it must have an **ir** Infinitive, *and* a Present Participle ending in **issant**.

The formation of the simple tenses is as follows:

1   The basic stem (Infinitive minus **ir**), is used (with the appropriate endings) for the first three persons singular of the Present Indicative, for the Past Historic, and for the 2nd person singular of the Present Imperative.
2   The whole of the Present Infinitive is used as a stem to form the Future and the Present Conditional.
3   The basic stem + **iss** is used to form the last three persons of the Present Indicative, the whole of the Imperfect, the two plural persons of the Present Imperative and the whole of the Present Subjunctive:

Compare:	Je réa**gis**	or:	Il invest**it**
	I react		*He invests*
with:	Je réa**girai**	or:	Il invest**irait**
	I shall react		*He would invest*
and:	Nous réa**gissions**	or:	Qu'ils invest**issent**!
	We used to react		*Let them invest!*

Note: Apart from the insertion of the syllable **iss** between the stem and the endings of certain tenses, the principles of tense formation are identical with those of the 1st group verbs.

This group is the least troublesome of the three but there are, nevertheless, a few other points to note:

1 **Bénir** (*to bless*) has two possible adjectival forms for its past participle:
– **bénit** when the meaning is *blessed by a priest*. For example
    Du pain **bénit**   *Consecrated bread*
    De l'eau **bénite**   *Holy water*
– **béni** in all other cases:
    Madame, soyez **bénie** pour ces bonnes paroles.   *Madam, may you be blessed for those kind words.*

2 **Fleurir** (*to blossom*) has two different stems for the Imperfect and the Present Participle:
(i) **fleur** if the action refers to trees or flowers;
(ii) **flor** if the action refers to a venture, a business, etc.
Compare: Le pommier **fleurissait**.
               The apple-tree was blossoming.
and: L'affaire **florissait**.
               The business was flourishing.
Note: No further distinction is made between the two throughout the rest of the conjugation.

3 **Haïr** (*to hate*) loses its diaresis (¨) in the first three persons of the Present Indicative and in the second person singular of the Present Imperative.
Compare: Je **hais** les dimanches. (and not *je haïs)
             I hate Sundays.
and: Vous **haïssez** la solitude.
            You hate loneliness.

As a point of interest, it may be noted that a number of 2nd group verbs have been formed from adjectives of colour: **blanchir** (*to turn white*), **brunir** (*to turn brown*), **jaunir** (*to turn yellow*), **rosir** (*to turn pink*), **rougir** (*to turn red, to blush*), **noircir** (*to turn black*), **pâlir** (*to turn pale*), **verdir** (*to turn green*). For example:
    Elle **rougissait** de plaisir.   *She was blushing with delight.*

3RD GROUP VERBS (**ir** category) — **partir** *to leave*

Simple Tenses	*Compound Tenses*
	Indicative
Present	*Perfect*
Je par**s**	Je suis parti
Tu par**s**	Tu es parti
Il par**t**	Il est parti
Nous part**ons**	Nous sommes partis
Vous part**ez**	Vous êtes partis
Ils part**ent**	Ils sont partis
Past Historic	*Past Anterior*
Je part**is**	Je fus parti
Tu part**is**	Tu fus parti
Il part**it**	Il fut parti
Nous part**îmes**	Nous fûmes partis
Vous part**îtes**	Vous fûtes partis
Ils part**irent**	Ils furent partis
Imperfect	*Pluperfect*
Je part**ais**	J'étais parti
Tu part**ais**	Tu étais parti
Il part**ait**	Il était parti
Nous part**ions**	Nous étions partis
Vous part**iez**	Vous étiez partis
Ils part**aient**	Ils étaient partis
Future	*Future Perfect*
Je partir**ai**	Je serai parti
Tu partir**as**	Tu seras parti
Il partir**a**	Il sera parti
Nous partir**ons**	Nous serons partis
Vous partir**ez**	Vous serez partis
Ils partir**ont**	Ils seront partis
	Conditional
Present	*Perfect*
Je partir**ais**	Je serais parti
Tu partir**ais**	Tu serais parti
Il partir**ait**	Il serait parti
Nous partir**ions**	Nous serions partis
Vous partir**iez**	Vous seriez partis
Ils partir**aient**	Ils seraient partis
	Imperative
Present	*Perfect* (Rare)
2nd pers. sing. Par**s**	2nd pers. sing. Sois parti
1st pers. plur. Part**ons**	1st pers. plur. Soyons partis
2nd pers. plur. Part**ez**	2nd pers. plur. Soyez partis

partir *cont.*

Simple Tenses	*Compound Tenses*
Subjunctive	
Present	*Perfect*
Que je part**e**	Que je sois parti
Que tu part**es**	Que tu sois parti
Qu'il part**e**	Qu'il soit parti
Que nous part**ions**	Que nous soyons partis
Que vous part**iez**	Que vous soyez partis
Qu'ils part**ent**	Qu'ils soient partis
Infinitive	
Present	*Perfect*
Part**ir**	Être parti
Participle	
Present	*Past*
Part**ant**	(Etant) parti

Note the different stems:
  (i) Mixed: **par**/**part** for the Present Indicative and the Present Imperative;
 (ii) **part** for the Past Historic, the Imperfect, the Present Subjunctive, the Past Participle;
(iii) **partir** for the Future and the Conditional.

3RD GROUP VERBS (**oir** category) – **recevoir** *to receive*

Simple Tenses	*Compound Tenses*
Indicative	
Present	*Perfect*
Je reçois	J'ai reçu
Tu reçois	Tu as reçu
Il reçoit	Il a reçu
Nous recev**ons**	Nous avons reçu
Vous recev**ez**	Vous avez reçu
Ils reçoiv**ent**	Ils ont reçu
Past Historic	*Past Anterior*
Je reç**us**	J'eus reçu
Tu reç**us**	Tu eus reçu
Il reç**ut**	Il eut reçu
Nous reç**ûmes**	Nous eûmes reçu
Vous reç**ûtes**	Vous eûtes reçu
Ils reç**urent**	Ils eurent reçu

recevoir-*cont.*

Simple Tenses	*Compound Tenses*
Imperfect	*Pluperfect*
Je recev**ais**	J'avais reçu
Tu recev**ais**	Tu avais reçu
Il recev**ait**	Il avait reçu
Nous recev**ions**	Nous avions reçu
Vous recev**iez**	Vous aviez reçu
Ils recev**aient**	Ils avaient reçu
Future	*Future Perfect*
Je recevr**ai**	J'aurai reçu
Tu recevr**as**	Tu auras reçu
Il recevr**a**	Il aura reçu
Nous recevr**ons**	Nous aurons reçu
Vous recevr**ez**	Vous aurez reçu
Ils recevr**ont**	Ils auront reçu

Conditional

Present	*Perfect*
Je recevr**ais**	J'aurais reçu
Tu recevr**ais**	Tu aurais reçu
Il recevr**ait**	Il aurait reçu
Nous recevr**ions**	Nous aurions reçu
Vous recevr**iez**	Vous auriez reçu
Ils recevr**aient**	Ils auraient reçu

Imperative

Present	*Perfect*
2nd pers. sing. reç**ois**	2nd pers. sing. Aie reçu
1st pers. plur. recev**ons**	1st pers. plur. Ayons reçu
2nd pers. plur. recev**ez**	2nd pers. plur. Ayez reçu

Subjunctive

Present	*Perfect*
Que je reç**oive**	Que j'aie reçu
Que tu reç**oives**	Que tu aies reçu
Qu'il reç**oive**	Qu'il ait reçu
Que nous recev**ions**	Que nous ayons reçu
Que vous recev**iez**	Que vous ayez reçu
Qu'ils reç**oivent**	Qu'ils aient reçu

Infinitive

Present	*Perfect*
Recev**oir**	Avoir reç**u**

recevoir-*cont.*

Simple Tenses	Participle	Compound Tenses
Present		*Past*
Recev**ant**		(Ayant) re**çu**

Note the different stems:
(i)   mixed: **reçoi**/**recev** for the Present Indicative, the Present Subjunctive and the Present Imperative;
(ii)   **reç** for Past Historic and Past Participle;
(iii)   **recev** for Imperfect and Present Participle;
(iv)   **recevr** for Future and Present Conditional.

Points regarding the use of 3rd group verbs (**ir**/**oir** categories):
1   Although the following verbs: **couvrir** (*to cover*), **ouvrir** (*to open*), **offrir** (*to offer*), **souffrir** (*to suffer*) belong to the 3rd group, they form their Present Indicative (and Present Imperative) in the same way as **er** verbs:

>   Je couvre;   tu ouvres;   il souffre
>   *I cover*;   *you open*   *he suffers*

2   The following verbs: **acquérir** (*to acquire*), **courir** (*to run*), **mourir** (*to die*), drop the **i** of their Infinitive (stem) in the Future and Present Conditional Tenses. For example:

>   J'**acquerr**ai; tu **courr**as; il **mourr**a
>   *I shall acquire; you will run; he will die*

3   **Mentir** (*to lie*), **partir** (*to leave*), **sentir** (*to feel*), **sortir** (*to go out*) drop the **t** of their stem in the first persons singular of the Present Indicative and in the second person singular of the Present Imperative:

>   Je mens;   tu sens;   sors!
>   *I lie;   you feel;   get out!*

4   **Tenir** (*to hold*) follows the same pattern as **venir** (*to come*) (see Irregular Verbs Charts on page 172).
5   **Fuir** (*to run away*) has two stems:

In the Present Indicative   { 1st, 2nd, 3rd sing. + 3rd plur. = **fui**
                             { 1st, 2nd plur. = **fuy**

In the Present Imperative   { 2nd sing. = **fui**
                            { 1st, 2nd plur. = **fuy**

In the Present Subjunctive   { 1st, 2nd, 3rd sing. + 3rd plur. = **fui**
                             { 1st, 2nd plur. = **fuy**

6 **Pouvoir** (*to be able to/can*) and **voir** (*to see*) have an irregular stem in the Future and Conditional:

Je **pourr**ai
I will be able to

Nous **verr**ions
We would see

3RD GROUP VERBS (**re** category) — **vendre** *to sell*

Simple Tenses	*Compound Tenses*
Indicative	
Present	*Perfect*
Je vend**s**	J'ai vendu
Tu vend**s**	Tu as vendu
Il vend	Il a vendu
Nous vend**ons**	Nous avons vendu
Vous vend**ez**	Vous avez vendu
Ils vend**ent**	Ils ont vendu
Past Historic	*Past Anterior*
Je vend**is**	J'eus vendu
Tu vend**is**	Tu eus vendu
Il vend**it**	Il eut vendu
Nous vend**îmes**	Nous eûmes vendu
Vous vend**îtes**	Vous eûtes vendu
Ils vend**irent**	Ils eurent vendu
Imperfect	*Pluperfect*
Je vend**ais**	J'avais vendu
Tu vend**ais**	Tu avais vendu
Il vend**ait**	Il avait vendu
Nous vend**ions**	Nous avions vendu
Vous vend**iez**	Vous aviez vendu
Ils vend**aient**	Ils avaient vendu
Future	*Future Perfect*
Je vend**rai**	J'aurai vendu
Tu vend**ras**	Tu auras vendu
Il vend**ra**	Il aura vendu
Nous vend**rons**	Nous aurons vendu
Vous vend**rez**	Vous aurez vendu
Ils vend**ront**	Ils auront vendu
Conditional	
Present	*Perfect*
Je vend**rais**	J'aurais vendu
Tu vend**rais**	Tu aurais vendu
Il vend**rait**	Il aurait vendu

vendre *cont.*

Simple Tenses		*Compound Tenses*
Nous vendr**ions**		Nous aurions vendu
Vous vendr**iez**		Vous auriez vendu
Ils vendr**aient**		Ils auraient vendu

Imperative

Present		*Perfect* (Rare)
2nd pers. sing. Vend**s**		2nd pers. sing. Aie vendu
1st pers. plur. Vend**ons**		1st pers. plur. Ayons vendu
2nd pers. plur. Vend**ez**		2nd pers. plur. Ayez vendu

Subjunctive

Present		*Perfect*
Que je vend**e**		Que j'aie vendu
Que tu vend**es**		Que tu aies vendu
Qu'il vend**e**		Qu'il ait vendu
Que nous vend**ions**		Que nous ayons vendu
Que vous vend**iez**		Que vous ayez vendu
Qu'ils vend**ent**		Qu'ils aient vendu

Infinitive

Present		*Perfect*
Vend**re**		Avoir vend**u**

Participle

Present		*Past*
Vend**ant**		(Ayant) vend**u**

Note the different stems:
(i) **vendr** for the Future and Present Conditional Tenses;
(ii) **vend** for all other Tenses.

Points regarding the use of 3rd group (**re** category) verbs:
1   **Rompre** (*to break*) and its compounds: **corrompre** (*to corrupt*) and **interrompre** (*to interrupt*), take a **t** in the 3rd person singular of the Present Indicative:

Il corrompt	*or*: Elle interrompt
He corrupts	*She interrupts*

2   Verbs ending in **dre** *normally* take a **d** in the 3rd person singular of the Present Indicative:

Il prend (Inf. = **Prendre**)	*or*: Elle attend (Inf. = **attendre**)
He takes	*She waits*

But: Verbs ending in **indre** and **soudre** take a **t** instead of a **d** in the same context:

Il pein**t** (Inf. = **peindre**)   *or*: Il résou**t** (Inf. = **résoudre**)
He paints   *He solves*

3   **Dire** (*to say*) and **redire** (*to repeat*) become **dites** and **redites** (and not *disez and *redisez) in the 2nd person plural of the Present Indicative and Imperative.

But: **Contredire** (*to contradict*), **interdire** (*to forbid*), **médire** (*to slander*), **prédire** (*to foretell*) become contre**disez**, inter**disez**, mé**disez** and pre**disez** in the same context.

4   **Faire** becomes **faites** (and not *faisez) in the 2nd Person plural of the Present Indicative and Imperative.

5   Verbs ending in **aître** and **oître** (e.g. **connaître** *to know* and **croître** *to grow/increase*) preserve their circumflex accent over the **i** whenever that **i** is followed by a **t** in the conjugation.

Compare: Je connai**s**sais   *or*: Ils croissent
            I used to know   *They are growing*
and: Il conna**î**t   *or*: Ils cro**î**tront
            He knows   *They will grow*

6   **Croître** (*to grow/increase*) takes a circumflex accent ^ over the **u** of its Past Participle but its compounds do not.

Compare: Il a cr**û**   and: Il a décr**u**
            It has increased   *It has decreased*

Irregular Verbs

PRÉSENT de l'indicatif *Present indicative*	PASSÉ SIMPLE *Past historic*	IMPARFAIT *Imperfect*	FUTUR *Future*	CONDITIONNEL *Conditional*	Present du SUBJONCTIF *Present subjunctive*	IMPÉRATIF *Imperative*

Aller (+ **être**) *to go:* Past participle: allé *Present participle:* allant

je vais	allai	allais	irai	irais	aille	
tu vas	allas	allais	iras	irais	ailles	va
il va	alla	allait	ira	irait	aille	
nous allons	allâmes	allions	irons	irions	allions	allons
vous allez	allâtes	alliez	irez	iriez	alliez	allez
ils vont	allèrent	allaient	iront	iraient	aillent	

S'asseoir (+ **être**) *to sit:* assis — asseyant

je m'assieds	m'assis	m'asseyais	m'assiérai	m'assiérais	m'asseye	
tu t'assieds	t'assis	t'asseyais	t'assiéras	t'assiérais	t'asseyes	assieds-toi
il s'assied	s'assit	s'asseyait	s'assiéra	s'assiérait	s'asseye	
nous nous asseyons	nous assîmes	nous asseyions	nous assiérons	nous assiérions	nous asseyions	asseyons-nous
vous vous asseyez	vous assîtes	vous asseyiez	vous assiérez	vous assiériez	vous asseyiez	asseyez-vous
ils s'asseyent	s'assirent	s'asseyaient	s'assiéront	s'assiéraient	s'asseyent	

Present indicative	Past historic	Imperfect	Future	Conditional	Present subjunctive	Imperative

Boire (+ **avoir**) *to drink*: bu — buvant

je bois	bus	buvais	boirai	boirais	boive	
tu bois	bus	buvais	boiras	boirais	boives	bois
il boit	but	buvait	boira	boirait	boive	
nous buvons	bûmes	buvions	boirons	boirions	buvions	buvons
vous buvez	bûtes	buviez	boirez	boiriez	buviez	buvez
ils boivent	burent	buvaient	boiront	boiraient	boivent	

Conduire (+ **avoir**) *to drive*: conduit — conduisant

je conduis	conduisis	conduisais	conduirai	conduirais	conduise	
tu conduis	conduisis	conduisais	conduiras	conduirais	conduises	conduis
il conduit	conduisit	conduisait	conduira	conduirait	conduise	
nous conduisons	conduisîmes	conduisions	conduirons	conduirions	conduisions	conduisons
vous conduisez	conduisîtes	conduisiez	conduirez	conduiriez	conduisiez	conduisez
ils conduisent	conduisirent	conduisaient	conduiront	conduiraient	conduisent	

Connaître (+ **avoir**) *to know*: connu — connaissant

je connais	connus	connaissais	connaîtrai	connaîtrais	connaisse	
tu connais	connus	connaissais	connaîtras	connaîtrais	connaisses	connais
il connaît	connut	connaissait	connaîtra	connaîtrait	connaisse	
nous connaissons	connûmes	connaissions	connaîtrons	connaîtrions	connaissions	connaissons
vous connaissez	connûtes	connaissiez	connaîtrez	connaîtriez	connaissiez	connaissez
ils connaissent	connurent	connaissaient	connaîtront	connaîtraient	connaissent	

Courir (+ **avoir**) *to run*: couru — courant

je cours	courais	courus	courrai	courrais	coure	
tu cours	courais	courus	courras	courrais	coures	cours
il court	courait	courut	courra	courrait	coure	
nous courons	courions	courûmes	courrons	courrions	courions	courons
vous courez	couriez	courûtes	courrez	courriez	couriez	courez
ils courent	couraient	coururent	courront	courraient	courent	

Craindre (+ **avoir**) *to fear*: craint — craignant

je crains	craignais	craignis	craindrai	craindrais	craigne	
tu crains	craignais	craignis	craindras	craindrais	craignes	crains
il craint	craignait	craignit	craindra	craindrait	craigne	
nous craignons	craignions	craignîmes	craindrons	craindrions	craignions	craignons
vous craignez	craigniez	craignîtes	craindrez	craindriez	craigniez	craignez
ils craignent	craignaient	craignirent	craindront	craindraient	craignent	

Croire (+ **avoir**) *to believe*: cru — croyant

je crois	croyais	crus	croirai	croirais	croie	
tu crois	croyais	crus	croiras	croirais	croies	crois
il croit	croyait	crut	croira	croirait	croie	
nous croyons	croyions	crûmes	croirons	croirions	croyions	croyons
vous croyez	croyiez	crûtes	croirez	croiriez	croyiez	croyez
ils croient	croyaient	crurent	croiront	croiraient	croient	

Cueillir (+ **avoir**) *to pick:* cueilli — cueillant

Present indicative	Past historic	Imperfect	Future	Conditional	Present subjunctive	Imperative
je cueille	cueillis	cueillais	cueillerai	cueillerais	cueille	
tu cueilles	cueillis	cueillais	cueilleras	cueillerais	cueilles	cueille
il cueille	cueillit	cueillait	cueillera	cueillerait	cueille	
nous cueillons	cueillîmes	cueillions	cueillerons	cueillerions	cueillions	cueillons
vous cueillez	cueillîtes	cueilliez	cueillerez	cueilleriez	cueilliez	cueillez
ils cueillent	cueillirent	cueillaient	cueilleront	cueilleraient	cueillent	

Devoir (+ **avoir**) *to have to/to owe:* dû — devant

Present indicative	Past historic	Imperfect	Future	Conditional	Present subjunctive	Imperative
je dois	dus	devais	devrai	devrais	doive	
tu dois	dus	devais	devras	devrais	doives	dois
il doit	dut	devait	devra	devrait	doive	
nous devons	dûmes	devions	devrons	devrions	devions	devons
vous devez	dûtes	deviez	devrez	devriez	deviez	devez
ils doivent	durent	devaient	devront	devraient	doivent	

Dire (+ **avoir**) *to say:* dit — disant

Present indicative	Past historic	Imperfect	Future	Conditional	Present subjunctive	Imperative
je dis	dis	disais	dirai	dirais	dise	
tu dis	dis	disais	diras	dirais	dises	dis
il dit	dit	disait	dira	dirait	dise	
nous disons	dîmes	disions	dirons	dirions	disions	disons
vous dites	dîtes	disiez	direz	diriez	disiez	dites
ils disent	dirent	disaient	diront	diraient	disent	

Dormir (+ **avoir**) *to sleep:* dormi — dormant

je dors	dormis	dormais	dormirai	dormirais	dorme	
tu dors	dormis	dormais	dormiras	dormirais	dormes	dors
il dort	dormit	dormait	dormira	dormirait	dorme	
nous dormons	dormîmes	dormions	dormirons	dormirions	dormions	dormons
vous dormez	dormîtes	dormiez	dormirez	dormiriez	dormiez	dormez
ils dorment	dormirent	dormaient	dormiront	dormiraient	dorment	

Ecrire (+ **avoir**) *to write:* écrit — écrivant

j'écris	écrivis	écrivais	écrirai	écrirais	écrive	
tu écris	écrivis	écrivais	écriras	écrirais	écrives	écris
il écrit	écrivit	écrivait	écrira	écrirait	écrive	
nous écrivons	écrivîmes	écrivions	écrirons	écririons	écrivions	écrivons
vous écrivez	écrivîtes	écriviez	écrirez	écririez	écriviez	écrivez
ils écrivent	écrivirent	écrivaient	écriront	écriraient	écrivent	

Envoyer (+ **avoir**) *to send:* envoyé — envoyant

j'envoie	envoyai	envoyais	enverrai	enverrais	envoie	
tu envoies	envoyas	envoyais	enverras	enverrais	envoies	envoie
il envoie	envoya	envoyait	enverra	enverrait	envoie	
nous envoyons	envoyâmes	envoyions	enverrons	enverrions	envoyions	envoyons
vous envoyez	envoyâtes	envoyiez	enverrez	enverriez	envoyiez	envoyez
ils envoient	envoyèrent	envoyaient	enverront	enverraient	envoient	

Eteindre (+ **avoir**) *to extinguish:* éteint — éteignant

	Present indicative	Past historic	Imperfect	Future	Conditional	Present subjunctive	Imperative
j'	éteins	éteignis	éteignais	éteindrai	éteindrais	éteigne	
tu	éteins	éteignis	éteignais	éteindras	éteindrais	éteignes	éteins
il	éteint	éteignit	éteignait	éteindra	éteindrait	éteigne	
nous	éteignons	éteignîmes	éteignions	éteindrons	éteindrions	éteignions	éteignons
vous	éteignez	éteignîtes	éteigniez	éteindrez	éteindriez	éteigniez	éteignez
ils	éteignent	éteignirent	éteignaient	éteindront	éteindraient	éteignent	

Faire (+ **avoir**) *to do/to make:* fait — faisant

	Present indicative	Past historic	Imperfect	Future	Conditional	Present subjunctive	Imperative
je	fais	fis	faisais	ferai	ferais	fasse	
tu	fais	fis	faisais	feras	ferais	fasses	fais
il	fait	fit	faisait	fera	ferait	fasse	
nous	faisons	fîmes	faisions	ferons	ferions	fassions	faisons
vous	faites	fîtes	faisiez	ferez	feriez	fassiez	faites
ils	font	firent	faisaient	feront	feraient	fassent	

Falloir (+ **avoir**) *to be necessary (impersonal only) Past participle:* fallu *No present participle*

Present indicative	Past historic	Imperfect	Future	Conditional	Present subjunctive	Imperative
il faut	il fallut	il fallait	il faudra	il faudrait	qu'il faille	

Lire (+ **avoir**) *to read*: lu — lisant

je lis	lus	lisais	lirai	lirais	lise	lis
tu lis	lus	lisais	liras	lirais	lises	
il lit	lut	lisait	lira	lirait	lise	
nous lisons	lûmes	lisions	lirons	lirions	lisions	lisons
vous lisez	lûtes	lisiez	lirez	liriez	lisiez	lisez
ils lisent	lurent	lisaient	liront	liraient	lisent	

Mettre (+ **avoir**) *to put*: mis — mettant

je mets	mis	mettais	mettrai	mettrais	mette	mets
tu mets	mis	mettais	mettras	mettrais	mettes	
il met	mit	mettait	mettra	mettrait	mette	
nous mettons	mîmes	mettions	mettrons	mettrions	mettions	mettons
vous mettez	mîtes	mettiez	mettrez	mettriez	mettiez	mettez
ils mettent	mirent	mettaient	mettront	mettraient	mettent	

Mourir (+ **être**) *to die*: mort — mourant

je meurs	mourus	mourais	mourrai	mourrais	meure	meurs
tu meurs	mourus	mourais	mourras	mourrais	meures	
il meurt	mourut	mourait	mourra	mourrait	meure	
nous mourons	mourûmes	mourions	mourrons	mourrions	mourions	mourons
vous mourez	mourûtes	mouriez	mourrez	mourriez	mouriez	mourez
ils meurent	moururent	mouraient	mourront	mourraient	meurent	

Present indicative	Past historic	Imperfect	Future	Conditional	Present subjunctive	Imperative

Naître (+ **être**) *to be born*: né — naissant

Present indicative	Past historic	Imperfect	Future	Conditional	Present subjunctive	Imperative
je nais	naquis	naissais	naîtrai	naîtrais	naisse	
tu nais	naquis	naissais	naîtras	naîtrais	naisses	nais
il naît	naquit	naissait	naîtra	naîtrait	naisse	
nous naissons	naquîmes	naissions	naîtrons	naîtrions	naissions	naissons
vous naissez	naquîtes	naissiez	naîtrez	naîtriez	naissiez	naissez
ils naissent	naquirent	naissaient	naîtront	naîtraient	naissent	

Ouvrir (+ **avoir**) *to open*: ouvert — ouvrant

Present indicative	Past historic	Imperfect	Future	Conditional	Present subjunctive	Imperative
j'ouvre	ouvris	ouvrais	ouvrirai	ouvrirais	ouvre	
tu ouvres	ouvris	ouvrais	ouvriras	ouvrirais	ouvres	ouvre
il ouvre	ouvrit	ouvrait	ouvrira	ouvrirait	ouvre	
nous ouvrons	ouvrîmes	ouvrions	ouvrirons	ouvririons	ouvrions	ouvrons
vous ouvrez	ouvrîtes	ouvriez	ouvrirez	ouvririez	ouvriez	ouvrez
ils ouvrent	ouvrirent	ouvraient	ouvriront	ouvriraient	ouvrent	

Partir (+ **être**) — see Model Chart on pages 154–5.

Plaire (+ **avoir**) *to please*: plu — plaisant

Present indicative	Past historic	Imperfect	Future	Conditional	Present subjunctive	Imperative
je plais	plus	plaisais	plairai	plairais	plaise	
tu plais	plus	plaisais	plairas	plairais	plaises	plais
il plaît	plut	plaisait	plaira	plairait	plaise	
nous plaisons	plûmes	plaisions	plairons	plairions	plaisions	plaisons
vous plaisez	plûtes	plaisiez	plairez	plairiez	plaisiez	plaisez
ils plaisent	plurent	plaisaient	plairont	plairaient	plaisent	

Pleuvoir (+ **avoir**) *to rain* (*impersonal only*): plu — pleuvant

il pleut	il plut	il pleuvait	il pleuvra	il pleuvrait	qu'il pleuve	

Pouvoir (+ **avoir**) *to be able to* (*can*): pu — pouvant

je peux	pus	pouvais	pourrai	pourrais	puisse	
tu peux	pus	pouvais	pourras	pourrais	puisses	
il peut	put	pouvait	pourra	pourrait	puisse	
nous pouvons	pûmes	pouvions	pourrons	pourrions	puissions	
vous pouvez	pûtes	pouviez	pourrez	pourriez	puissiez	
ils peuvent	purent	pouvaient	pourront	pourraient	puissent	

Prendre (+ **avoir**) *to take*: pris — prenant

je prends	pris	prenais	prendrai	prendrais	prenne	
tu prends	pris	prenais	prendras	prendrais	prennes	prends
il prend	prit	prenait	prendra	prendrait	prenne	
nous prenons	prîmes	prenions	prendrons	prendrions	prenions	prenons
vous prenez	prîtes	preniez	prendrez	prendriez	preniez	prenez
ils prennent	prirent	prenaient	prendront	prendraient	prennent	

Present indicative	Past historic	Imperfect	Future	Conditional	Present subjunctive	Imperative

Recevoir (+ **avoir**) — see Model Chart on pages 155–7.

Rire (+ **avoir**) *to laugh:* ri — riant

Present indicative	Past historic	Imperfect	Future	Conditional	Present subjunctive	Imperative
je ris	ris	riais	rirai	rirais	rie	
tu ris	ris	riais	riras	rirais	ries	ris
il rit	rit	riait	rira	rirait	rie	
nous rions	rîmes	riions	rirons	ririons	riions	rions
vous riez	rîtes	riiez	rirez	ririez	riiez	riez
ils rient	rirent	riaient	riront	riraient	rient	

Savoir (+ **avoir**) *to know:* su — sachant

Present indicative	Past historic	Imperfect	Future	Conditional	Present subjunctive	Imperative
je sais	sus	savais	saurai	saurais	sache	
tu sais	sus	savais	sauras	saurais	saches	sache
il sait	sut	savait	saura	saurait	sache	
nous savons	sûmes	savions	saurons	saurions	sachions	sachons
vous savez	sûtes	saviez	saurez	sauriez	sachiez	sachez
ils savent	surent	savaient	sauront	sauraient	sachent	

Sentir (+ **avoir**) *to feel/smell:* senti — sentant

Present indicative	Past historic	Imperfect	Future	Conditional	Present subjunctive	Imperative
je sens	sentis	sentais	sentirai	sentirais	sente	
tu sens	sentis	sentais	sentiras	sentirais	sentes	sens
il sent	sentit	sentait	sentira	sentirait	sente	
nous sentons	sentîmes	sentions	sentirons	sentirions	sentions	sentons
vous sentez	sentîtes	sentiez	sentirez	sentiriez	sentiez	sentez
ils sentent	sentirent	sentaient	sentiront	sentiraient	sentent	

Servir (+ **avoir**) *to serve:* servi — servant

je sers	servis	servais	servirai	servirais	serve	sers
tu sers	servis	servais	serviras	servirais	serves	
il sert	servit	servait	servira	servirait	serve	
nous servons	servîmes	servions	servirons	servirions	servions	servons
vous servez	servîtes	serviez	servirez	serviriez	serviez	servez
ils servent	servirent	servaient	serviront	serviraient	servent	

Sortir (+ **être**) *to go out:* sorti — sortant

je sors	sortis	sortais	sortirai	sortirais	sorte	sors
tu sors	sortis	sortais	sortiras	sortirais	sortes	
il sort	sortit	sortait	sortira	sortirait	sorte	
nous sortons	sortîmes	sortions	sortirons	sortirions	sortions	sortons
vous sortez	sortîtes	sortiez	sortirez	sortiriez	sortiez	sortez
ils sortent	sortirent	sortaient	sortiront	sortiraient	sortent	

Suivre (+ **Avoir**) *to follow:* suivi — suivant

je suis	suivis	suivais	suivrai	suivrais	suive	suis
tu suis	suivis	suivais	suivras	suivrais	suives	
il suit	suivit	suivait	suivra	suivrait	suive	
nous suivons	suivîmes	suivions	suivrons	suivrions	suivions	suivons
vous suivez	suivîtes	suiviez	suivrez	suivriez	suiviez	suivez
ils suivent	suivirent	suivaient	suivront	suivraient	suivent	

Present indicative	Past historic	Imperfect	Future	Conditional	Present subjunctive	Imperative

Valoir (+ **avoir**) *to be worth:* valu — valant

je vaux	valus	valais	vaudrai	vaudrais	vaille	
tu vaux	valus	valais	vaudras	vaudrais	vailles	
il vaut	valut	valait	vaudra	vaudrait	vaille	*(not used)*
nous valons	valûmes	valions	vaudrons	vaudrions	valions	
vous valez	valûtes	valiez	vaudrez	vaudriez	valiez	
ils valent	valurent	valaient	vaudront	vaudraient	vaillent	

Venir (+ **être**) *to come:* venu — venant

je viens	vins	venais	viendrais	viendrai	vienne	
tu viens	vins	venais	viendrais	viendras	viennes	viens
il/elle vient	vint	venait	viendrait	viendra	vienne	
nous venons	vînmes	venions	viendrions	viendrons	venions	venons
vous venez	vîntes	veniez	viendriez	viendrez	veniez	venez
ils/elles viennent	vinrent	venaient	viendraient	viendront	viennent	

Vivre (+ **avoir**) *to live:* vécu — vivant

je vis	vécus	vivais	vivrai	vivrais	vive	
tu vis	vécus	vivais	vivras	vivrais	vives	vis
il vit	vécut	vivait	vivra	vivrait	vive	
nous vivons	vécûmes	vivions	vivrons	vivrions	vivions	vivons
vous vivez	vécûtes	viviez	vivrez	vivriez	viviez	vivez
ils vivent	vecurent	vivaient	vivront	vivraient	vivent	

Voir (+ **avoir**) *to see:* vu — voyant

je vois	vis	voyais	verrai	verrais	voie	
tu vois	vis	voyais	verras	verrais	voies	vois
il voit	vit	voyait	verra	verrait	voie	
nous voyons	vîmes	voyions	verrons	verrions	voyions	voyons
vous voyez	vîtes	voyiez	verrez	verriez	voyiez	voyez
ils voient	virent	voyaient	verront	verraient	voient	

Vouloir (+ **avoir**) *to want:* voulu — voulant

je veux	voulus	voulais	voudrai	voudrais	veuille	
tu veux	voulus	voulais	voudras	voudrais	veuilles	veuille
il veut	voulut	voulait	voudra	voudrait	veuille	
nous voulons	voulûmes	voulions	voudrons	voudrions	voulions	veuillons
vous voulez	voulûtes	vouliez	voudrez	voudriez	vouliez	veuillez
ils veulent	voulurent	voulaient	voudront	voudraient	veuillent	

Key points

1   The verb is considered the most important word in a sentence: it enables us *to express* actions, states of mind or body, feelings; *to situate* them along the time axis through its various Tenses and, through the various Moods, *to add* particular overtones (doubt, possibility, etc.).

2   There are significant differences in the conjugation systems of the two languages. In French, verb endings are far more significant than in English to determine the *Tense* (Present, Imperfect, etc.) and the *Person* of the verb (1st, 2nd, 3rd, singular or plural).

3   Verbs fall into several categories according to the endings of their infinitives *and* of their present participle. Those categories are themselves organised into the three following groups:

– 1st group: Infinitive = **er** — Present Participle = **ant**
– 2nd group: Infinitive = **ir** — Present Participle = **issant**
– 3rd group: Infinitive = **ir/oir/re** — Present participle = **ant**

4   With very few exceptions, notably **aller** (*to go*), the verbs of the 1st and 2nd groups are regular, i.e. they follow a fixed pattern as regards tense formation. Close examination of the Model Charts for those 2 groups will reveal the way the stem is selected *and* the endings used within each Tense.

5   Some of the 'exceptions' encountered in the first group are *phonetic* and not grammatical: the stem of the verb only changes to preserve the same sound-pattern throughout the conjugation. Such is the case for verbs ending in **cer** and **ger**.

– *the first* change **c** to **ç** before **a** or **o**;
– *the second* insert an **e** between the **g** and any subsequent ending beginning with **a** or **o**.

6   *Normally*, verbs use two stems in their conjugation

(*a*)   the Infinitive *minus* the ending (**er/ir/re**) for the present, Past Historic, Imperfect Indicative; the Present Imperative and the Present Subjunctive

(*b*)   the *full* Infinitive (ending included) — except for the **e** of **re** verbs — for the Future Indicative and the Present Conditional.

7   There are, however, some *notable exceptions* to this rule, particularly in the 3rd group, which is the smallest but also the most troublesome. A Model Chart of three of its verbs (**partir**, **recevoir**, **vendre**) has been given so as to present the most likely variations in *stem and endings* for that group.

8   The most frequently used irregular verbs have been presented in the Irregular Charts.

9   In order to form compound tenses, auxiliaries are needed. The main auxiliaries are **avoir** (*to have*) and **être** (*to be*); the Past Participle of the main verb is then added to the selected tense of the appropriate auxiliary.

Remember: Verbs conjugated with **être** are: pronominal verbs (e.g. reflexives) and the 'famous 14' (**aller**, **venir**, etc.). All other verbs form their compound tenses with **avoir**.

10   It is possible to create a whole new category of *double compound tenses* which may be used in *spoken French* to replace some of the more 'highbrow'

or 'old fashioned' tenses (Past Historic or Past Anterior). They are called **temps surcomposés** and are constructed as follows:

(*a*)   For verbs using **avoir** as an auxiliary:
        – appropriate compound tense of **avoir** + Past Participle of main verb.

(*b*)   For tenses using **être** as an auxiliary:
        – appropriate compound tense of **avoir** + Past Part. of **être** (= **été**) + Past Part. of main verb

11   For the conjugation of verbs (i.e. formation of tenses with stems and endings), some of the 'detective work' outlined in the introduction will prove invaluable.

14 Adverbs

Adverbs are words — or expressions — which in French as in English modify (i.e. refine) the meaning of verbs, adjectives, other adverbs or their equivalents. For example:

> Je *chante* **mal**.   *I sing badly*. (Here the adverb modifies a verb.)
> Cette photo est **très** *jolie*.   *This photo is very pretty*. (Here the adverb modifies an adjective.)
> Vous dansez **extrêmement** *bien*.   *You dance extremely well*. (Here the adverb modifies another adverb.)

In the above examples, the adverb is indicated in bold type, and the word the adverb modifies in italic bold.

In a way, adverbs are to the words they modify, the equivalent of what adjectives are to nouns. The similarity is further highlighted by the following facts:

1 Some adjectives can be used as adverbs (this point is also mentioned on page 53 in the chapter dealing with adjectives).

> Je vais le dire **haut** et **clair**.   *I am going to say it loud(ly) and clear(ly)*.
> Elle chante **faux**.   *She sings off-key*.
> Ils tiennent **ferme**.   *They are holding on firmly/fast*.

2 A great many French adjectives can be turned into adverbs by addition of the ending **ment**. The adverbs thus obtained are often labelled 'adverbs of manner'. In fact, some of them can also be adverbs of time, quantity, etc. (see categories below).

Unlike adjectives, however, adverbs do not vary in gender or number.

Compare: Il marche **droit**.   *He walks straight = in a straight line*.
and: Elle marche **droit**.   *She walks straight = in a straight line*.

Rules governing the formation of adverbs in *ment*

The rules of formation of such adverbs are as follows:

1 *Normally*, the adverb is obtained by adding **ment** to the feminine-singular form of the adjective. Examples are shown in the table below.

masc. sing.	*fem. sing.*	*adverb*	*meaning*
fort	forte	fortement	*strongly*
normal	normale	normalement	*normally*
partiel	partielle	partiellement	*partially*
sage	sage	sagement	*wisely/quietly*
vif	vive	vivement	*quickly/swiftly*

2   In certain cases, however, there are some modifications to this 'normal' formation rule:

(*a*)   If the masculine singular form of the adjective ends in **i**, **e** or **u**, the adverb will be formed directly from it, and the **e** of the feminine omitted, as shown in the table below:

masc. sing.	*fem. sing.*	*adverb*	*meaning*
absolu	absolue	absolument	*absolutely*
*cru	crue	crûment	*crudely*
*gai	gaie	gaîment	*gaily*
joli	jolie	joliment	*prettily*
vrai	vraie	vraiment	*truly*

Notes:
(i)   In the case of **beau** (*beautiful*), **nouveau** (*new*), **fou** (*mad*) and **mou** (*limp*), the adverbs will be formed in the normal way: **bellement** (*beautifully*), **nouvellement** (*newly*), **follement** (*madly*) and **mollement** (*limply*).
(ii)   In two of the above examples (marked *), the absence of the **e** of the feminine is signified by a circumflex accent. The circumflex accent often indicates in this way the disappearance of a letter which used to be present in old French.

(*b*)   If the masculine singular form of the adjective ends in **ant**, the adverb will be formed by deleting that ending and replacing it with **amment**. Adjectives ending in **ent** in the masculine singular will lose that ending and replace it with **emment**:
Vous vous battez **vaillamment**.   *You fight valiantly.* (from adj. **vaillant**)
Elles se disputaient **constamment**.   *They used to argue constantly.* (from adj. **constant**)
Elle le frappa **violemment** au visage.   *She hit him violently in the face.* (from adj. **violent**)
Avançons **prudemment**.   *Let's proceed cautiously.* (from adj. **prudent**)

Note: **lent** (*slow*), **présent** (*present*) and **véhément** (*vehement*) follow the normal pattern of formation (i.e. fem. sing. adj. + **ment**). For example:

> La voiture avançait **lentement**. *The car was moving slowly forward.*
>
> *Ils refusèrent* **véhémentement** de partir. *They vehemently refused to leave.*

(*c*) A small number of adjectives, whilst following the normal pattern of formation, take an acute accent (´) on the **e** before adding the ending **ment**:

masc. sing.	fem. sing.	adverb	meaning
aveugle	aveugle	aveuglément	*blindly*
commode	commode	commodément	*conveniently*
commun	commune	communément	*commonly*
confus	confuse	confusément	*vaguely*
énorme	énorme	énormément	*enormously*
immense	immense	immensément	*immensely*

(*d*) A limited number of adjectives undergo a change in spelling before adding the ending **ment**:

masc. sing.	fem. sing.	adverb	meaning
bref	brève	*or* brièvement / brèvement	*briefly*
grave	grave	*or* grièvement / gravement	*gravely (ill)*
traître	traîtresse	traîtreusement	*treacherously*

Position of adverbs

The position of French adverbs is not always absolutely fixed and can, at times, be quite different from that of English adverbs. (In the following examples the adverb is shown in bold with the word it modifies in italic bold:

Compare: He **often** *comes* to see us.
and: Il *vient* **souvent** nous voir.
or   We shall **never** *forget* you.
and: Nous ne vous *oublierons* **jamais**.

It is, however, possible to formulate general rules concerning the position of French adverbs. They are as follows:

1   Adverbs modifying simple tense verbs (i.e. without an auxiliary) are normally placed after those verbs:

> Ils reviendront **souvent** nous voir.   *They will often come back to see us.*
>
> Nous parlons **rarement** du passé.   *We rarely talk about the past.*

2   Adverbs modifying compound tense verbs (i.e. with an auxiliary) are normally placed between the auxiliary and the past participle:

> J'ai **souvent** parlé à cet homme.   *I have often talked to that man.*
>
> Vous êtes **quelquefois** arrivés en retard au bureau.   *You sometimes arrived late at the office.*

3   Adverbs modifying adjectives, past participles, other adverbs or expressions of similar value, are generally placed before those words or expressions:

> Votre chien est **très** fidèle mais **peu** obéissant.   *Your dog is very faithful but not very obedient.*
>
> Les deux hommes parlaient **trop** fort.   *The two men were speaking too loudly.*

Notes:

(a)   The position of the adverb can sometimes be changed to create a special effect. In the two examples which follow, the brackets indicate the place the adverb should normally occupy.

> **Soudain**, il se tourna (   ) vers moi.
>
> *Suddenly he turned towards me.* (dramatic effect)
>
> Tu as (   ) été trompé, **incontestablement**.
>
> *You have been swindled, no doubt about it.* (emphasis)

(b)   Adverbs of place and many adverbs of time (see categories below) modifying a compound tense verb are placed after the past participle and not immediately after the auxiliary:

> Ils ont dîné **ici** hier soir.   *They dined here last night.*
>
> Nous étions arrivés **là** par hasard.   *We had arrived there by chance.*
>
> Je l'ai revue **souvent**.   *I have often seen her again.*

(c)   If the adverb, because of its meaning, links two sentences together, it will be placed between them:

> Il a refusé de nous voir. **Néanmoins**, il a accepté de lire notre lettre.   *He refused to see us. Nevertheless, he accepted to read our letter.*
>
> L'argent a disparu. **Pourtant** il était là il y a deux minutes!   *The money has disappeared. Yet it was here two minutes ago!*

Types of adverbs

Adverbs are generally grouped by meaning into seven broad categories. It is, of course, possible for the same adverb to occur in more than one category with a different meaning:

Compare: Il travaille **bien**.

He works well. (adverb of manner)

and: Il est **bien** malade.

He is very ill. (adverb of quantity)

The seven categories are given below.

1 Adverbs of manner:

ainsi *thus*, **à tort** *wrongly*, **bien** *well*, **comme** *as/how*, **exprès** *on purpose*, **mal** *badly*, **mieux** *better*, **pis** *worse*, **plutôt** *rather*, **vite** *quickly*, **volontiers** *willingly*, etc. (To these must be added a great many adverbs ending in **ment** which are derived from adjectives.) For example:

Je suis sûr que vous le faites **exprès** dit-il **méchamment**. *I am sure you do it on purpose, he said viciously.*

Les choses vont **de mal en pis**. (set expression) *Things are going from bad to worse.*

Il est accusé **à tort**. *He is wrongfully accused.*

2 Adverbs of quantity:

à peine *hardly*, **assez** *enough*, **aussi** *as much*, **beaucoup/bien** *a great deal/much*, **comme** *how much*, **davantage** *more*, **guère** *little*, **moins** *less*, **pas mal** *a good deal* (familiar), **peu** *little*, **plus** *more*, **quelque** *approximately*, **si** *so*, **tant/tellement** *so much*, **tout** *totally*, **très** *very*, **trop** *too much*, etc. For example:

Nous avons **beaucoup** marché et nous sommes **très** fatigués. *We have walked a great deal and we are very tired.*

Ils ont **tant** souffert! *They have suffered so much!*

J'ai **assez** mangé, merci **bien**. *I have eaten enough, thank you very much.*

Notes:

(*a*) Do not confuse the adverb **quelque** (*approximately*) and the indefinite adjective **quelques** (*some/a few*). The adverb is invariable, whereas the adjective can vary in number (see chapter on indefinite adjectives)

Compare: Le train est resté **quelque** dix minutes en gare. *The train stayed approximately ten minutes in the station.* (adverb = no agreement)

and: Le train est resté **quelques** minutes en gare. *The train stayed a few minutes in the station.* (indefinite adjective = agreement)

(*b*) As mentioned previously, adverbs are invariable. **Tout**, however, violates the rule in the following cases: *if* **tout** modifies a
feminine adjective, *and if* that adjective begins with a consonant
or with an aspirated 'h' (on this point see appendix I), **tout** will
agree in gender and number with that adjective.

Compare: Elle était **tout** émue.
             She was quite moved. (followed by vowel = no
             agreement)
and: Elle était **toute** contente.
             She was quite pleased. (followed by consonant =
             agreement)
or: Elles sont **toutes** honteuses.
             They are quite ashamed. (followed by aspirated
             'h' = agreement)
and: Elles sont **tout** étonnées.
             They are quite astonished. (followed by vowel = no
             agreement)

3 Adverbs of time:

d'abord *firstly*, **alors** *then*, **après** *afterwards*, **aujourd'hui** *today*,
auparavant *previously*, **aussitôt** *immediately/at once*, **autrefois** *pre-
viously/formerly*, **avant** *before*, **bientôt** *soon*, **déjà** *already*, **demain**
tomorrow, **depuis** *since*, **désormais** *from now on/henceforth*, **de suite**
straight afterwards, **encore** *again/still*, **enfin** *finally*, **ensuite** *afterwards*, **hier** *yesterday*, **jadis** *a long time ago*, **jamais** *ever/never*,
longtemps *for a long time*, **immédiatement** *at once*, **maintenant** *now*,
parfois/quelquefois *sometimes*, **soudain/tout à coup** *suddenly*,
toujours *always/still*, **tout de suite** *at once*.

For example:
             Téléphonez **d'abord**; vous partirez **ensuite**.   *Telephone first, you
             will go afterwards.*
             La neige ne reste **jamais** bien **longtemps**.   *The snow never stays
             (for) very long.*
             Ils ont **quelquefois** reçu des nouvelles de leur fils.   *They
             sometimes heard from their son.*

Notes:
(*a*) Some of the above adverbs have two distinct meanings or nearly
identical forms which may lead to confusion. Extra care will be
needed when dealing with those:

Compare: Il finira ce travail et il viendra **de suite**.
             He will finish this job and will come afterwards.
and: Il vient **tout de suite**!
             He is coming at once!

or: Elle est insupportable; elle est **toujours** en colère.
           She is unbearable; she is always cross.
and: Elle n'était pas contente; elle est **toujours** en colère.
           She wasn't pleased; she is still angry.
or: Vous n'avez **jamais** répondu.
           You have never replied.
and: Avez-vous **jamais** répondu?
           Have you ever replied?

(*b*) **tout à coup** (*suddenly*) has a near-equivalent in the 'adverbs of manner' category. Care should be taken not to confuse the two.

Compare: Il ouvrit **tout à coup** la porte.
           He suddenly opened the door.
and: Il ouvrit **tout d'un coup** la porte.
           He opened the door all in one go. (adverb of manner)

4   Adverbs of place/position:

Ailleurs *elsewhere*, **alentour/autour** *around*, **ça et là** *here and there*, **-ci** *here*, **contre** *against*, **dedans** *inside*, **dehors** *outside*, **derrière** *behind*, **dessous** *below/underneath*, **ici** *here*, **-là** *there*, **loin** *far*, **nulle part** *nowhere*, **où** *where*, **partout** *everywhere*, **près** *near*, **quelque part** *somewhere*. For example:

Les rescapés couraient **ça et là**.   *The survivors were running here and there.*

Attendez **dehors**!   *Wait outside!*

Ils voient des espions **partout**!   *They see spies everywhere!*

In the last example, note the unusual position of the adverb (for emphasis)

Note: **ici** (*here*) can also be an adverb of time meaning *up to now*
so: Jusqu'**ici** la route a été bonne. could mean:
either: *Up to now* (adv. of time) *the road has been good.*
or: *Up to this point* (adv. of place) *the road has been good.*

5   Adverbs of affirmation:

Assurément *assuredly*, **aussi** *also/too*, **bien/fort bien** *very well*, **certainement** *certainly*, **certes** *indeed*, **oui** *yes*, **précisément** *precisely*, **sans aucun doute** *without any doubt*, **sans doute** *probably/certainly*, **si** *yes*, **soit** *alright/granted*, **vraiment** *indeed/definitely*. For example:

Je crois **vraiment** qu'ils ont raison.   *I definitely believe they are right.*

Pensez-vous que vous réussirez? **Certes!**   *Do you think you will succeed? Indeed (I do)!*

Sortirez-vous seul? **Sans aucun doute!**   *Will you go out alone? Without a doubt!*

Aussi, placed at the beginning of a sentence/clause, is a 'sentence connector' meaning *consequently/therefore*. In that case it is normally followed by an inversion.

Compare: Vous avez donné votre parole. **Aussi** irons-nous les voir. *You have given your word. Consequently we shall go and see them.*

and: Vous avez donné votre parole. Nous irons **aussi** les voir. *You have given your word. We will go and see them too.*

Note: Although they *both* mean *yes*, **oui** and **si** must be clearly distinguished:

– **Oui** is used to reply to a straight-forward question:

Il est malade? **Oui**. *Is he ill? Yes (he is).*

Est-ce que le film est fini? **Oui**. *Is the film over? Yes (it is).*

– **Si** is used as a reply to a question *formulated in the negative*:

Tu n'as pas froid? **Si**! *Aren't you cold? Yes (I am).*

Les agents ne vous ont jamais arrêté? **Si**, une fois! *Have the police ever stopped you? Yes once!*

6 Adverbs of negation:

The main adverbs of negation are **non** (*no*) and **ne** (*not* . . .). A clear distinction should be made between them.

– *Non* can be used on its own to express the negation, whether the sentence is affirmative or interrogative:

Descends! **Non**! *Come down! No (I shan't)!*

Prendrez-vous l'avion? **Non**! *Will you take the plane? No (I won't)!*

Vous n'avez pas froid? **Non**! *Aren't you cold? No (I'm not)!*

– **Non** can also be used with some other adverbial expression like **pas**, **point**, **point du tout**, **pas le moins du monde** to emphasise the negative meaning (= *not in the least/not in the slightest*):

Avez vous soif? **Non, pas le moins du monde**. *Are you thirsty? (No) not in the least.*

Note: In modern French, the English expression *why not*? is translated by **Pourquoi pas**? rather than **pourquoi non**?

Irons-nous en Espagne cet été? Pourquoi **pas**? *Shall we go to Spain this summer? Why not?*

– **Ne** is *normally* unable to express the negative idea on its own and is therefore used in connection with other suitable words or expressions. The most common are listed below.

NB Words in brackets can be used with the word they appear next to. If so, they must appear in the position shown.

1 *followed by*		2 *accompanying phrase*	3 *meaning*
ne	+ verb/aux	+ aucun/aucune	*not a single one* (masc/fem.)
		+ aucunement	*not in the least*
		+ (plus) guère	*hardly (any more)*
		+ jamais	*not . . . ever*
		+ jamais plus	*not . . . ever again*
		+ jamais (plus) personne	*not anyone (ever) again*
		+ jamais (plus) rien	*not anything (ever) again*
		+ ni . . . ni	*neither . . . nor*
		+ non plus	*not . . . either*
		+ nul	*not . . . anyone/anything*
		+ nullement	*not . . . in the slightest*
		+ pas	*not . . . any*
		+ pas du tout	*not . . . at all*
		+ personne	*not . . . anybody*
		+ plus	*not . . . any longer*
		+ plus personne	*not . . . anyone any more*
		+ plus que	*not any more/no more than . . .*
		+ que	*. . . only*
		+ (plus) quiconque	*not . . . anyone (any longer)*
		+ (plus) rien	*not . . . anything (any more)*

For example:

> Vous **ne** payez **plus** votre loyer.   *You no longer pay your rent.*
> Laissez-moi tranquille! Je **n**'ai **rien** fait!   *Leave me alone! I have done nothing!*
> Que se passe-t-il? Il **n**'y a **plus personne** sur la plage.   *What is happening? There is no longer anybody on the beach.*
> Nous **ne** resterons **que** cinq minutes.   *We shall only stay five minutes.*
> Pourquoi **ne** dites-vous **plus rien**?   *Why are you not saying anything any more?*

Note: Except for those appearing *on the same line*, the expressions in column 2 are mutually exclusive:

Do not say or write:

> *Nous **ne** dormons **pas jamais** avec les fenêtres fermées.

Say or write instead:

> Nous **ne** dormons **jamais** avec les fenêtres fermées.   *We never sleep with the windows closed.*

Do not say or write:

> *Vous **ne** mangez **pas plus**.

Say or write instead:

> Vous **ne** mangez **plus**.   *You no longer eat.*

> However, if the sense of **plus** is comparative (= *more*) rather than
> negative (= *no longer*) the association **pas plus** is possible:
> Compare: Il **ne** paie **plus**! *He no longer pays!*
> and: Il **ne** paie **pas plus** (que moi).
>   *He does not pay any more (than I do).*

Note:
(*a*)   In colloquial French **ne** is very often omitted:
       Tu travailles **pas**. (for: tu **ne** travailles **pas**)
       You do not work.
       Elle arrête **jamais**. (for: elle **n'**arrête **jamais**)
       She never stops.
       As a learner you should use such constructions with great care to
       avoid possible ambiguities:
       Compare: Je fume **plus**. (for: je **ne** fume **plus**)
                   I no longer smoke. (in this case the **s** of **plus** is *never*
                   sounded)
       and: Je fume **plus**!
                   I smoke more! (in this case the **s** of **plus** is *usually*
                   sounded)
(*b*)   Conversely, **ne** can sometimes be used on its own in re-
       fined/literary French for **ne pas** or **ne point**, i.e. to express a
       negative idea:
       Je **ne** sais si vous comprenez. (for: je **ne** sais **pas** . . .)
       I do not know if you understand.
       Partez donc! Je **ne** peux! (for: je **ne** peux **pas**)
       Do go! I cannot!

> A small number of verbs or expressions are, in good French,
> used with a **ne** called 'expletive ne' which is *not* a negative. The
> most common of those verbs/expressions are: **avoir peur que** *to
> be afraid that*, **craindre que** *to fear that*, **à moins que** *unless* . . . ,
> **avant que** *before*, **de crainte que/de peur que** *for fear that* . . . For
> example:
>   Finis ton chocolat **avant que** ton frère **n'**arrive.   *Finish
>   your chocolate before your brother arrives.*
>   **J'ai peur qu'**il **ne** refuse.   *I fear he may refuse.*
> Compare: Nous craignons qu'il **n'**accepte.
>   *We fear that he may accept.*
> and: Nous craignons qu'il **n'**accepte **pas**.
>   *We fear he may not accept*

(c) The following negative adverbial expressions can be placed at the beginning of a sentence/clause, provided the order of the two words is reversed: **ne . . . aucun** *none/no one*, **ne . . . jamais** *never*, **ne . . . nul** *no one*, **ne . . . personne** *nobody*, **ne . . . rien** *nothing*. In such cases the negative **ne** will be placed before the verb.

> **Jamais** les gens **ne** signeront ce document. *People will never sign this document.*
>
> **Rien** n'avait **plus** d'importance. *Nothing mattered any longer.*
>
> **Personne ne** souhaite vous offenser. *Nobody wishes to offend you.*

(d) When modifying an infinitive, the following expressions are placed before it in one block instead of being, as is normal, separated by the verb: **ne pas** *not to*, **ne jamais** *not ever*, **ne plus** *not any longer*, **ne rien** *not anything*. For example:

> Le vieux monsieur décida de **ne plus** sortir. *The old man decided not to go out any more.*
>
> Prière de **ne pas** marcher sur la pelouse. *You are requested not to walk on the grass.*
>
> Je t'ai dit de **ne jamais** m'écrire. *I told you never to write to me.*

But: La vieille dame décida de **ne** voir **personne**. *The old lady decided not to see anyone.*

7 Adverbs of doubt:

Apparemment *apparently*, **peut-être** *perhaps*, **probablement/sans doute** *probably*, **vraisemblablement** *in all probability*. For example:

> Il faudrait **peut-être** faire quelque chose. *Perhaps we should do something.*
>
> **Apparemment**, les étrangers ont besoin d'un visa. *Apparently, foreigners need a visa.*

Note: If **peut-être**, **probablement** and **sans doute** are placed at the beginning of the sentence and are *not* followed by **que**, a change in the word-order (i.e. inversion) is necessary.

Compare: Le docteur a **peut-être** tort.

and: **Peut-être** le docteur a-t-il tort.

> *The doctor may be wrong.*

or: Les prix vont **sans doute** baisser.

and: **Sans doute** les prix vont-ils baisser.

> *Prices are probably about to go down.*

If the subject of such sentences is a noun, it must appear immediately after the adverb; the corresponding subject pronoun will then be used to form the inversion (in other words the subject will appear twice).

Compare: **Peut-être** vont-ils réussir. (pronoun only)
              They may succeed.

and: **Peut-être** les journalistes vont-ils réussir.
              The journalists may succeed.(noun + pronoun)

Note: ***Peut-être vont les journalistes réussir** (noun only) is unacceptable.

Key points

1   Adverbs are words or expressions which can modify verbs, adjectives, past participles, other adverbs, or phrases of similar value.

2   Adverbs are invariable: they do not alter in gender or number.

3   A great many adverbs are formed by adding the ending **ment** to the feminine (and in some cases to the masculine) form of the required adjective.

4   Although the position of adverbs is not absolutely fixed and can sometimes be changed for stylistic reasons, there are some general rules concerning their placement which can be of help to the learner.

5   Adverbs modifying *simple tense* verbs (i.e. without an auxiliary) follow the verb; adverbs modifying *compound tense* verbs (i.e. with an auxiliary) are normally placed between the auxiliary and the past participle; adverbs modifying adjectives and other adverbs generally precede them.

6   There are 7 main categories of adverbs; they express the following notions: manner; quantity; time; place/position; affirmation; negation; doubt.

7   Some adverbs, when placed at the beginning of a sentence or clause, undergo a change in meaning and/or require a change in word order.

8   A small number of adverbs may appear in more than one of the 7 categories. In such cases, their meaning will obviously be different in each of the categories in which they appear.

9   A very small number of pairs of adverbial expressions look almost identical but have different meanings. They should be carefully distinguished and remembered.

SECTION III
Building the Complete Picture

15 Prepositions

Note: Making proper use of prepositions is probably the most difficult stage in the acquisition of a foreign language, but it is by no means impossible. In this case, as in any other, be attentive to the examples given and to any new material you will come across, and refine your knowledge accordingly.

Prepositions are words, or groups of words, which are used to express a relationship (usually of time, space, purpose, etc.) between two phrases. The first phrase may have the shape or the value of a noun, an adjective, a verb or an adverb, and the second that of a noun, a pronoun or a verb:

> Les clients attendent **devant** le magasin. *The customers are waiting in front of the shop.*
>
> C'est à cause **de** lui qu'elle a décidé de partir. *It is because of him that she decided to leave.*

Notes:

(*a*) Prepositions may be made of one word only (simple prepositions) or several (compound prepositions or prepositional phrases). In the second case, the last words will very often be **à** (*at, to, in*, etc. or **de** (*of, from*, etc.), which are the two most common prepositions in the language.

(*b*) **à** (*at, to, in*, etc.) and **de** (*of, from*, etc.) combine with the definite articles **le** and **les** (*the*) in the following way:

à + **le** ⟶ **au**
à + **les** ⟶ **aux**
de + **le** ⟶ **du**
de + **les** ⟶ **des**

For example:

> Les employés allaient **au** travail. *The employees were going to work.*
>
> Les spectateurs sortent **du** cinéma. *The spectators are coming out of the cinema.*

(*c*) In an attempt to facilitate learning, the prepositions introduced in the chapter have been grouped into broad categories: position; movement; constraint-restriction-exclusion; inclusion or participation; manner or purpose. But it should be noted that such a classification, although useful, can be somewhat arbitrary.

(*d*) The same preposition may be found in more than one of the above-mentioned categories, each time with a different shade of meaning. For example:

Il est **à** Paris. *He is in Paris.* (position in space)

Il va **à** Paris. *He is going to Paris.* (movement)

C'est une machine **à** coudre. *It is a sewing machine.* (lit: *a machine for sewing* — purpose)

Le car arrivera **à** six heures. *The coach will arrive at 6 o'clock.* (position in time)

The main prepositions are given below in their categories.

Position or location

1 *In space*: **à** *at, in,* **à côté de** *beside,* **à l'arrière de** *at the back of,* **à l'avant de** *at the front of,* **à l'intérieur de** *inside,* **à l'exterieur de** *outside,* **à l'extrémité de** *at the far end of,* **au bout de** *at the end of,* **au-dessous de** *below,* **au-dessus de** *above,* **au milieu de** *in the middle of,* **auprès de** *close to,* **autour de** *around,* **aux environs de** *in the vicinity of,* **avant** *before,* **chez** *at someone's,* **contre** *against,* **derrière** *behind,* **devant** *in front of,* **en** *in,* **en arrière de** *further back from,* **en avant de** *ahead of,* **en travers de** *across,* **entre** *between,* **hors de** *outside,* **le long de** *along,* **parmi** *among,* **sur** *on,* **sous** *under,* etc. For example:

Ton fils est **au** lit. *Your son is in bed.*

Il est tombé **au milieu de** la rue. *He fell in the middle of the street.*

Il y a un arbre **en travers de** la route. *There is a tree lying across the road.*

2 *In time*: **à** *at,* **après** *after,* **au milieu de** *in the middle of,* **au moment de** *at the time of,* **aux environs de** *around,* **avant** *before,* **dès** *from/as early as,* **en début de** *at the beginning of,* **en dehors de** *outside,* **en fin de** *at the end of,* **entre** *between,* **pendant** *during,* **vers** *towards,* etc. For example:

Ils ont sonné **au milieu de** la nuit. *They rang (the bell) in the middle of the night.*

Je vous écrirai **dès** demain. *I shall write to you no later than tomorrow.*

Est-ce que vous fermez **avant** ou **après** huit heures? *Do you close before or after 8 o'clock?*

Movement

1 *In space*: à *to*, **après** *after*, **au-dehors de** *outside*, **au-delà de** *beyond*, **au-devant de** *before/towards*, **au travers de** *through*, **en** *in/to*, **le long de** *along*, **passé** *after/past*, **par** *through*, **pour** *to/towards*, **vers** *towards*, **via** *via*, etc. For example:

N'allez pas **au-delà de** la rivière! *Do not go beyond the river!*
Il est toujours **par** monts et **par** vaux. (saying) *He is always gallivanting about.* (lit: *through mountains and valleys*)
Elle se tourna **vers** lui. *She turned towards him.*

2 *In time*: à *to*, **à partir de** *from*, **après** *after* **au-delà de** *beyond*, **avant** *before*, **de** *from*, **durant** *during*, **en** *within*, **jusqu'à** *up to/until*, **passé** *after*, **pour** *for*, **vers** *towards*, etc. For example:

A partir d 'aujourd' hui, je prends les décisions. *As from today, I make the decisions.*
Ne m'appelez pas **avant** dix heures ce soir. *Do not call me before ten o'clock tonight.*
Restez **jusqu'à** dimanche! *Stay until Sunday!*

Constraint-restriction-exclusion

A cause de *because of*, **à force de** *by dint of*, **à défaut de** *for want of*, **à l'exception de** *except for*, **à l'exclusion de** *excluding*, **à l'insu de** *unbeknown to*, **à moins de** *unless*, **au péril de** *at the risk of*, **aux dépens de** *at the expense of*, **au lieu de** *instead of*, **de peur de** *for fear of*, **contre** *against*, **en dépit de** *in spite of*, **en raison de** *by reason of*, **étant donné** *given*, **excepté** *except*, **faute de** *through lack of*, **hormis** *except*, **malgré** *in spite of*, **quant à** *as for*: idea of opposition, **sans** *without*, **sauf** *except*, **selon** *according to*, **vu** *in view of*, etc. For example:

Ne restez pas trop longtemps **de peur de** le fatiguer. *Do not stay too long for fear of tiring him.*
En dépit de nos efforts, il a échoué. *In spite of our efforts, he has failed.*
Vous pouvez partir; **quant à** moi, je reste. *You may go; (as for me) I am staying.*

Participation — inclusion

A l'aide de *with the help of — something*, **avec** *with*, **avec l'aide de** *with the help of — someone*, **dans** *in*, **en** *in*, **en compagnie de** *in the company of*, **en plus de** *besides*, **grâce à** *thanks to*, **parmi** *among*, **outre** *besides*, **y compris** *including*, etc. For example:

Reste **avec** moi! *Stay with me!*

Il est **dans** la marine. *He is in the Navy.*

Tout a disparu, **y compris** l'argent. *Everything has gone, including the money.*

Manner — purpose

A *to/for*, **avec** *with*, **afin de** *in order to*, **à la mode de** *in the manner of*, **au moyen de** *by means of*, **contre** *against*, **dans le but de** *with a view to*, **de façon à/de manière à** *so as to*, **en vue de** *with a view to*, **par** *by/through*, **pour** *in order to*, **sans** *without*, **suivant** *according to*, etc. For example:

C'est une machine **à** laver. *It is a washing machine.* (lit: *a machine for washing*)

Je vous dis cela **afin de** vous aider. *I tell you that in order to help you.*

Il est sorti **sans** chapeau. *He went out without a hat.*

Use of prepositions

1 A limited number of prepositions can be followed by a verb. In each case, the verb must be in the infinitive (present or past). Those prepositions are:

à *to/for*, **de** *to/of/from*, **pour** *for/to*, **sans** *without*, **après** *after*, **par** *by*. For the last two, see notes below.

For example:

Préparez-vous **à** partir. *Get ready to go.*

Ça ne coûte rien **de** dire merci. *It does not cost anything to say thank you.*

Il se baissa **pour** ramasser la pièce. *He bent down to pick up the coin.*

Vous partirez **sans** le voir. *You will leave without seeing him.*

Notes:

(*a*) When a verb occurs after **après**, it must be in the past infinitive (infinitive of the auxiliary + past participle) *except* if it can take the value of a noun:

Après manger, il est sorti. (**manger** = **le repas**) *After the meal he went out.*

Il est amusant **après** boire. (**boire** = **la boisson**) *He is amusing after he has had a few drinks.*

But: **Après avoir fini** le travail, il sort.

and not: *Après finir le travail, il sort.

After finishing work he goes out.

or: **Après être descendue**, elle ferma la porte.

and not: *Après descendre elle ferma la porte.
After going down, she closed the door.

Avoir fini and **être descendue** are the past infinitives of **finir** (*to finish*) and **descendre** (*to go down*) respectively.

(*b*) **Par** (*by*) can be followed by an infinitive in *two set phrases only*: **commencer par** (*to begin by*) and **finir par** (*to end up by*).

Nous commencerons **par** prendre un apéritif.   *We shall begin by taking an aperitif.*

Je vais finir **par** perdre patience.   *I am going to end up by losing my patience.*

2   Elimination of certain prepositions:

Since prepositions are supposed to link two words or phrases within a sense-group, it is not generally acceptable to leave them out in French. Otherwise, the link may not be obvious and an ambiguity may be created. In the following examples the words in bold are linked, and the sign // indicates the end of a sense group.

Compare: Je parle **à mon voisin** et **à sa femme**// . . .

   I speak to my neighbour and (to) his wife . . .

and: Je parle **à mon voisin** // et sa femme . . .

In the second example, the reader or listener expects a verb to follow **femme** explaining what that lady is doing while I'm speaking to her husband!

Remember: In English it is acceptable to avoid repeating the preposition. In French it is generally unwise to do so.

Exceptions:

(*a*)   With set expressions made up of several elements, but considered as one word, the preposition is not repeated:

Il habite en **Seine-et-Marne**. *He lives in Seine-et-Marne.* (region near Paris)

Je passe mon temps à **aller et venir**. *I spend my time going to and fro.*

(*b*)   If the word **ou** (*or*) is used to indicate an alternative, the preposition is not normally repeated:

Un voyage **de** deux **ou** trois jours. (*and not* *de deux ou de trois jours*) *A two or three-day journey.*

La maison est **à** trois **ou** quatre cents mètres (*and not* *à trois ou à quatre cents mètres*). *The house is three or four hundred metres away.*

(*c*)   **Pour** (*for*) is often not repeated:

Voici la note **pour** la chambre et le repas. (*and not* *pour la chambre et pour le repas*). *Here is the bill for the bedroom and the meal.*

(*d*)   **Entre** (*between*) is never repeated:
  Entre vous et moi, il n'est pas très doué.(*and not* *entre vous et entre moi . . .*)   *Between you and me, he is not very gifted.*

3   Prepositions indicating 'position in' or 'movement to or from' a country:

(*a*)   Position and movement to a feminine singular country: **en**:
  Nous allons **en** France. (movement)   *We are going to France.*
  Il habite **en** Espagne. (position)   *He lives in Spain.*

(*b*)   Position and movement to a masculine country: **au** (sing.), **aux** (plur.):
  Il va au Canada? Non, **aux** Etats-Unis. (movement)   *Is he going to Canada? No, to the United States.*
  Elle vit **au** Japon. (position)   *She lives in Japan.*

(*c*)   Movement from a feminine country: **de** (sing.), **des** (plur.):
  Cette vague de froid arrive **d**'Allemagne.   *This cold wave is coming from Germany.*
  Voici une lettre **des** Seychelles.   *Here is a letter from the Seychelles.*

(*d*)   Movement from a masculine country: **du** (sing.), **des** (plur.):
  J'aime le café **du** Brésil.   *I like coffee from Brazil.*
  J'ai reçu un coup de téléphone **des** USA.   *I have received a phone call from the States.*

Notes:

(i)   The general rules stated for countries also apply for regions, 'départements' and counties, with the following modifications:
  – In the case of 'movement to' or 'position in' a 'masculine' area, region, county or 'département', **au** (sing.) will be replaced by **dans le**, and **aux** (plur.) by **dans les**:
  Il a une villa **dans le** Midi de la France.   *He has a villa in the South of France.*
  Je fais du ski **dans les** Alpes.   *I go skiing in the Alps.*

(ii)   English counties are masculine in French:
  Nous avons passé cinq jours **dans le** Kent.   *We spent five days in Kent.*

4   Prepositions indicating 'position in', 'movement to', or 'movement from' a town:

(*a*)   Position or movement to = **à** (or **au**, if the name of the town includes the article **le**):
  Ils resteront deux jours **à** Marseille. (position)   *They will stay two days in Marseilles.*
  Nous irons **à** Paris. (movement)   *We shall go to Paris.*

Le bateau arrive **au** Havre à midi. (movement)   *The boat arrives in Le Havre at 12 noon.*

(*b*)   Movement from = **de** (or **du**, if the name of the town includes the article **le**):

Je viens **de** Londres.   *I am coming from London.*

C'est le train **du** Touquet.   *It is the train from Le Touquet.*

5   Prepositions used to introduce the name of the material(s) or substance(s) constituting an object. **De** and **en** are used for this purpose.

Note: In modern French, **en** has become relatively more frequent than **de**. Although there is little difference in meaning between the two, it is generally agreed that **en** emphasises the material/substance slightly more than **de**:

Compare: Une table **de** chêne = *an oak table*

and: Une table **en** chêne = *a table made of oak*

or: Un vase **de** cristal = *a crystal vase*

and: Un vase **en** cristal = *a vase made of crystal*

6   The prepositions **entre** (*between*) and **parmi** (*among*) are not interchangeable.

– **entre** suggests a position or movement *between* two things or beings;

– **parmi** suggests a position or movement *among* a larger number of things or beings.

Compare: Je vois la maison **entre** la rivière et la route.

   I see the house between the river and the road.

and: Je vois la maison **parmi** les arbres.

   I see the house among the trees.

When the preposition **de** precedes, **parmi** is replaced by **entre**:
Plusieurs **d'entre** eux ont visité le château. *Several of them* (i.e. *among them*) *visited the castle.*

---

7   The preposition **pour** may be used to indicate:

(*a*)   *destination*:

Nous partons **pour** Londres ce soir.   *We leave for London tonight.*

(*b*)   *anticipated duration*:

Nous partons **pour** une semaine.   *We are going for a week.*

Note: In this latter sense, **pour** must be distinguished from **pendant**, which insists on the actual duration or time span (and which can often be omitted).

Compare: J'y vais **pour** trois semaines.
            I am going there for three weeks.
and: J'y resterai (pendant) trois semaines.
            I shall stay there (for) three weeks.

(*c*) *purpose*:
       Je voudrais des cachets **pour** calmer la douleur.   *I would like
          pain-killing tablets.* (lit: *to calm pain*)

8   The preposition **depuis** (*since/for*) may be used to indicate a time
span (duration):

Compare: Il habite ici **depuis** 1945. (precise date).
            He has been living here since 1945.
            Il habite ici **depuis** la fin de la guerre. (precise event)
            He has been living here since the end of the war.
            Il habite ici **depuis** 40 ans. (duration)
            He has been living here for 40 years.

Note: If **depuis** is followed by an expression denoting duration, as in
the last of the above examples, it will normally be used with a tense
also emphasising duration (i.e. Present or Imperfect Indicative).
Do not say: *Il travailla ici depuis 10 ans.
say instead: Il **travaillait** ici **depuis** 10 ans.
               He had been working here for 10 years.

9   The preposition **de** is often used with the meaning of **avec** (*with*) or
par (*by*):
      Je l'ai vu **de** mes propres yeux. (**de** = **avec**)   *I saw it with my own
         eyes.*
      Elle est aimée **de** tous. (**de** = **par**)   *She is loved by all.*

10   The preposition **de** is also used in French to express possession:
      Où est le stylo **de** Jean?   *Where is John's pen?*
      Le frère **de** Robert est malade.   *Robert's brother is ill.*

11   The preposition **chez** may have the following meanings:
(*a*) *to* or *at* someone's house, apartment, shop, etc.
       Va **chez** le boucher!   *Go to the butchers!*
(*b*) *among* when referring to the attitudes, habits, etc. of a group of
       people:
       La délinquance **chez** les jeunes.   *Delinquency among young
          people.*
Note: If a firm, shop, etc. bears the name of the founder(s) **chez** will
be used:
       Il travaillait **chez** Citroën.   *He was working for the Citroen
          Company.*

Elle s'habille **chez** Christian Dior. *She buys her clothes at Christian Dior's.*

12 When used with an expression of the type **l'un l'autre** (*one another*) the preposition will be placed between the two elements:

Ils se battent les uns **contre** les autres. *They are fighting against each other.*

Key points

1 Prepositions are words or expressions used to link together certain words or phrases, to indicate the relationship (time, space, manner, purpose, etc.) which exists between them.

2 Prepositions are invariable: they do not agree in gender or number with the words they link together.

3 It is possible for a given preposition to have a variety of meanings and therefore express different relationships.

4 In general, it is essential to repeat prepositions as required, since failure to do so may cause confusion in the mind of the reader or listener. There are, however, cases when the preposition *must not* be repeated: set expressions, presence of **ou** (*or*) or **entre** (*between*).

5 Certain prepositions are subject to *elision* (removal of the final vowel) whenever there is the danger of a vowel-vowel clash, or *fusion* (combination with the definite articles **le** or **les**).

6 The preposition **de** can be used in certain circumstances to express possession.

7 The prepositions **entre** (*between*) and **parmi** (*among*) are not normally interchangeable; the former expresses a position or movement *between* two things or beings, the latter a position or movement *among* a greater number of things or beings. There are, however, some cases when **entre** is used with the meaning of *among*.

8 The preposition **chez** is used to indicate 'movement to' *or* 'position in' the abode or shop of a person. In this case, *either* the name *or* the profession of the person concerned may be used. **Chez** is also used to express the attitudes, habits, etc. of a given group of people.

16 Conjunctions

Conjunctions are invariable expressions composed of one or more words which are used to link:

1 Words or phrases of equal grammatical status:

<u>Il est entré</u> **et** <u>Il a commandé une bière.</u>

    (1)   (2)

He went in and ordered a beer.

<u>J'ai refusé</u> **mais** <u>ma femme a accepté.</u>

    (1)   (2)

I refused but my wife accepted.

The elements 1 and 2 are linked by **et** (*and*) and **mais** (*but*) but they could both stand as sentences in their own right.

2 Phrases or clauses (i.e. sense groups with subject, verb, etc.) of unequal status, but closely related; one being the *main clause* (m.c.) and the other, the *subordinate clause* (s.c.), serving to 'complete the picture', as it were, by underlining the relationship (time-opposition-restriction) which exists between the two clauses and by giving extra information:

<u>Il vient me voir</u> **bien que** <u>je sois malade.</u>   (opposition)

    m.c.   s.c.

He comes to see me although I am ill.

<u>Elle doit prendre ce sirop</u> **jusqu'à ce qu**'elle ne tousse plus

    m.c.   s.c.

She must take this mixture until she stops coughing.

The conjunctions of type 1 are called *coordinating conjunctions* and those of type 2 are known as *subordinating conjunctions*. The two types will now be examined in turn. In order to facilitate learning, broad categories have been created to outline the relationships the conjunctions create between the elements they join together.

Coordinating conjunctions

Time: **comme** *as*, **ensuite** *afterwards*, **et** *then*, **lorsque** *when*, **puis** *then = afterwards*, **quand** *when*. For example:

Finissez cette lettre; **ensuite**, venez dans mon bureau. *Finish this letter; then come into my office.*

Vous ferez la vaisselle **quand** vous aurez fini de manger. *You will wash up when you have finished eating.*

Comme je me levais, on frappa à la porte. *As I was getting up, someone knocked on the door.*

Cause/consequence: **ainsi** *so = thus*, **aussi** *so = therefore*, **car** *for = because*, **donc** *therefore*, **en effet** *indeed = that is so*, **partant** *consequently*. For example:

Ainsi il est d'accord! Vous m'étonnez. *So he agrees! You astonish me.*

Je vais au restaurant **car** j'ai une faim de loup. *I'm going to the restaurant because I am starving.* (lit: *I have a wolf's hunger*)

Je pense, **donc** je suis. *I think, therefore I am.*

Il perdra sa réputation et, **partant**, son emploi. *He will lose his reputation and consequently his job.*

Constraint/restriction/exclusion: **au contraire** *on the contrary*, **cependant** *yet*, **et** *but*, **néanmoins** *nevertheless*, **ni . . . ni** *neither . . . nor*, *or yet*, **ou/ou bien** *or*, **pourtant** *however*, **quoique** *although*, **si** *if*, **sinon** *except/if not*, **soit . . . soit** *either . . . or*. For example:

Vous le détestez et **cependant** vous restez? Bizarre! *You detest him and yet you stay? Strange!*

Tu te reposes **et** je fais tout le travail. *You are resting and* (i.e. *whilst*) *I do all the work.*

Quoique riche il vivait simplement. *Although rich, he lived simply.*

Emphasis: **à savoir** *namely*, **bien** *jolly well*, **donc** *so, therefore*, **en effet** *indeed*. For example:

Pourquoi n'y allez-vous pas? J'y suis **bien** allé, moi! *Why don't you go? I jolly well went (didn't I)!*

Vous voilà **donc**! *So there you are!*

Je crois que vous êtes au courant. **En effet**! *I think you know Indeed I do!*

Points to bear in mind regarding the use of co-ordinating conjunctions:

1 **Et**, which is normally used to indicate association (*and = with*), may also be used to express:

(*a*) *Opposition*:

Je sais tout **et** je ne dis rien. *I know everything and (= but) I say nothing.*

(*b*)   *Simultaneity*:

Papa fume **et** maman lit.   *Father is smoking and (= whilst) Mother is reading.*

(*c*)   *Posteriority*:

Fermez le magasin **et** venez prendre un verre.   *Close the shop and (= then) come for a drink.* (lit: *to take a glass*)

2   **Si**, which is normally used to express a condition (= *if*), may also express:

(*a*)   *Doubt*:

Je ne sais pas **si** elle répondra.   *I do not know whether she will reply.*

(*b*)   *Hope or wish*:

Ah **si** j'étais jeune!   *Ah, if only I were young (again)!*

(*c*)   *Supposition*:

Et **s'**ils avaient eu un accident?   *And what if they'd had an accident?*

(*d*)   *Repetition*:

Si elle allait au bal, tout le monde l'admirait.   *Whenever she went dancing, everyone admired her.*

3   Whenever **quand** (*when*) is used to refer to a future action, it will be followed by the Future (simple or Perfect) and not the Present as in English.

Compare: **Quand** vous aurez fini, vous fermerez.

and: *When you have finished, you will lock up.*

or: **Quand** ils arriveront laissez-les entrer.

and: *When they arrive let them come in.*

4   The English word *then* has two distinct meanings: *afterwards* and *in that case*. You must take care to distinguish clearly between them:

(*a*)   *then = afterwards* will be translated by:

(i)   **puis** if there is no significant time-lapse between the two actions referred to:

J'ai fait la vaisselle, **puis** j'ai essuyé la poussière.   *I washed up, then I dusted.*

(ii)   **ensuite** if there is a significant time-lapse between the two actions referred to:

J'ai fait la vaisselle, **ensuite** j'ai essuyé la poussière.   *I washed up, afterwards I dusted.*

(*b*)   *then = in that case* is an adverb and must be translated by **alors, dans ce cas** or **dans ces conditions**:

Tu ne dis rien? **Alors** je m'en vais.   *Aren't you saying anything? In that case I am going.*

5 **Ni . . . Ni** (*neither . . . nor*) is normally accompanied by the negative particle **ne** (*not*) *but not* by **pas.** You must say or write:

Il n'est **ni** riche **ni** célèbre. *He is neither rich nor famous.*

and not: * Il n'est pas ni riche ni célèbre.

However, when used in a negative sentence **ni . . . ni** will be reduced to **ni**.

Tu n'es pas bête, **ni** paresseux. *You are not stupid, nor (are you) lazy.*

6 **Comme** (*as*), **lorsque quand** (*when*), **puisque** (*since*), **si** (*if*), etc. are not normally repeated in the same sentence; if necessary, they can be replaced by **que.**

It should be noted that if **que** replaces **quand, comme, lorsque** or **puisque** it will *not* be followed by a verb in the subjunctive:

Quand vous serez riche et **que** je serai vieux . . . *When you are rich and (when) I am old . . .*

However, if **que** replaces **si**, the verb which follows will be in the subjunctive:

Si vous tombez malade et **que** vous ayez besoin de moi, appelez-moi. (**ayez** = 2nd pers. plur. subjunctive of **avoir**). *If you fall ill and you need me, call me.*

Subordinating conjunctions

They, too, have been grouped into broad categories according to the relationship they create between the clauses they link together.

Note: Certain subordinating conjunctions *always* require the verb which follows to be in the subjunctive mood; in such cases, the conjunction will be accompanied by the mark **+ S**. Some other conjunctions may *sometimes* be followed by a subjunctive; this will be expressed by the mark **(+ S)** placed immediately after the conjunction.

Time = **alors que** *as/while*, **à mesure que** *as*, **après que** *after*, **aussitôt que** *as soon as*, **avant que** + *S before*, **cependant que** *while*, **depuis que** *since*, **dès que** *as soon as*, **en attendant que** + *S until*, **jusqu'à ce que** + *S until*, **maintenant que** *now that*, **pendant que** *while*, **sitôt que** *as soon as*, **tandis que** *while*, **tant que** *so long as*, etc.

For example:

Ils l'ont arrêté **alors qu**'il ouvrait le coffre. *They arrested him as he was opening the safe.*

Je veux vous dire deux mots **avant qu**'ils n'arrivent. *I want to say a few words to you before they arrive.*

Dès que midi sonne, il s'en va! *As soon as it is twelve o'clock, he is off!*

Restez assis **jusqu'à ce que** l'avion s'arrête. *Remain seated until the aircraft stops.*

Constraint-restriction-exclusion = **afin que** + S *so that*, **alors que** *whereas*, **à moins que** + S *unless*, **attendu que** *bearing in mind that*, **au lieu que** + S *whereas*, **bien que** + S *although*, **de crainte que** + S *for fear that*, **de façon que** + S *in such a way that*, **de manière que** + S *so that*, **de peur que** + S *for fear that*, **de sorte que** (+ S) *in such a way that*, **encore que** + S *although*, **étant donné que** *given that*, **parce que** *because*, **plutôt que** + S *rather than*, **pour que** + S *so that*, **pour . . . que** + S *however*, **puisque** *since*, **quoique** + S *although*, **quoi que** + S *whatever*, **sans que** + S *without*, **sauf que** *except that*, **selon que** *depending*, **si ce n'est que** *except for the fact that*, **soit que** (+ S) *whereas*, **suivant que** *depending whether*, **supposé que** + S *assuming that*, **tandis que** *whereas*, **vu que** *in view of the fact that*, etc. For example:

Venez plus près, **afin que** je vous voie. *Come closer so that I may see you.*

Bien qu'il soit vieux, il n'est pas gâteux. *Although he is old, he is not senile.*

Travaille bien **de sorte qu'**ils soient contents. *Work well so that they will be pleased.*

Il ne l'épousera pas, **parce qu'**il ne l'aime pas. *He will not marry her, because he does not love her.*

Vu que vous êtes directeur, vous pouvez prendre cette décision. *In view of the fact that you are a director you can take this decision.*

Comparison: **ainsi que** *as*, **autant que** + S *so far as*, **comme si** *as though*, **d'autant plus que** *all the more so that*, **de même que** *in the same way as*, **moins que** *less than*, **non moins que** *no less than*, **plus que** *more than*. For example:

Le plan a réussi, **ainsi que** nous l'avions prévu. *The plan succeeded, as we had forecast.*

Faisons **comme si** tout allait bien. *Let us act as if everything was going well.*

Ils ont dépensé **moins que** nous. *They spent less than we did.*

Points to bear in mind regarding the use of subordinating conjunctions:

1 In the lists given above, there are many words which also appear in the chapters dealing with adverbs or prepositions. This is because there is a close relationship between those grammatical categories:

alors (*then* = adv.) ←—→ alors que (*while* = conjunction)
après (*after* = prep.) ←—→ après que (*after* = conjunction)
avant (*before* = prep.) ←—→ avant que (*before* = conjunction)

In most cases, those words are followed by **que** (*that*) which is the most commonly encountered subordinating conjunction.

2   As well as being a conjunction in its own right, **que** is also used in the following ways:

(*a*)   As an elliptic (shorter) version of other conjunctions: **afin que** *so that*, **avant que** *before*, **de telle façon que**/**de telle sorte que** *so that*, **pour que** *in order that*, etc. For example:

Viens ici **que** je te voie. (= **afin que**)   *Come here so that I can see you.*

Faites du bon travail, **qu**'il soit content. (= **de sorte que**)   *Do a good job so that he'll be pleased.*

(*b*)   Almost systematically as an 'alternative' to avoid the repetition of an already-used subordinating conjunction. For example:

Je l'ai fait **afin que** tu comprennes et **que** tu acceptes.   *I did it so that you understand and accept.*

Tu resteras ici **jusqu'à ce que** le brouillard se lève et **que** la pluie cesse.   *You will stay here until the fog lifts and the rain stops.*

3   Care must be taken not to confuse the following two conjunctions (both followed by a subjunctive):

(i)   **quoique** = *although*:

Quoiqu'il soit souffrant il est allé au bureau.   *Although he was unwell, he went to the office.*

(ii)   **quoi que** = *whatever*/*no matter what*:

Quoi que vous disiez, je refuse de vous croire.   *Whatever you say, I refuse to believe you.*

4   The conjunctions **à moins que** *unless*, **avant que** *before*, **de crainte que**/**de peur que** *for fear that which* are all followed by the subjunctive, are normally constructed with the expletive particle **ne**. In such cases, the particle **ne** has no negative value whatever.

Compare: Attendez ici de peur qu'il **ne** vous voie. (expletive).
            Wait here for fear he may see you.
and: Attendez ici de peur qu'il **ne** vous voie **pas** (negation).
            Wait here for fear he may not see you.

5   As previously stated, many subordinating conjunctions must be followed by a verb in the subjunctive. However, since that tense is felt to be stylistically 'heavy', French people will try to avoid, it if at all possible. To that end, *and so long as the subject (performer) is the same in the main clause (m.c.) and the subordinate clause (s.c.);* a preposition equivalent in meaning to the conjunction and often

containing **de** will be used. This will allow the replacement of the subjunctive by an infinitive:

Compare: Nous avons attendu afin que nous puissions vous parler.

same subject

m.c.   s.c.

and: Nous avons attendu **afin de** pouvoir vous parler.
        We have waited in order to speak to you (i.e. *so that we may speak to you*).

or: Vous mangerez un sandwich avant que vous partiez.

same subject

m.c.   s.c.

and: Vous mangerez un sandwich **avant de** partir.
        You will eat a sandwich before going (i.e. *before you go*).

or: Je n'ai rien ajouté de peur que je dise une bêtise.

same subject

m.c.   s.c.

and: Je n'ai rien ajouté **de peur de** dire une bêtise.
        I did not add anything for fear of saying something stupid (i.e. *for fear I may say something stupid*).

> If the subject is not the same in the two clauses, the subjunctive must be used if the conjunction requires it.

Note: If the subject of the main clause is the impersonal pronoun **il** (*it*), it will be possible for the subordinate clause to be constructed with an infinitive.

Compare: Il faut que vous partiez.

m.c.   s.c.

and: Il vous faut **partir.**
        You must go.

or: Il est important que nous acceptions

m.c.   s.c.

and: Il est important pour nous d'**accepter**.
        It is important for us to accept

Any ambiguity about the subject (performer) can be removed by using an additional pronoun: **moi, toi**, etc. (*me, you*, etc.)

6   The conjunctions **pendant que** and **tandis que** (*while*) have two possible meanings.

(*a*) They can indicate the straightforward occurrence of two actions *at the same time*. For example

Elle lit le journal $\begin{cases} \text{tandis que} \\ \text{pendant que} \end{cases}$ j'écoute la radio.

She is reading the paper while I am listening to the radio.

(*b*) They can introduce an idea of opposition (*while = whereas*).

Il se repose $\begin{cases} \text{tandis que} \\ \text{pendant que} \end{cases}$ je me tue au travail.

He is resting while I am working my fingers to the bone. (lit: . . . *while I am killing myself working*)

7   After certain verbs (constructed with the preposition **à**) **que** must be preceded by the expression **à ce** (lit: *to that*). The most common of those verbs are: **s'attendre à** *to expect*, **consentir à** *to agree to*, **se décider à** *to make up one's mind to*, **s'habituer à** *to get used to*, **s'opposer à** *to be opposed to*, **se refuser à** *to refuse to* and **renoncer à** *to give up*. For example:

Je m'attends **à ce qu'**il refuse. (and not *je m'attends qu'il refuse) *I expect he will refuse.*

Nous nous opposons **à ce qu'**ils entrent. (and not * nous nous opposons qu'ils entrent) *We are opposed to them coming in.*

8   As well as introducing subordinate clauses, **que** can also be found:

(*a*) At the beginning of a main clause:

$\underbrace{\text{Qu'il parle,}}_{\text{m.c.}}$ $\underbrace{\text{s'il en a le courage.}}_{\text{s.c.}}$

Let him talk if he has the courage to do so.

(*b*) At the beginning of an independent clause (i.e. not followed by a subordinate one):

Que dieu vous garde! *May God be with you.* (lit: *let God keep you*)

9   Although the presence of **que** often indicates that the verb of the subordinate clause it introduces will be in the Subjunctive, it is by no means always the case. This is very important and should always be borne in mind.

Compare: Nous pensons **que** vous **refuserez**. (Future Indicative)
            We think you will refuse.

and: Nous ne pensons pas **que** vous **refusiez**. (Present Subjunctive)
        We do not think you will refuse.

or: Je crois que vous **avez** raison. (Present Indicative)
           I think you are right.
and: Je ne crois pas que vous **ayez** raison. (Perfect
           Subjunctive).
           I do not think you are right.

Key points

1   Conjunctions are invariable words or expressions which are used to link:

(*a*)   Words or expressions of equal grammatical status (nouns, adjectives,
        verbs, adverbs). Such conjunctions are called *coordinating conjunctions.*
(*b*)   Phrases or clauses of unequal status, one being a *main clause* and the
        other(s) giving useful additional information about the first and called
        subordinate clause(s). Such conjunctions are called *subordinating
        conjunctions.*

2   Conjunctions serve to indicate the relationship which exists between the
elements they link together (time; cause/consequence; constraint/restric-
tion/exclusion; opposition; emphasis; etc.)
3   It is possible for a given conjunction to have several distinct meanings
according to context.
4   There is a close relationship between conjunctions, prepositions and even
adverbs: similar expressions can sometimes be found in more than one of
those categories.
5   Certain subordinating conjunctions introduce clauses in which the verb
must be in the subjunctive mood; others do not.
6   Because of its 'ponderous' quality, the subjunctive can sometimes be
avoided in subordinate clauses. In such cases, the conjunction is replaced by
the corresponding preposition which is then followed by an infinitive or by a
noun.
7   Normally, the repetition of a given subordinating conjunction in one
sentence is not acceptable. This can easily be avoided by using **que** as a
substitute, as many times as required.
8   Although the conjunction **que** often indicates the presence of a subjunctive in the subordinate clause it introduces, this is by no means systematic.
Careful note should be made of which conjunctions require which mood.

17 Interjections

Interjections are invariable words or expressions which can be slipped into the speech chain, either to convey certain commands, emotions or moods, or to represent, as faithfully as practicable, noises made by things or beings (onomatopoeias). Interjections may be nouns, adjectives, adverbs, verbs, etc. They can also be modifications of blasphemous expressions referring to God, the Virgin Mary or even Satan. For example:

Parbleu! (*You bet!*) comes from **Par Dieu** (*by God*)

Diantre! (*By Jove!*) comes from **Par le Diable** (*by the devil*)

Dame! (Of course!) comes from **Par Notre-Dame** (*by Our Lady*)

Note: Very often, the interjection is an elliptical (shortened) sentence:

Patience! = Prenez patience!

Patience! Have patience!

Attention! = Faites attention!

Careful! Be careful!

The interjections presented in this chapter have, for the sake of convenience, been divided into three groups: interjections proper, oaths and onomatopoeias.

Interjections proper

1 *Appreciation*: **A la bonne heure!** *None too soon!*, **bon!** *good!*, **bien!** *well done!*, **bravo!** *hurrah!*, **chic!** *great!*, **enfin!** *at last*, **fichtre!** *by God!*, **hip hip hip hourra!** *hip hip hooray!*, **ô!** *oh!*

2 *Disappointment*: **Bah!** *too bad!*, **bof!** *what the heck!*, **flûte!** *blast!*, **fichtre!** *blast!*, **hélas** *alas*, **mince!** *drat!*, **zut!** *blast!*

3 *Encouragement*: **Allez!** *Go on!*, **allons!** *come on!*, **chiche!** *I dare you!*, **courage!** *take heart!*, **hardi!** *go on!*, **hue!** *gee-up!*, **patience!** *patience!*

4 *Greeting*: **Adieu!** *Goodbye!*, **allô!** *hallo!*, **bonjour** *hallo!*, **bonsoir** *good evening!*, **hé!** *hey!*, **salut!** *Hi!*, etc.

5 *Relief*: **Ah!** *Well done!*, **enfin!** *at last!*, **ouf!** *phew!*

6 *Sadness or pain*: **Ah! Oh!**, **aïe** *ouch!*, **hélas!** *alas!*, **oh là là!** *oh dear!*, **ouille!** *ouch!*

7   *Surprise*:   **Ah!** *Oh!*, **bonté divine!** *good gracious!*, **grand dieu!**
good God!, **juste ciel!** *good heavens!*, **sapristi!** *gosh!*, **tiens!** *I say!*
8   *Warning*:   **Attention!/gare!** *Watch out!*, **au secours!** *help!*, **chut!**
hush!, **halte!** *halt/stop!*, **hé bien!** *watch out!*, **ho!** *hey!*, **holà!** *watch out!*,
silence! *silence!*, **tout doux!** *take it easy!*

For example:

Voilà le garçon! **A la bonne heure!**   *Here is the waiter! And
about time too!*
Flûte! J'ai oublié de téléphoner.   *Blast! I forgot to telephone.*
Allez! Avancez!   *Go on! Move!*
Allô! Je voudrais parler au gérant.   *Hallo! I'd like to speak to
the manager.*
Attention! Vous allez tomber!   *Watch out! You are going to fall!*

Oaths

Dame! *Of course!*, **diable/diantre!** *by Jove!*, **nom de dieu!** *by God!*,
parbleu! *of course*, **sacrebleu!/ventrebleu!** *by God!*
Note: Most of the oaths containing **bleu** (a deformation of
dieu = *God*) are now old-fashioned and humorous; modern versions
have been created to replace them. For example:

Nom d'une pipe! (lit: *in the name of a pipe!*) = *Good God!*
Nom d'un chien! (lit: *in the name of a dog!*) = *Damn!*
Nom d'un petit bonhomme! (lit: *in the name of a small
man!*) = *Blast!*

Onomatopoeias

Some of the most commonly used onomatopoeias are given below
along with the context in which they normally occur, or the thing or
being associated with them:
Badaboum *noisy and spectacular fall*, **clic-clac** *key locking a door*, **clac**
sharp noise or slap, **cocorico** *cock crowing*, **crac** *wood snapping*, **cui-cui**
small bird chirping, **ding-dong** *big bell*, **drelin-drelin** *small bell*, **flic-floc**
noise in mud or water, **hi-han** *donkey*, **hi-hi** *laugh*, **meuh** *cow*, **miaou**
cat, **ouah-ouah** *dog*, **paf** *hard slap or thud*, **pan** *shot-like noise*, **patatras**
fall, **pif** *sharp slap-like noise*, **plouf** *object falling in water*, **teuf-teuf** *an
old engine*, **tic-tac** *clock or watch*, **toc-toc** *knocking on a door*, **vlan**
slamming noise:

Ses chaussures faisaient **flic-floc** dans la boue!   *His shoes were
making squelching noises in the mud!*
Elle le gifla violemment, **paf!**   *She slapped him very hard!*

J'ai glissé dans l'herbe mouillée et **plouf!** *I slipped on the damp grass and fell into the water!*

Note: Some of the above may also be used figuratively.

Compare: La porte se referme. Vlan!
            The door closes, bang!
and: Je le lui ai dit tout net! Vlan!
            I told him! Straight between the eyes!

As with slang words, it is extremely important to be aware of the context (social and linguistic) in which interjections are used. So, whenever you hear them, pay particular attention to who is saying them and the circumstances in which they are used.

Key points

1   Interjections are invariable words or phrases used in speech to convey a command, a feeling, a mood or to imitate the sounds made by a thing or being.
2   Some interjections are disguised oaths. They should be used with care. In modern French, oaths ending in **bleu** (a deformation of **dieu** = *God*) are generally seen as old-fashioned and humorous.
3   If used properly (and sparingly), interjections can liven up a conversation, but it is essential to be sensitive to the social and linguistic context in which they occur.
4   Although interjections can be found in written form, they were (and are) essentially a means of expressing feelings in the spoken language.

18 Comparatives and Superlatives

In certain circumstances, we need to express a comparison between two or more things, beings or actions, to state which of them possess(es) a given characteristic, to a lesser degree (inferiority), to the same degree (equality), to a higher degree (superiority) or even to the highest degree possible (superlative).

In general, comparisons involve adjectives or adverbs, but they can also involve nouns and verbs:

> Il y avait **plus** de monde **que** d'habitude. (noun)   *There were more people than usual.*

> Tu travailles **moins que** moi. (verb)   *You work less than I do.*

In English, those various degrees are expressed in the following way:

Inferiority = lesser degree:	*less . . . than (not so . . . as)*
Equality = same degree:	*as . . . as (no more . . . than)*
Superiority = higher degree:	more . . . than (. . . er than . . .)
Superlative highest degree:	the most . . . (the . . . est)
very high degree:	*extremely . . . , infinitely . . . , very . . .*

Note: A small number of adjectives and adverbs do not follow the regular pattern of formation. This is also the case in French. They will be studied separately.

The French comparative and superlative structures are presented below. For each example, the part of speech affected by the comparison is given in brackets.

Inferiority

Moins . . . que *(less . . . than)*. For example:

> Nous sommes **moins** riches **qu'** eux. (adjective)   *We are less rich than they are.*

> Il y a **moins** de travail **qu'**hier. (noun)   *There is less work than yesterday.*

> Sa voiture va **moins** vite **que** la nôtre. (adverb)   *His car goes less fast than ours.*

Il a **moins** bu **que** d'habitude. (verb) *He drank less than usual.*

Notes:

1   It is possible to convey the same meaning (inferiority) by using the negative structure **ne . . . pas (aus) si . . . que** (*not as . . . as*)

Compare: Il est **moins** intelligent **que** toi. (adjective)

and: Il **n**'est **pas (aus)si** intelligent **que** toi.

       He is less intelligent than you.

If this comparison is constructed with a noun or a verb instead of an adjective, **ne pas (aus)si** will become **ne pas (au)t ant**:

    Le vieux monsieur **n**'avait **pas autant** de courage qu'autrefois. *The old man did not have as much courage as in the old days.*

2   To express an idea of continuous reduction, the phrase **de moins en moins** (*less and less*) can be used:

    J'ai **de moins en moins de** courage. (noun) *I have less and less courage.*

    C'est **de moins en moins** facile. (adjective) *It's getting less and less easy.*

Equality

Aussi . . . que (*as . . . as*). For example:

    Elle est **aussi** charmante **que** sa mère. (adjective) *She is as charming as her mother.*

    Nous crierons **aussi** fort **que** vous. (adverb) *We shall shout as loud(ly) as you.*

Notes:

1   If this degree of comparison is used with a noun or a verb, **aussi** *must* be replaced by **autant**:

    Il y a **autant** de bruit **que** ce matin. (noun) *There is as much noise as this morning.*

    Ils ont **autant** travaillé **que** moi. (verb) *They have worked as much as I have.*

2   It is possible to convey the idea of equality by using the negation **ne pas** (*not*) with a construction expressing superiority or inferiority:

    Elle **n**'est **pas plus** riche **que** toi. (adjective) *She is no richer than you (= as rich as).*

    Je **ne** suis **pas moins** prudent **que** lui. (adjective) *I am no less careful than he is (= as careful as).*

3   The idea of equality can also be conveyed by using the adverb **comme** (*as*):

    Il est têtu **comme** une mule. *He is (as) stubborn as a mule.*

    Des cheveux blancs **comme** neige. *Hair (as) white as snow.*

Superiority

Plus . . . que (*more . . . than/ . . . er than*). For example:

Son voisin est **plus** raisonnable **que** lui. (adjective)   *His neighbour is more reasonable than he is.*

Il parle **plus** vite **que** moi. (adverb)   *He speaks faster than I do.*

Elle a **plus** de soucis **que** vous. (noun)   *She has more cares than you have.*

Tu manges **plus que** nous deux. (verb)   *You eat more than both of us.*

Notes:

1   In cases when a noun or a verb are used in this type of comparison, **plus** is normally replaced by **davantage**:

Ils ont **davantage** d'idées **que** leur patron. (noun)   *They have more ideas than their boss.*

2   When the point of reference for the comparison is a noun, **de** or **d'** (as applicable) is inserted immediately after **plus** or **davantage**:

Ils ont **plus d'**argent **que** nous.   *They have more money than we have.*

3   To express an idea of continual increase, the expression **de plus en plus** (*more and more*) can be used.

Nous recevons **de plus en plus** de lettres. (noun)   *We are receiving more and more letters.*

Il est **de plus en plus** déçu. (adj.)   *He is getting more and more disappointed.*

A similar meaning can be obtained by using **toujours plus** (or **toujours davantage** when required) or **chaque jour plus** (or **chaque jour davantage** when required):

Les trains vont **chaque jour plus** vite. (adverb)   *Trains are getting faster every day.*

La tension augmente **toujours davantage**. (verb)   *Tension is ever increasing.*

Superlative degree

Highest degree

le plus . . . (*the . . . est* or *the most . . .*). For example:

C'est **le plus** beau jour de ma vie. (adjective)   *It is the best day of my life.*

C'est ce remède qui agit **le plus** vite. (adverb)   *It is this remedy which works the fastest.*

Note: When this structure is used with an adjective, the article which is part of the superlative expression must vary in gender *and* number with the noun which the adjective qualifies. In addition, the required agreement must be made at the end of the adjective.

Compare: Elle avait **la plus** jolie robe et **le plus** beau collier.
She had the prettiest dress and the most beautiful necklace.

and: Elle avait **les plus** jolies robes et **les plus** beaux colliers.
She had the prettiest dresses and the most beautiful necklaces.

In all other cases (i.e. with nouns, adverbs, verbs), the superlative expression will be invariable:

Elle a **le plus** de travail. (noun) *She has the most work.*

Ce sont eux qui ont **le plus** mangé. (verb) *It is they who ate the most.*

Very high degree

For the expression of *a very high degree*, the adjective or adverb will be preceded by an adverb such as: **bien** or **fort** (*very*), **extraordinairement** (*extraordinarily*), **extrêmement** (*extremely*), **infiniment** (*infinitely*), etc. For example:

Nous avons **extrêmement** peur. (noun) *We are extremely frightened.*

Je suis **infiniment** touché. (adjective) *I am extremely touched.*

Notes:

1 This second category of superlatives can sometimes be expressed by a prefix: **extra**, **super**, **hyper**, **ultra** or by a suffix: **issime** usually welded to the appropriate adjective:

Elle est **hypersensible**. (adjective) *She is hypersensitive.*

Ce vin est **extra sec**. (adjective) *This wine is extra dry.*

Cet homme est **richissime** (adjective) *This man is incredibly rich.*

2 This superlative meaning can also be expressed by the repetition of the adjective or adverb concerned:

C'est **dur-dur**. (adjective) *Things are very hard.*

Il faut partir **vite-vite.** (adverb) *We must leave very quickly.*

3 The same effect can also be achieved by using **des plus** (*most*):

La décision est **des plus** importante. *The decision is most important.*

(Note the absence of agreement!)

4 In many cases, the construction of a French comparative or superlative sentence will involve a word order which is different from the one used in English.

Compare: *A more important discovery has been made.*

and: Une découverte **plus** importante a été faite.
or: *Here is the strongest man in the world.*
and: Voici l'homme **le plus fort** du monde.
or: *The most stringent experiments are carried out.*
and: Les expériences **les plus** rigoureuses sont effectuées.

NB   In such sentences, the noun-phrase is placed *before* the comparative or superlative and *not after* it as in English.

Exceptional forms

A small number of adjectives and adverbs do not follow the regular rules of formation for comparatives and superlatives. Their list is given below.

Category	*Positive form*	*Meaning*	*Comparative*	*Superlative*
adjective	bon mauvais petit	*good* *bad* *slight*/small	meilleur pire moindre	le meilleur le pire le moindre
adverb	beaucoup bien mal peu	*much* *well* *badly* *little*	plus mieux pis moins	le plus le mieux le pis le moins

For example:
>   Ici le climat est **meilleur** que là-bas. (adjective)   *Here the climate is better than over there.*
>   C'est **mieux** que la dernière fois. (adverb)   *It's better than last time.*
>   Tout va de **mal** en **pis**. (adverbs) *Everything is getting from bad to worse.*

Notes:
1   In the case of the adjectives, it must be remembered that the appropriate agreements must be made according to the gender and number of the noun concerned:
>   Prenez **la meilleure** chambre et **le meilleur** lit.   *Take the best room and the best bed.*

2   **Mauvais** (*bad*), **petit** (*slight*/*small*) and **mal** (*badly*), can also be constructed in the normal way. The two forms are used in different circumstances:

(i) the regular form is used particularly when a concrete characteristic is expressed. It is the most frequent;
(ii) the irregular form is used in abstract cases.

Compare: De deux maux il faut choisir **le moindre**. (abstract)
We must choose the lesser of two evils.

and: De ces deux hôtels je préfère **le plus petit**. (concrete)
Of those two hotels I prefer the smaller.

or: La situation est **pire qu'**hier. (abstract)
The situation is worse than yesterday.

and: La soupe est **plus mauvaise qu'**hier. (concrete)
The soup is worse than it was yesterday.

Idiomatic uses of comparative structures

1 { **plus . . . plus** (*the more . . . the more*)
{ **moins . . . moins** (*the less . . . the less*):
   Plus je joue, **plus** je gagne.   *The more I play, the more I win.*
   Plus on est (de fous) **plus** on rit. (saying)   *The more, the merrier.*
   Moins je le vois, **plus** je suis heureux.   *The less I see him, the happier I am.*

2 { **de plus en plus** (*more and more*)
{ **de moins en moins** (*less and less*):
   Elle devient **de plus en plus** forte.   *She is becoming stronger and stronger.*
   Votre travail est **de moins en moins** acceptable.   *Your work is getting less and less acceptable.*

3 { **Plus de** (*more than*)
{ **moins de** (*less than*):
Those two expressions are used in sentences where the idea of a limit
is formulated (distance, time, age, weight, etc.), to indicate that the
limit has been exceeded (**plus de**), or has not been reached (**moins de**):
   Ils sont restés **plus de** trois jours.   *They stayed more than three days.*
   Elle a **moins de** 18 ans.   *She is under 18.*

Certain adjectives cannot normally be used in comparative or
superlative constructions because their meaning *already* implies a
comparative or superlative value. Such is the case for:
aîné *elder*, **cadet** *younger*, **dernier** *last*, **excessif** *excessive*, **majeur**
major, **mineur** *minor*, **ultime** *ultimate*, **unique** *unique*, etc.

Key points

1   There are in French, as in English, phrases which enable us:
(a)   to express various degrees of comparison between things, beings or actions; or
(b)   to state that certain things, beings, etc., possess a certain characteristic to the highest degree or to 'a very high degree'.
      The first are known as comparatives, the second as superlatives.

2   There are 3 degrees of comparison: (i) *inferiority*, (ii) *equality* and (iii) *superiority*. They are rendered in French by (i) **moins . . . que** (*less than*) (ii) **aussi . . . que** (*as . . . as*) (iii) **plus . . . que** (*more than*).
3   There are alternatives to express two of the degrees mentioned:
(a)   *inferiority* can also be expressed as 'negative equality' with **ne . . . pas aussi que** (*not so . . . as*), or **ne . . . pas comme** (*not . . . like . . .*)
(b)   *equality* can also be expressed as 'negative superiority': **ne . . . pas plus . . . que** (*not any more than*) or 'negative inferiority': **ne . . . pas . . . moins . . . que** (*not any less than . . .*). Equality can also be expressed by using **comme** (*as, like*).
4   If a comparison involves an adjective, the necessary agreements (gender and number) must be made as required.
5   If a comparison involves a nominal or verbal phrase instead of an adjective or adverb, the expressions used will have to be modified in the following way:
   aussi . . . que (equality) must be replaced by **autant . . . que:**
   plus . . . que (superiority) should be replaced by **davantage . . . que**.
6   There are two main types of superlatives:
   a superlative conveying the idea of 'the highest degree';
   a superlative conveying the idea of 'a very high degree'.
–   The first one is expressed in French by: **le plus . . .** (*the . . . est/the most . . .*).
–   The second by placing before the appropriate element (adjective/adverb) an adverb such as: **excessivement** (*excessively*), **extrêmement** (*extremely*), **infiniment** (*infinitely*), **merveilleusement** (*wonderfully*), **très** (*very*), etc.
7   It is important to remember that in many sentences where a comparative (or superlative) is present, the word-order may be different in French and English. In particular, nouns which are placed after the comparative or superlative in English will be placed before it in French.
8   Although most adjectives and adverbs follow the normal rules for the formation of comparatives and superlatives, a small number of them are irregular; they are: *adjectives* = **bon** (*good*), **mauvais** (*bad*) and **petit** (*small/slight*). *adverbs* = **beaucoup** (*much*), **bien** (*well*), **mal** (*badly*) and **peu** (*little*).
9   The irregular comparatives and superlatives of adjectives *must agree* in gender and number as required by the grammatical context.

10   The regular method of formation for comparatives and superlatives can also be used with **mauvais** (*bad*), **petit** (*small/slight*), and **mal** (*badly*). The two forms (regular and irregular) have a slightly different use:
− the regular form is used in a concrete context;
− the irregular form is used in an abstract context.

11   Certain adjectives cannot normally be used in comparative or superlative constructions, because they already express a comparative or superlative idea on their own.

19   The Agreement of Tenses in Main and Subordinate Clauses

When speaking and writing in French, it is important to have the opportunity to situate a series of actions in relation to one another. In other words, it is useful to indicate whether:

1   One action occurred *before* the other(s) (= *anteriority*);
2   All actions occurred *at the same time* (= *simultaneity*);
3   One action occurred *after* the other(s) (= *posteriority*).

This can be done through careful use of tenses. The problem of tense agreement becomes particularly acute in the case of a sentence composed of a main clause (m.c.) and one (or more) subordinate clause(s) (s.c.) which, as previously stated, help(s) to give a fuller picture of the situation through added information.

Compare:

	perfect	perfect
C'est l'homme	que j'ai rencontré à la gare	qui m'a donné la lettre
m.c.	s.c. 1	s.c. 2

It is the man (whom) I met at the station who gave me the letter.

and:

	perfect	future
C'est l'homme	que j'ai rencontré à la gare	qui me donnera la lettre
m.c.	s.c. 1	s.c. 2

It is the man (whom) I met at the station who will give me the letter.

There are three types of possibilities

1   The main clause is in the Indicative mood and the subordinate clause does *not* require a verb in the subjunctive. In this case the verb of the subordinate clause may be in the Indicative, the Conditional, or even the Infinitive. An example is shown on pages 222–3 overleaf.

2   The main clause is in the Indicative, but the subordinate clause requires a subjunctive, because it expresses a possibility, a hypothesis, a doubt, etc. or because it is introduced by a conjunction requiring the subjunctive (see chapter on conjunctions).

There are two cases to envisage:

(i)   the action expressed in the subordinate clause *may already have occurred*;

(ii)   the action expressed in the subordinate clause *may yet occur* (now or later).

Main clause	Subordinate clause in the subjunctive	
(Indicative)	(i) *The action may have occurred*	(ii) *The action may yet occur*
Present je doute *I doubt* **Future** je douterai *I shall doubt* **Perfect** j'ai douté *I doubted* **Past Historic** je doutai *I doubted* **Imperfect** je doutais *I was doubting*	**Perfect subjunctive** qu'il soit venu *that he has/had come*	**Present subjunctive** qu'il vienne *that he is coming* *that he will come* *that he would come*

Note: There are other subjunctive tenses (Imperfect and Pluperfect) which could be used. But because of their increasing rarity in everyday French, it was deemed unnecessary to include them here.

3   The subordinate clause is introduced by **si** (*if*) *expressing a condition*. At this level, you are advised to consider that the three possibilities given below are *the only acceptable ones* for a sentence *in which a condition is expressed*. In each case the arrow indicate the only possible combination.

Note: Very often, the subordinate clause beginning with **si** is *placed first* and followed by the main clause.

Main Clause	Subordinate Clause (Indicative or Conditional)		
(Indicative mood)	*1* *Anteriority*	*2* *Simultaneity*	*3* *Posteriority*
Present Je pense *I think* →	**Perfect Indicative** qu'il est venu *he has come*	**Present Indicative** qu'il vient *he is coming*	**Future Indicative** qu'il viendra *he will come*
Future je penserai *I shall think* →	**Perfect Indicative** (as above)	**Present Indicative** (as above)	**Future Indicative** (as above)
Perfect j'ai pensé *I thought* →	**Pluperfect Indicative** qu'il était venu *he had come*	**Imperfect Indicative** qu'il venait *he was coming*	**Present conditional** qu'il viendrait *he would come*
Past Historic → je pensai	**Pluperfect Indicative** (as above)	**Imperfect Indicative** (as above)	**Present Conditional** (as above)
Imperfect → je pensais	**Pluperfect Indicative** (as above)	**Imperfect Indicative** (as above)	**Present Conditional** (as above)

		Perfect Infinitive	Present Infinitive	Present Infinitive
Present je pense *I think*	→	**Perfect Infinitive** être venu *I have come*	**Present Infinitive** venir *I am coming*	**Present Infinitive** venir *I shall come*
Future je penserai	→	**Perfect Infinitive** (as above)	**Present Infinitive** (as above)	**Present Infinitive** (as above)
Perfect j'ai pensé *I thought*	→	**Perfect Infinitive** être venu *I had come*	**Present Infinitive** venir *I was coming*	**Present Infinitive** venir *I would come*
Past Historic je pensai	→	**Perfect Infinitive** (as above)	**Present Infinitive** (as above)	**Present Infinitive** (as above)
Imperfect je pensais	→	**Perfect Infinitive** (as above)	**Present Infinitive** (as above)	**Present Infinitive** (as above)

Notes:

1 The use of an infinitive in a subordinate clause implies that the subject of the two clauses is the same. For example:

Je pense **être** venu = Je pense que je suis venu.
I think I came.

Tu espères venir = Tu espères que tu viendras.
You hope that you will come.

2 If an infinitive clause is used, there is no way of distinguishing simultaneity or posteriority with the help of the infinitive alone: **J'espère venir** could mean either *I hope I am coming* or *I hope I will be coming*. The context should however make matters clear in most cases.

	Subordinate Clause	Main Clause
1	(Indicative) **Present Indicative** ⟶ Si tu refuses *If you refuse*	(Indicative or Conditional) **Present Indicative/Future** je pars/je partirai *I am leaving /I shall leave*
2	**Imperfect Indicative** ⟶**Present Conditional** Si tu refusais *If you refused*	je partirais *I would go*
3	**Pluperfect Indicative** ⟶**Perfect Conditional** Si tu avais refusé *If you had refused*	je serais parti *I would have gone*

In addition to the above possibilities, there are other instances when tenses need to be modified to comply with the 'agreement of tenses' rules. Two such instances are given below.

Direct and indirect speech

As already mentioned, *direct speech* is someone's speech presented as if the listener or reader were face to face with the person uttering the words in question. The quotation marks are used as well as exclamation or question marks. Indirect speech is someone's speech *reported* as though by a witness. No speech marks and no question or exclamation marks are used. In the table below the arrows indicate which way the changes should be made.

Direct speech		Indirect speech	
introducing clause	*quotation*	*introducing clause*	*reported speech*
Present Il dit: *He says*:	+ **Present** "je sors" *"I am going out"*	↔**Present** Il dit *He says*	+ **Present** qu'il sort *he is going out*
Present Il dit: *He says*:	+ **Perfect** "je suis sorti" *"I have gone out"*	↔**Present** Il dit *He says*	+ **Perfect** qu'il est sorti *he has gone out*
Future Il dira: *He will say*:	+ **Present** "je sors" *"I am going out"*	↔**Future** Il dira *He will say*	+ **Present** qu'il sort *he is going out*
Perfect Il a dit: *He said*:	+ **Present** "je sors" *"I am going out"*	↔**Perfect** Il a dit *He said*	+ **Imperfect** qu'il sortait *he was going out*

Direct speech (cont.)		*Indirect speech* (cont.)	
introducing clause	*quotation*	*introducing clause*	*reported speech*
Perfect	+ **Perfect**	↔**Perfect**	+ **Pluperfect**
Il a dit:	"je suis sorti"	Il a dit	qu'il était sorti
He said:	*"I have gone out"*	*He said*	*he had gone out*
Perfect	+ **Future**	↔**Perfect**	+ **†Present conditional**
Il a dit:	"je sortirai"	Il a dit	qu'il sortirait
He said:	*"I shall go out"*	*He said*	*he would go out*
Imperfect	+ **Present**	↔**Imperfect**	+ **Imperfect**
Il disait:	"je sors"	Il disait	qu'il sortait
He was saying:	*"I am going out"*	*He was saying*	*he was going out*
Imperfect	+ **Perfect**	↔**Imperfect**	+ **Pluperfect**
Il disait:	"je suis sorti"	Il disait	qu'il était sorti
He was saying:	*"I have gone out"*	*He was saying*	*he had gone out*

† This tense is not, properly speaking, a Present Conditional but a *Future of the Past* which is the indirect speech equivalent of a *direct speech Future* uttered in the past.

Compare:	Il **a dit** (Perfect):	"Je **sortirai**" (Future)
	He said	*"I will go out"*
and:	Il **a dit** (Perfect)	qu'il **sortirait** (Future of the Past)
	He said	*he would go out*

For the sake of convenience, and because both tenses are identical, only the appellation Present Conditional has so far been given.

Modal attraction (the 'chameleon effect')

In sentences where the main clause is followed by several other clauses introduced by a relative pronoun: **qui** (*who*), **que** (*that*), **dont** (*whose*), **où** (*where*), etc. (see relative pronouns on pages 94–5), the first subordinate clause (s.c. 1), may require a subjunctive because of its meaning (doubt, hypothesis, etc.). In such cases the second relative clause (s.c. 2), may also take the subjunctive (by a sort of 'chameleon effect') even though the sense may not require it; this phenomenon is called *Modal attraction*. For example:

Je veux un ouvrier ⏜ qui **fasse** bien son travail,

      m.c.   s.c. 1   (Present Subjunctive)

I want a worker who will do his work well,

et { qui **sera** ponctuel. (Future Indicative)
    { qui **soit** ponctuel. (Present Subjunctive)

      s.c. 2

and who will be punctual.

Donnez–moi un remède ⏜ qui **soit** efficace, (Present subjunctive)

      m.c.   s.c. 1

Give me a remedy, which will be efficient,

et $\left\{\begin{array}{l} \text{que je } \textbf{pourrai} \text{ prendre facilement. (Future Indicative)} \\ \text{que je } \textbf{puisse} \text{ prendre facilement. (Present subjunctive)} \end{array}\right.$

s.c. 2

and which I can take easily.

Key points

1   Tense agreement enables the speaker or writer to express the timing of a given action in relation to other actions.

2   If a subordinate clause does not require a verb in the Subjunctive, the range of tenses which can be used is very large and may include the indicative as well as the Conditional Mood.

3   If a subordinate clause requires the Subjunctive, two tenses can be used depending on sense:
− the Perfect Subjunctive to express actions that may have occurred
− the Present Subjunctive to express actions that may yet occur.

4   In the case of a sentence composed of a subordinate clause (s.c.) beginning with **si** (*if*) expressing a condition, and a main clause (m.c.), 3 combinations only are possible.

    s.c. = Present/Perfect   ⟶   m.c. = Present/Future
    s.c. = Imperfect   ⟶   m.c. = Present Conditional
    s.c. = Pluperfect   ⟶   m.c. = Perfect Conditional

5   The rules governing changes of tense from direct to indirect speech (or vice versa) are fairly rigid and should be learned with care.

6   In certain sentences where the main clause is followed by several relative clauses (introduced by **qui**, **que**, etc.), the first of which requires the subjunctive, the other(s) may also take the subjunctive by virtue of modal attraction ('chameleon effect').

20 Problems and Solutions

When studying a language, one always comes across problems which are hard to solve, or mistakes which are difficult to eliminate. This chapter has been written with this point in mind.

Some of the most commonly encountered problems are examined. The entries are made in alphabetical order. For a fuller treatment of the grammatical categories involved, you should refer to the relevant chapter when appropriate.

Adjectives

With very few exceptions, adjectives agree in gender and number with the noun they qualify. The following, however, are exceptions and remain invariable.

1 Adjectives of colour derived from nouns: **aurore** *dawn*, **cerise** *cherry*, **chocolat** *chocolate*, **orange** *orange*, **marron** *chestnut*, **mastic** *putty*, **noisette** *hazel*:

  Elle a les yeux **noisette**. *She has hazel eyes.*

2 Compound adjectives of colour:

  J'aime les chemises **bleu-clair**. *I like light-blue shirts.*

3 **Nu** (*bare*) and **demi** (*half*), when placed before the noun (note the hyphen!):

  Il est **nu-tête** et **nu-pieds**. *He is bare-headed and barefoot.*

4 **Grand** (*great/main*), when used in a feminine (singular or plural) compound:

  Voilà la **grand-route**! *Here is the main road.*

5 Adjectives placed after a verb and used as adverbs: **bas** *low*, **bon** *good*, **cher** *dear*, **dur** *hard*, **fort** *very/loud*, etc.

  Ces fleurs sentent **bon**. *These flowers smell good.*

Adverbs

Adverbs are invariable. They are *normally* placed as follows.

1 After the verb in a simple tense:

  Il travaille **bien**. *He is working well.*

2 Between the auxiliary and the past participle in compound tenses:

  Il a **bien** travaillé. *He has worked well.*

3   Before an adjective or an adverb:
Elle est **très** jeune.   *She is very young.*
Tu vas **trop** vite.   *You are going too fast.*

After (*Après*)

Après (preposition) can be followed by:
1   A noun or a pronoun:
Il est arrivé **après** le repas.   *He arrived after the meal.*
Après vous!   *After you!*
2   A Perfect Infinitive (Infinitive of **être** (*to be*) or **avoir** (*to have*) + Past
Participle) and *not* a Present Participle as in English:
Il est parti **après avoir payé** sa note. (and not* . . . après payant
sa note)   *He left after paying his bill.*

Age

In French, the verb **avoir** (*to have*) is used to express age. It must be
followed by the cardinal number *and* the word **an(s)** (*year(s)*):
Il **a** vingt-cinq **ans**. (lit: *he has twenty-five years*)   *He is twenty-
five.*

Attributive verbs

The following verbs: **demeurer** (*to remain*), **devenir** (*to become*), **être**
(*to be*), **paraître** (*to seem*), **rester** (*to remain*) and **sembler** (*to seem*) are
called 'attributive verbs'. They cannot, unlike other verbs, be
modified by an adverb but they can be qualified by an adjective which
will *vary in gender and number* as required:
Ils **semblent** tristes et fatigués. (masc. plur. agreement)   *They
seem sad and tired.*
La porte **reste** ouverte. (fem. sing. agreement)   *The door remains
open.*
Compare: Ils **sont** rapides. (and not *ils sont vite) *They are quick.*
(adjective)
and: Ils vont vite. *They go quickly.* (adverb)
Notes:
1   In sentences of the type Il est **très** rapide (*He is very fast*), the
adverb **très** modifies the adjective and not the verb.
2   Expressions like **C'est bien** (*it is good = it is well done*) and **C'est
mal** (*it is bad = it is badly done*) are not exceptions but are merely
elliptical (shortened) sentences where the Past Participle **fait** (*done*) is
missed out.

Auxiliaries

Être (*to be*) and **avoir** (*to have*) are the verbs which are used in the formation of *compound tenses* (Perfect, Pluperfect, etc.); the rule is as follows:

1 **être** is used to form the compound tenses of:

(*a*) the 'famous 14': **aller** *to go*, **venir** *to come*, **arriver** *to arrive*, **partir** *to leave*, **descendre** *to go down*, **monter** *to go up*, **entrer** *to go in*, **sortir** *to go out*, **mourir** *to die*, **naître** *to be born*, **passer** *to go by*, **retourner** *to return*, **rester** *to stay*, **tomber** *to fall*:

Ils **sont partis** mais je **suis resté**. *They went but I stayed.*

(*b*) pronominal verbs (reflexive and reciprocal):

Je **me suis coupé**. *I cut myself.* (reflexive)

Nous **nous sommes battus**. *We fought each other.* (reciprocal)

2 **Avoir** is used in all other cases (including the compound tenses of passive verbs):

Ils **ont été insultés** par vous. *They have been insulted by you.*

For the agreement of past participles with **avoir** and **être**, see *Past Participle agreement* on page 240.

Because

It can be translated in two ways:

1 **à cause de**, if it is followed by a noun or a pronoun:

L'accident est arrivé **à cause de** cet idiot. *The accident happened because of this fool.*

2 **parce que**, if it introduces a subordinate clause (s.c.) with subject, verb, etc.:

Je vous téléphone parce que je ne suis pas satisfait.
                     s.c.

I am ringing you because I am not satisfied.

By

It can be translated by:

1 **en** + Present Participle of a verb if, in English, it was followed by an *ing* form:

C'est **en travaillant** qu'il réussira. *It's by working that he will succeed.*

2 **par**, when a noun follows:

Prenez-moi **par** la main. *Take me by the hand.*

Note: If the meaning of *by* is *at the side of* or *near*, it should be translated by **près de**:

Je me promène **près de** la rivière. *I am walking by the river.*

3   **en**, when the idea of transport is present:
Ils sont allés aux Etats-Unis **en** avion.   *They went to the United States by plane.*

Collective nouns

Nouns such as: **l'armée** (*the army*), **l'église** (*the Church*), **la famille** (*the family*), **le gouvernement** (*the government*), **la police** (*the police*), **le public** (*the public*), etc. *must* be used in the singular, despite the fact that they represent a large collection of beings, and the verb they are associated with *must* be in the 3rd person singular. For example:

Le gouvernement est tombé. (and not *sont tombés)   *The government has fallen.*

Le public est content. (and not *sont contents)   *The public is pleased.*

La famille est arrivée. (and not *sont arrivés)   *The family has arrived.*

Dates and days

Dates, with the exception of the first day of the month, require the *cardinal number* in French.

Compare: Le **premier** mai
May 1st

and: Le **deux** mai (and not *le deuxième mai)
May 2nd

Du **premier** janvier au **trente et un** décembre. (and not * . . . au trente et unième . . .)   *All the year round.* (lit: *from January 1st to December 31st*)

Note: Neither the name of the day nor that of the month begin with a capital letter (unless they are at the start of a sentence).

Definite articles

The definite article, which varies according to the gender and number of the noun it relates to, serves as an *advance warning system*. It is therefore used more systematically than in English, not only to indicate very precise and clearly defined categories of things or beings, but also to refer to broad categories or concepts.

Compare: **Les** loups sont féroces.
Wolves (as a species) *are ferocious.*

and: **Les** loups du zoo sont superbes.
The wolves at the zoo (very precise group) *are superb.*

The fact that, with very few exceptions, the plural form of French nouns sounds exactly the same as their singular form, *makes it imperative* to use the definite article (or another determiner) to signal the difference:

Compare:	Il adore **le** cadeau.	The only sound difference
	He loves the present.	between those two French
		sentences is
and:	Il adore **les** cadeaux.	**le** [lə] v. **les** [le]
	He loves presents.	(see appendix I)

Note: The definite article must also be used with the name of a country, or the rank or title of a person (whether or not followed by the name of that person):

Compare: *General de Gaulle did a lot for France.*

and: **Le** Général de Gaulle a beaucoup fait pour **la** France.

Direct (accusative) and indirect (dative) object pronouns

1 If a verb is constructed in the *accusative*, i.e. admits an answer to the question **qui?** (*who(m)?*) or **quoi?** (*what?*), one of the object pronouns — **me** (*me*), **te** (*you* fam.), **le/la** (*him/her/it*), **nous** (*us*) **vous** (*you* sing. or plur.), **les** (*them*) — must be used. For example:

Nous **le** regardons. (nous regardons qui? = **le**)

We are watching him/it.

Je **les** vois. (je vois qui? = **les**)

I see them.

Note: **me** (*me*) changes to **moi** in the 2nd person (sing./plur.) of the Present Imperative (*positive*) tense.

Compare:	Regarde-**moi**! (positive)
	Watch me!
and:	Ne **me** regarde pas! (negative)
	Do not watch me!

2 If a verb is constructed in the *dative*, i.e. is followed by à and admits an answer to the question **à qui?** (*to whom?*) or **a quoi?** (*to what?*), one of the object pronouns -**me** (*to me*), **te** (*to you* fam.), **lui** (*to him/her*), **nous** (*to us*), **vous** (*to you* sing. or plur.), **leur** (*to them*) -must be used:

Nous **lui** téléphonons. (nous téléphonons à qui? = à **lui**)

We are telephoning (to) him/her.

Je **leur** parle. (je parle à qui? = à eux = **leur**)

I am talking to them.

Note: **me** (*to me*) changes to **moi** in the 2nd person (sing./plur.) of the Present Imperative (*positive*) tense:

Compare: Ecrivez-**moi**! (positive)
                Write to me!
and: Ne **m**'écrivez pas! (negative)
                Do not write to me!

The two sets of pronouns (direct and indirect object) presented above, are almost identical *except for the 3rd persons* (singular and plural). Be particularly careful about constructions involving those 3rd persons.

Disjunctive pronouns

Those pronouns are: **moi** (*me*), **toi** (*you* fam.), **lui** (*him/it*), **elle** (*she/it*), **nous** (*us*), **vous** (*you* sing. or plur.), **eux** (*them* masc. plur.), **elles** (*them* fem. plur.). They are used:

1   After a preposition: **à** (*at/to*), **de** (*of/from*), **pour** (*for*), **sans** (*without*), **vers** (*towards*), etc. For example:

      Elle se tourna vers **eux**.   *She turned towards them.*

2   As emphatic reinforcement of the corresponding subject pronoun:

      Moi, je pense que vous avez tort.   *I (for one) think you are wrong.*

3   To replace the corresponding subject pronoun in constructions involving a coordinating conjunction: **et** (*and*), **mais** (*but*), **ni** (*neither/nor*), **ou** (*or*):

      Nous travaillons dur **lui** et **moi**.   *He and I work hard.*

      Ni **eux** ni **moi** n'avons rien vu.   *Neither they nor I saw anything.*

4   In reply to a question where, in English, an auxiliary would follow the subject pronoun:

      Qui a parlé? **Moi**!   *Who spoke? I did!*

      Qui est coupable? **Eux**!   *Who is guilty? They are!*

Faire

Apart from its straightforward meanings (*to do/to make*), **faire** also occurs in a number of useful idiomatic constructions. The most common are presented below.

1   To translate the expressions *to have something done* or *to cause something to be done*. In this case, **faire** is followed by another Infinitive:

      Nous **faisons construire** une maison.   *We are having a house built.*

      Il **a fait fermer** le magasin.   *He had the shop closed* (i.e. *he caused the shop to be closed*).

Notes:
(*a*) It is possible to have a construction where **faire** is used twice: once as the auxiliary and once in its own right:

> Elle a **fait faire** sa robe a Paris. *She had her dress made in Paris.*

(*b*) In certain expressions, particularly in cooking recipes, **faire** is often used as an auxiliary where in English only the main verb would be present.

> **Faire** cuire à feu doux. *Cook on a low heat.*
> **Faites** monter la crème. *Whisk up the cream.*

(*c*) **Faire** is also used in orders or requests to indicate that a person other than the one you are addressing should perform the action requested:

> **Faites** ouvrir la porte. *Have someone open the door.*
> **Fais** appeler le docteur. *Have somebody call the doctor.*

2 To translate impersonal expression relating to the weather:

	beau	*fine*
	du brouillard	*foggy*
	chaud	*hot*
Il fait	frais	*cool*
The weather is	froid	*cold*
It is	humide	*damp*
	orage	*stormy*
	sec	*dry*
	soleil	*sunny*
	du vent	*windy*

3 To translate the expression of assent **do!** in reply to a request (this use is informal):

> Je peux fumer? **Faites,** je vous en prie! *May I smoke? Please do!*
> Vous permettez? **Faites** donc! *Do you mind . . . ? By all means!*

4 In a pronominal construction to translate the English *to get*:

> Il **se fait** tard. *It is getting late.*
> Ta voix **se fait** dure. *Your voice is getting harsh.*

5 To translate the following English expressions:

> *to hurt somebody* = faire mal à quelqu'un
> *to frighten somebody* = faire peur à quelqu'un
> *to shame somebody* = faire honte à quelqu'un
> *to please somebody* = faire plaisir à quelqu'un
> *to mollify somebody* = faire pitié à quelqu'un

Note: The above verbs can also be used pronominally:

> Je **me fais** peur. *I frighten myself.* (reflexive)
> Ils **se** sont **fait** mal. *They hurt themselves.* (reflexive)
> *They hurt each other.* (reciprocal)

6   In certain constructions with 'passive' overtones:

> Il s'est **fait** tuer.   *He was killed* (i.e. *someone killed him*).
>
> Je me suis **fait** voler.   *I was robbed* (i.e. *someone robbed me*).
>
> Ils se sont **fait** prendre.   *They have been caught* (i.e. *someone caught them*).

In all the above constructions, **fait** bears no gender or number agreement.

7   To translate expressions like *to play . . . , to act . . .* For example:

> Vous **faites** l'idiot!   *You are playing the fool!*
>
> Arrêtez de **faire** le singe!   *Stop acting the goat!* (lit. *the monkey*)

For (duration)

This word can be translated in different ways, according to its precise meaning.

1   If it indicates a period (in the past, present or future) seen from the point of view of its *actual* duration, it may be translated as **pendant** (*for = during*), or totally omitted. You may say:

either:	Il a vécu **pendant** vingt ans à Londres.
or:	Il a vécu vingt ans à Londres.
	He lived in London for twenty years.
either:	Je resterai ici **pendant** trois jours.
or:	Je resterai ici trois jours.
	I shall stay here for three days.

2   If it indicates an *anticipated duration*, particularly with a verb of movement -**aller**/**se rendre** (*to go*), **arriver** (*to arrive*), **partir** (*to leave*), **venir** (*to come*), etc.-it will be translated as **pour**:

> Nous partons **pour** un mois.   *We are leaving for a month.*

Note: *for* expressing a duration in the past can be translated by the expression **il y a . . . que** with one of the appropriate tenses emphasising duration (i.e. present, imperfect, etc. *but not* past historic):

> **Il y a** deux heures **que** j'attends. (present)   *I have been waiting for two hours.*
>
> **Il y avait** deux ans **qu**'il était parti. (imperfect)   *He had been gone for two years.*

For example

This is translated by **par exemple** (and not * pour exemple).

Note: In an exclamative sentence **par exemple** is used in familiar French to express incredulity or great surprise:

> Vous ici? Ça **par exemple**!   *You are here? Well I never!*

Generally/in general

This is translated in French by:

1 **En général** (often used in informal situations):
   En général, il est assez compréhensif. *Generally, he is fairly understanding.*
2 **Généralement** (often used is slightly more elevated style):
   Je le vois **généralement** le mercredi. *Generally, I see him on Wednesdays.*

Note: *Generally speaking* can be translated by **Généralement parlant**:
   Généralement parlant, ça marche bien. *Generally speaking, things are going well.*

Imperfect v. Perfect (or Past Historic)

This is one of the most common sources of errors.

1 The Perfect or the Past Historic indicate that an action occurred as an isolated event in the past *regardless of its duration*. It permits the faithful recording of a sequence of *separate* events (A, B, C) along the time axis, as shown below:

```
                          Present
Past ──────── × ──── × ──── × ──────────────→ Future
              A     B     C
```

Il s'est assis, a appelé le garçon et a commandé son déjeuner.
         A   B   C
He sat down, called the waiter and ordered his lunch.

Il fréquenta l'Université pendant trois ans.
He attended University for 3 years.

Note: Here, the duration is irrelevant to the tense; the action is seen as a finite, isolated event.

2 The imperfect emphasises:

(*a*) The habitual recurrence of an action in the past, seen from the point of view of its *duration* or *repetition*:
   Tous les lundis il **allait** au cinéma. *Every Monday he used to go to the pictures.*

(*b*) The fact that an action was in progress when another *isolated* action occurred:
   Je finissais mon travail quand elle est arrivée.
      Imperf.   Perf.
   I was finishing my work when she arrived.

(*c*) The fact that an action used to occur *every time* another did:

Chaque fois qu'il sortait il prenait, un taxi.
    Imperf.   Imperf.
Every time he went out, he used to take a taxi.

(*d*) The fact that an action used to be the 'hallmark' of a period in which another used to occur:

Quand j'étais jeune, je vivais à la campagne.
    Imperf   Imperf.
When I was young, I used to live in the country.

Infinitives

The Infinitive is the 'nominal' form of a verb. In French, it is recognisable by its ending: **er, ir** or **re**. The following important points should always be borne in mind:

1   Some infinitives can be used as nouns: **l'avoir** (*'nest egg'* or *credit note*), **l'être** (*the being*), **le devoir** (*duty*), **le manger** (*food*), **le pouvoir** (*power to act*), **le savoir** (*knowledge*), etc.

2   After the prepositions **à** (*at/to*), **de** (*of/from*), **pour** (*to*) and **sans** (without) the verb *must be in the infinitive*:

Il vient de **partir** sans **dire** merci. *He has just left without saying thank you.*

3   If two verbs follow each other the second one *must be in the infinitive* unless the first is an auxiliary (**avoir** or **être**):

J'aime **marcher**. (and not* j'aime marchant) *I like walking.*

Elle déteste **sortir**. (and not * elle déteste sortant) *She hates going out.*

Note: The English Present Participle found in such constructions must only be translated *either* by an infinitive (as above) *or* by a noun equivalent in meaning. For example:

J'aime marcher.
= J'aime **la marche**.
Elle déteste sortir.
= Elle déteste **les sorties**.

4   The infinitive can be used with the value of an imperative in written instructions:

Assembler avec soin. *Assemble with care.*
Ouvrir ici. *Open here.*

It is

This expression can be translated in a variety of ways according to the context in which it occurs. The main possibilities are given below.

1   If *it* is impersonal (i.e. does not refer to any thing or being) and is constructed as follows:

$$ it\ is + \text{adjective} + \begin{cases} \text{subordinate clause beginning} \\ \text{with } that \\ \qquad\qquad or \\ \text{infinitive clause introduced by } to \end{cases} $$

For example:

$$ It\ is\ important \begin{cases} that\ you\ work. \\ or \\ (for\ you)\ to\ work. \end{cases} $$

The French structure will be:

$$ \textbf{Il est} + \text{adjective} + \begin{cases} \text{subordinate clause (usually subjunctive)} \\ \text{beginning with } \textbf{que} \\ or \text{ infinitive clause beginning with '}\textbf{de}\text{'} \end{cases} $$

For example:

$$ Il\ est\ important \begin{cases} \text{que tu travailles.} \\ or \\ \text{(pour toi) de travailler.} \end{cases} $$

Note: The real subject of such sentences is not **il** but the subordinate or infinitive clauses themselves. You could therefore say:

Either: (Le fait de) travailler est important.
          Working is important.
or: (Le fait) que tu travailles est important.
          (The fact) that you should work is important.

2   If *it* refers to a precise masculine or feminine noun already mentioned in the same or a previous sentence, the translation will be **il** or **elle** as required by the noun's gender:

Lisez cette lettre qui vient d'arriver. **Elle** est urgente.   *Read this letter which has just arrived. It* (i.e. this letter) *is urgent.*

J'ai examiné votre dossier. **Il** est impressionnant.   *I have examined your dossier. It* (i.e. your dossier) *is impressive.*

3   If *it* refers to something which cannot directly be assimilated to a masculine or feminine noun quoted before, but has nevertheless been hinted at 'in substance', the translation will be: **c'**, **ceci**, **cela**, **ça** (*this/that*) and the adjective will be in the masculine singular:

Lisez cette lettre. C'est urgent. *Read this letter. It* (i.e. the fact that you should read this letter) *is urgent.*

J'ai examiné votre dossier. C'est impressionnant!   *I have examined your dossier. It* (i.e. what you have achieved or what is in it . . .) *is impressive!*

Compare: Ce cheval ne gagne jamais. **Il** est ridicule.
           This horse never wins. It (i.e. this horse) *is ridiculous.*

and: Ce cheval ne gagne jamais. C'est ridicule.
             This horse never wins. It (i.e. the fact that it never wins) *is ridiculous.*

4   If *it is* is followed by a noun or a pronoun, the translation will be **c'est** (or **ce sont** if the verb which follows is in the 3rd person plural):

C'est la plage que je préfère.   *It is the beach I prefer.*

Ce sont les invités qui arrivent.   *It is the guests who are arriving.*

It is cannot be used on its own in reply to a question, as in English. The adverbs **oui** or **si** (as appropriate) will have to be used and, if required, accompanied by a repetition of the relevant adjective, noun or pronoun.

Compare: *Is it your car? (Yes) it is!*
and: C'est votre voiture? Oui! (c'est la mienne).
and *not just*: *oui c'est!

More and less

Those words are used in a variety of constructions:

1   *More than/less than* (or equivalent) = comparative; this is translated as: **plus . . . que/moins . . . que**:

Il court **plus** vite **que** moi.   *He runs faster than I.*

2   *The more . . . the more/the less . . . the less* (or equivalent) = augmentative; this is translated as: **plus . . . plus . . . /moins . . . moins . . .** (and not* le plus . . . le plus or le moins . . . le moins):

Plus nous avançons, **plus** il fait sombre.   *The more we advance, the darker it gets.*

3   *More than/less than* + a limit expressed by a figure (i.e. over-/under): this is translated by **plus de . . . /moins de . . .** (and not* plus que . . . /moins que . . .).

Il nous reste **moins de** trois jours.   *We have less than three days left.*

Une absence de **plus de** six mois.   *An absence of over six months.*

4   *More and more/less and less* (or equivalent) = idea of progression or deterioration. This is translated in French by **de plus en plus . . . /de moins en moins . . .** (and not *plus et plus/moins et moins):

Ils ont **de plus en plus** de temps libre.   *They have more and more free time.*

5   *More or less*. This is translated by **plus ou moins**:

Je crois qu'il a **plus ou moins** compris.   *I think he has more or less understood.*

Notes:

(*a*)   *More* expressing a request/order for a greater amount is translated by **encore!**

(*b*)   *More* followed by a noun can be translated by **davantage de** as well as **plus de**:

Nous avons **plus de** temps.

= Nous avons **davantage de** temps.

We have more time.

In certain sentences **plus que** . . . followed by a noun or equivalent may have the meaning of *only . . . left!:*

Plus que deux heures à attendre!   *Only two more hours to wait.*

Il ne reste **plus que** lui.   *He is the only one left* (lit: *There is only him left*).

Neuter

Although it is accepted that there are only two genders in French, there are a number of expressions which do not refer specifically to any masculine or feminine thing or being, e.g. **ce** or **c'** (*this/that*), **ça** (*that*), **ceci** (*this*), **cela** (*that*), **quelque chose** (*something*), **quelqu'un** (*someone*), etc. They are considered neutral in value, but any agreement will be made in the *masculine singular*.

Such neutral expressions are used when the speaker or writer does not know (or want to tell) what the gender of the thing or being referred to is, or when the subject of the sentence is too vague to be clearly labelled masculine or feminine. For example:

Il est encore ici. C'est étrange.   *He is still here. That's strange.*
(i.e. the fact that he is still here is strange)

J'ai entendu **quelque chose** d'intéressant.   *I have heard something interesting.*

Quelqu'un frappe à la porte.   *Someone is knocking at the door.*
(it could be a man or a woman)

Note: If **quelque chose** and **quelqu'un** are followed by an adjective, the preposition **de** must be used:

Mangez **quelque chose de** bon.   *Eat something good.*

Je cherche **quelqu'un de** consciencieux.   *I am looking for somebody conscientious.*

Past participle agreement with *avoir* and *être*

1 With **être** there are two main cases:

(a) *If the verb concerned is not a 'reflexive' verb* (or more precisely a pronominal verb) the past participle will agree in gender and number with the subject, like an adjective:

Ils **sont** part**is** mais elle **est** rest**ée**.   *They* (masc. plur.) *went but she stayed.*

(b) *If the verb concerned is a pronominal verb,* the past participle will agree *if* the construction is an accusative one (i.e. if the performer of the action is also the answer to the questions **qui?** or **quoi?** posed after the past participle reconstructed with **avoir**).

Compare: **Elle** s'est coup**ée**. (elle a coupé qui? = elle)
She cut herself. (accusative = agreement)
and: **Elle** s'est **dit**. (elle a dit à qui? = à elle)
She said to herself. (dative = no agreement)

2 With **avoir** the principle of agreement is as follows:

(a) If the construction is not an accusative one (i.e. no answer to the question **qui?** or **quoi?**) there is no agreement:
Elle a fermé. (Elle a fermé quoi?-no answer available = no agreement)   *She locked up.*
Ils lui ont parlé (Ils ont parlé à qui? dative = no agreement)   *They talked to him/her.*

(b) If the construction is accusative but if the answer to the question **qui?** or **quoi?** comes too late (i.e. after the past participle), there is no agreement:
Ils ont **vu** la mer. (Ils ont vu quoi? = la mer)   *They saw the sea.*

(c) If the construction is accusative *and* if the answer to the question **qui?** or **quoi?** precedes the past participle, then the latter agrees *in gender and number* with the direct object.
La mer est là; ils l'ont **vue**.
(ils ont vu quoi? = l' = la mer = agreement)
The sea is there; they saw it.

People/persons

There are two possible translations of those words:
1 **Gens** (masc. plur.)   This word *cannot* be used to refer to one person only.
You can say: Il y a **des gens** sur la place. *There are people in the square.*

but not: *Il y a un gens sur la place.
This word *cannot* be used with an exact number.
You can say: Une centaine de **gens**. *Approximately a hundred people.*
but not: *Cent trente gens. One hundred and thirty people.
2 *Personnes* (fem. plur.) This word *can* be used to refer to one person only.

   Il y a une **personne** qui attend. *There is a person (who is) waiting.*
It *can* be used with a precise *or* approximate number of people:
   Cent **personnes** attendaient. *A hundred people were waiting.*
   Quelques **personnes** sont descendues. *Some people went down.*
Note: After **quelques** (*a few*) and **plusieurs** (*several*), it is **personnes**
and not **gens** which is used:
   Il a parlé à **plusieurs** personnes. (and not *. . . à plusieurs gens)

Adjectives used immediately before **gens** are put in the *feminine*,
although subsequent agreements remain masculine plural.
   Les **vieilles gens** sont isolés. (and not *isolées) *Old people
   are isolated.*
   Certaines gens sont furieux. (and not *furieuses) *Certain
   people are furious.*

Present participles

The Present Participle is the adjectival form of a verb. In English, it is
recognisable by its *ing* ending. It can appear in four types of
constructions in French.
1 *As an adjective.* In this case, it will agree in gender and number
with the noun it qualifies:
   Une étoile **filante**. *A shooting star.*
2 *As an invariable word*, often replacing a relative clause beginning
with **qui** (*who*):
   Elle aperçoit la voiture **roulant** à toute vitesse. (roulant = qui
   roule) *She sees the car going at full speed.*
3 *To indicate the simultaneity of two actions.* In this case the
French Present Participle will be preceded by **en**:
   Ils montent **en sifflant**. *They come up whistling.*
   Il est parti **en pleurant**. *He went away crying.*
4 *To express manner* (= by/through) The French equivalent is also
constructed with **en**:
   Vous réussirez **en travaillant** bien. *You will succeed by working
   well.*

> English Present Participles immediately following a verb and relating to the same subject *must*, in French, be translated by *an Infinitive*:
> Compare: J'aime **manger** des pommes.
> and: *I like eating apples.*
> or: Ils détestent **se lever** tôt.
> and: *They hate getting up early.*

Requests and orders

In French, as in English, there are many different ways of formulating a request or an order. The expression chosen may depend on the force of the request, the degree of urgency, the status of the person formulating the request, the social context, etc. Some examples are given below. Non standard usage will be mentioned where appropriate.

It should be noted, however, that in most cases a strong request may be 'toned down' by adding such expressions as **s'il te/vous plaît, je te/vous prie** (*please*), **si tu veux/vous voulez bien, si cela ne te/vous dérange pas** (*if you do not mind*), etc. The following categories may be considered:

1   *Strong requests or commands*
(*a*)   The Present Imperative can be used at all levels of language to convey such a meaning:
Fermez la porte (s'il vous plaît)!   *Close the door (please)!*
Ouvre la bouche (je te prie)!   *Open your mouth (please)!*
Note: In the case of a construction involving the second person plural of the Imperative, the corresponding form of **vouloir** (*to want*) may be used as a softener.
Compare: Attendez un moment, je vous prie.
     Wait a moment, please.
and: Veuillez attendre un moment, je vous prie.
     Would you mind waiting a moment please.
In certain situations, the verb may be omitted altogether; the tone of the command is then quite abrupt and can verge on rudeness:
Un moment, s'il vous plaît!   *Just a moment, if you please!*
Deuxième porte à droite!   *Second door on the right!*
(*b*)   The Present Indicative of verbs of request — **demander** (*to ask*), **désirer** (*to wish*), **exiger** (*to demand*), **ordonner** (*to order*)- followed, as appropriate, by an Infinitive or subjunctive clause

can also be used for the purpose:

J'exige que vous partiez immédiatement. *I demand that you go immediately.*

Il **désire** parler au directeur. *He wishes to talk to the director.*

Nous vous **demandons** de bien vouloir attendre. *We ask you to be good enough to wait.*

Note: In certain administrative circles, a distinction is sometimes drawn between the softeners **bien vouloir** and **vouloir bien** (*to be kind enough to. . .*): the former is used by a subordinate when making a request to a superior and the latter by a superior politely instructing a subordinate to do something.

Compare: Je vous demande de **bien vouloir** lire ce dossier. (subordinate to superior) *I would be pleased if you could read this dossier.*

and: Je vous demande de **vouloir bien** lire ce dossier. (superior to subordinate) *Would you be good enough to read this dossier?*

Both constructions are quite formal. In normal French, the distinction is often no longer made.

(*c*) Certain impersonal expressions such as **il faut/il est nécessaire de/que** (*it is necessary to/that*) can also be used to indicate an order or a strong request:

Il faut que j'aille à la banque. *I must go to the bank.*

Il est nécessaire d'obéir aux ordres. *It is necessary to obey orders.*

(*d*) Certain words or expressions may be used on their own to convey an order or strong request:

Halte! *Halt!*

Attention! *Beware!*

En avant, marche! *Forward, march!*

2 *Softened requests or toned-down orders*

(*a*) The Future Indicative of such verbs as **demander** (*to ask*), **devoir** (*to have to*), **falloir** (*to be necessary*), etc. can be used to tone down a request.

Compare: **Il faut** que je vous parle.
I must talk to you.

and: **Il faudra** que je vous parle.
I shall have to talk to you.

or: Je vous **demande** de ne rien dire.
I ask you not to say anything.

and: Je vous **demanderai** de ne rien dire.
I would ask you not to say anything.

(*b*)   The Present Conditional of some verbs may be used to soften a request even further:

Compare:	Vous **devez** accepter.
	You must accept.
and:	Vous **devriez** accepter.
	You should accept.
or:	Nous **voulons** sortir.
	We want to go out.
and:	Nous **voudrions** sortir.
	We would like to go out.

Note: The expression **je vous serais reconnaissant de . . .** (*I would be grateful if you would . . .*) belongs to the same category, but sounds more formal and could be interpreted as condescending.

(*c*)   Requests expressed in the form of a question are often used in French. Their level of stylistic acceptability will depend on the way the question is phrased.

Compare:	Pouvez-vous venir, s'il vous plaît (formal)
and:	Est-ce que vous pouvez venir, s'il vous plaît (standard)
and:	Vous pouvez venir, s'il vous plaît? (familiar)
	Could you come please?
or:	Venez-vous prendre l'apéritif? (formal)
and:	Est-ce que vous venez prendre l'apéritif? (standard)
and:	Vous venez prendre l'apéritif? (familiar)
	Will you come for an aperitif?

(*d*)   A reduced sentence beginning with **si** (*if*) can be used to convey a fomal request:

Si vous voulez bien me suivre . . .   *Would you care to follow me?*

Si Monsieur veut bien s'asseoir . . .   *Would you care to sit down, Sir?*

The following phrases, also expressing a command, are very colloquial and should be used with great care:

La ferme!   *Shut up!*

Ta gueule!   *Shut your trap!*

Since

This word can have two distinct meanings:

1   *As a preposition*, it can express a duration with a clear starting point (date or event). In this case, it is translated by **depuis**:

Ils habitent ici **depuis** la guerre.   *They have been living here since the war.*

Ils habitent ici **depuis** 1945. *They have been living here since 1945.*

2 *As a conjunction*, it can introduce a cause-consequence relation (i.e. *given the fact that . . .*). It is translated by **puisque**:

Puisque vous refusez, j'irai ailleurs. *Since you refuse, I shall go elsewhere.*

Note: Since, as a preposition expressing duration, should only be used with tenses also emphasising duration (e.g. Present, Imperfect), and *not* with tenses stressing the mere occurrence of an event (e.g. Perfect or Past Historic).

You should say:	Il **est** ici **depuis** trois mois.
	He has been here for three months.
or:	Il **était** ici **depuis** trois mois.
	He had been here for three months
and not:	* Il **a été** ici **depuis** trois mois.
or:	* Il **fut** ici **depuis** trois mois

Some

It is translated by **quelque**, but it can have three distinct meanings as indicated below.

1 *some . . . or other* + singular:

Quelque voisin l'aura averti. *One or other of his neighbours must have warned him.* (lit:. . *will have warned him*)

2 *a few/some* + plural:

Nous passerons **quelques** jours chez vous. *We shall spend a few days at your house.*

3 *approximately* (adverb = invariable):

Il a gagné **quelque** vingt courses. *He has won some (i.e. approximately) twenty races.*

There is/there are

Both expressions are translated by a single French form: **il y a**. Care must be taken *not to change anything to* the expression, *except* the tense of the verb **avoir** (as required):

Il y avait une vieille dame dans cette maison. *There used to be an old lady in this house.*

Il y aura beaucoup d'invités ce soir. *There will be many guests this evening.*

Soudain **il y eut** une terrible explosion. *Suddenly there was a terrible explosion.*

Notes:
(*a*) For the opening sentence of a fairy tale the expression **il était une fois** is used instead of **il y avait une fois**.
(*b*) **Il y a** is sometimes replaced by such expressions as **il existe** (*there exist(s)*), **il se trouve** (*there is/are to be found*):
Il existe des gens qui n'ont pas de scrupules.   *There exist (i.e. are) people who have no scruples.*

This/these — that/those

Those words can have two grammatical roles, either demonstrative adjectives (followed by a noun) or demonstrative pronouns (followed by a verb):
1 *As demonstrative adjectives*, they agree in gender and number with the noun which follows; they are: **ce** (masc. sing.), **cette** (fem. sing.), **ces** (masc./fem. plur.); in addition there exists the form **cet** (masc. sing.), used when the next word begins with a vowel or a mute 'h'. For example:
Regardez **cet** énorme embouteillage.   *Look at this (that) enormous traffic jam.*
Note: The above-mentioned words can have the meaning of *this* or *that*. If a distinction is needed, the words **-ci** (here) or **-là** (*there*) can be added to the noun concerned:
Je n'aime pas **ce** livre-**ci**.   *I do not like this book.*
Il adore **cette** plage-**là**.   *He loves that beach.*
2 *As demonstrative pronouns*, with the exception of **c', ça, ceci, cela** (which have a neutral value but are still considered to be masculine singular), they vary according to the gender and number of the noun they represent. They are:
celui + **-ci**/**-là** (masc. sing.); **celle** + **-ci**/**-là** (fem. sing.)
ceux + **-ci**/**-là** (masc. plur.); **celles** + **-ci**/**-là** (fem. plur.)
For example:
Vous qui aimez les chats, regardez **celui-ci**.   *You who love cats, look at this one.*

Towards

The word has two meanings and requires two different translations as indicated below.
1 If *towards* indicates a *movement* (in space or time) *towards a goal*, it will be translated by **vers**:
Ils vont **vers** la ville.   *They are going towards the town.*
Je vous appellerai **vers** six heures.   *I shall call you towards (i.e. around) six o'clock.*

2   If *towards* indicates *feelings* it will be translated by **envers**:

   Quels sont tes sentiments **envers** lui?   *What are your feelings towards him?*

Note: In this latter sense, its is the equivalent of the expression **vis à vis de**:

   Quels sont tes sentiments **vis à vis de** lui?   *What are your feelings towards him*?

Until

Two constructions are possible depending whether:

1   *Until* is followed by a noun *or* by **hier** (*yesterday*), **aujourd'hui** (*today*) or **demain** (*tomorrow*). In this case, its French equivalent is **jusqu'à**:

   Restez **jusqu'à** demain.   *Stay until tomorrow.*

2   *Until* introduces a subordinate clause (subject, verb, etc.). In this case it *must* be translated by **jusqu'à ce que** and the verb of the subordinate *must* be in the Subjunctive:

   Tenez bon **jusqu'à ce que** nous arrivions.   *Hold on tight until we arrive.*   s.c.

Verbs without prepositions

The following verbs do not require a preposition when followed by another verb (which *must be* in the infinitive): **compter** (*to bank on*), **croire** (*to believe*), **désirer** (*to wish*), **devoir** (*to have to*), **espérer** (*to hope*), **faire** (*to cause/to do*), **falloir** (impersonal = *must*), **oser** (*to dare*), **penser** (*to hope*), **pouvoir** (*to be able to*), **sembler** (*to seem*), **vouloir** (*to want*). For example:

   Nous **comptons** réussir.   *We bank on succeeding.*

   Il faut faire quelque chose. (lit: *It is necessary to do something*)   *Something must be done.*

   Vous **osez** me demander de l'argent?   *You dare to ask me for money?*

Note: The reason why some English learners tend to over-use prepositions in that context is because they have difficulty in accepting that *to* when placed before a verb in English is often merely a 'signal' for the infinitive and has, in that case, no value in French (which signals its infinitives by a special ending: **er, ir** or **re**). It must therefore be considered that a preposition is attached *to the verb that precedes* rather than to the verb that follows. In the following examples the verb and preposition appear in bold type:

   Je **commence à** comprendre.   *I am beginning to understand.*

   Ils **refusent de** manger.   *They refuse to eat.*

   Elle **s'est décidée à** sortir.   *She has made up her mind to go out.*

NB   Any good dictionary will give the list of acceptable prepositions (if any) which may be used with a given verb.

When

This word is generally translated by **quand** or **lorsque** and is used to introduce a clause clarifying a certain time-sequence. Several shades of meaning may be distinguished depending on the tenses used in the two clauses.

1   **Quand/lorsque** = *after* when the tense of the subordinate clause indicates that the action it describes has been fully completed *before* the start of the action expressed by the main clause.

Quand tu auras fini, tu partiras.
        s.c.   m.c.
When you have finished, you will go.
Lorsqu'il eut fini, il partit.
        s.c.   m.c.
When he had finished, he went.

2   **Quand/lorsque** = *as soon as* when the tenses in the subordinate and the main clause are the same, thereby indicating the absence of any time-lag between the two actions:

Quand je crie, tu lâches la corde.
     s.c.   m.c.
When (i.e. as soon as) I shout, you let go of the rope.
Lorsque je l'ai appelé il s'est enfui.
        s.c.   m.c.
When (i.e. as soon as) I called him, he ran away.

Notes:
(*a*)   If a tense expressing duration (Imperfect, Present) is used in both clauses **quand** indicates a repetition and can be translated by *whenever*:

Quand il me voyait, il tournait la tête.
        s.c.   m.c.
Whenever he saw me, he looked away.
Lorsque je vais au marché, j'achète des fleurs
           s.c.   m.c.
When I go to the market I (always) buy flowers

(*b*)   If the sense of *whenever* needs to be emphasised, the expression **chaque fois que** (*every time*) may be used instead of **quand** or **lorsque**:

Chaque fois qu'il me voyait, il souriait

 s.c.   m.c.

Every time he saw me he smiled.

It is not possible, as it is in English, to use a Present or Perfect Indicative in the subordinate clause, if the verb of the main clause is in the Future Indicative; you *must* say or write:

Quand je le verrai, je lui parlerai

 s.c.   m.c.

When I see him I shall talk to him.

and not* :   Quand je le vois, je lui parlerai.

Remember: Expressions such as *the day when*, *the time when*, etc. are translated into French as **le jour où**, **le moment où** (and not ***le jour/le moment quand**):

Compare: *I long for **the day when** we'll all be free.*

and: J'attends impatiemment **le jour où** nous serons tous libres.

If the sense of *when* is *as soon as*, it may be translated by **aussitôt que** or **dès que** with the tense-sequences outlined above.

Year

There are two ways of translating the word *year*:

1   If it refers to a precise or 'objective' number of years it will be translated by **an(s)**:

Nous avons passé **deux ans** au Pérou.   *We spent two years in Peru.*

2   If it refers to an imprecise number of years, or if there is an overtone of nostalgia, fondness, hate, etc. it will be translated by **année(s)**:

Il a habité quelques **années** en Italie. (and not * quelques ans . . .)   *He has lived a few years in Italy.*

Nous avons passé deux **années** au Maroc.   *We spent two* ('long' or 'happy') *years in Morocco.*

In this latter example (where one would expect **an**) **année** gives the idea of a subjective overtone (happiness, boredom, etc.).

Note:

(*a*)   *last year* and *next year* may be translated respectively by:

l'an dernier *or* **l'année dernière**

l'an prochain *or* **l'année prochaine**

without any particular overtone.

(*b*)   *this year*, however, must *always* be translated by **cette année** (* cet an is *not* acceptable).

Appendix 1
The Sounds of French

It may seem strange that, in a grammar book, there should be a section on pronunciation. Yet there are very good reasons why this should be so and that is why most modern grammars now include a chapter on phonetics. The first reason is that, when learning to speak French, many people find that a good potential performance is marred by bad pronunciation. The second is that, in modern reference books like dictionaries, useful information is available to those who are familiar with the International Phonetic Alphabet (IPA) symbols: each word is transcribed using those symbols, which are the ones introduced in this chapter. Thirdly, and most importantly, many so-called grammatical rules are, in fact, dictated by phonetic considerations. This point will be clearly and abundantly illustrated in this section. You should not try to take in every detail of it at once, but return to it as often as you wish or need to.

Although the letters used to write French words are the same as for English, the sounds that the French associate with these letters are sometimes quite different. You must therefore try not to carry the rules of English pronunciation into French.

The following example may make things clearer: take the English word *party* and the French one **parti** both meaning a political group. They look reasonably alike and you may well be tempted to pronounce the French word in the same way as the English one. By doing so you would break a whole series of 'rules' governing the French language. These are as follows:

Rule 1

In French, the sounds **p**, **t** and **k** are *not* followed by an escape of breath before the next sound. A simple trick will enable you to become aware of the fact. Take a piece of paper approximately 15 cm by 10 cm. Hold it down in front of your face so that the bottom part of the paper rests lightly on your lips. When you pronounce the *p* of the English word *party* the paper should move away from your lips. Learn to pronounce the French word in such a way that the paper hardly moves at all.

Rule 2

There are 2 **a** sounds in French. The one you need here is not the one you would expect, but an **a** closer to the one found in standard English *cat* and *bat* or the Northern pronunciation of such words as *bath* or *path*.

Rule 3

Whereas in most English accents the *r* is present in spelling but not normally sounded, the **r** is always pronounced in standard French. This is a very difficult sound for an English person to master, but another simple trick may help you: insert into your mouth the end of a pencil (preferably not the sharp one!) just far enough — one inch or so — to hold the tip of your tongue down. With your tongue tip in that position, try to make a friction noise by lifting the back of your tongue as if you were gargling. You should succeed in producing a French **r** or something fairly close to it.

Rule 4

The **i** sound in French is similar in quality to the *ee* sound in *beef* but shorter; in other words quite different from the sound of the *y* in *party*.

Rule 5

In English the emphasis is on the first section of the word: PArty, whereas in French it is on the last: parTI.

Do not be discouraged! The aim of the above example is to show you that French and English have each got their own identity. Be critical in your listening and then try to reproduce the sounds faithfully.

As we have seen, letters are sometimes misleading. So, in order to simplify matters, it is often very useful to have a special way of writing up words, a code which will be immediately recognisable and pronounceable by anyone who is familiar with it. This code is used in all good dictionaries and is now more or less standardised; it is called the International Phonetic Alphabet (IPA). We shall list the elements of it in two broad categories, *consonants* and *vowels*. Those units of sound, arranged in certain ways, make up the words we use. Whenever a phonetic transcription is given, it will appear in square brackets: [ ].

Important remarks

Unless otherwise stated, 'English pronunciation' should be taken as meaning 'standard English pronunciation' and 'French pronunciation' as meaning 'Educated Parisian French'.

252   *The Sounds of French*

Consonants

see note

[p]	la **p**orte	*door*	
[t]	la **t**our	*tower see Rule* 1 above	
[k]	la **c**our	*courtyard*	
[b]	le **b**ain	*bath*	
[d]	le **d**oute	*doubt*	
[g]	le **g**arde	*guard*	
[m]	la **m**ère	*mother*	
[n]	**n**ous	*we*	
[ɲ]	l'a**gn**eau	*lamb*	1
[l]	le **l**ivre	*book*	2
[f]	le **f**our	*oven*	
[s]	le **s**ac	*bag*	
[ʃ]	le **ch**ou	*cabbage*	3
[v]	le **v**erre	*glass*	
[z]	le **z**èbre	*zebra*	
[ʒ]	le **j**our	*day*	4
[R]	le **r**oi	*king* (see Rule 3 above)	5
[w]	**ou**i	*yes*	
[ɥ]	t**u**er	*to kill*	6
[j]	le **y**oga	*yoga*	

Notes: The following notes correspond to the numbers appearing in the right-hand column above.

1 It is very rare to pronounce the two letters **gn** as [g+n] (as in *to ignore*). Normally, **gn** sounds like the first section of *new* and is transcribed [ɲ].

2 [l] In English this *l* has two values (which you may not even be aware of), according to its position. If you say the word *lull* and think about how you pronounce it, you will notice that the qualities of the first *l* and of the last two (pronounced as one) are quite different. If you tried to reverse their position the word *lull* would sound 'foreign'. In French, whatever its position in the word, the **l** sounds like the first sound in *lull*, *late*, *line*, etc. There is no 'dark' quality to it.

3 [ʃ] In French, except in rare cases, the combination **c**+**h** is pronounced [ʃ]. This sound is similar to that of the first element of the words *sh*ape, *sh*eep and *sh*oe: la **ch**asse (*hunting*), le **ch**at (*cat*), le **ch**ien (*dog*).

4 [ʒ] This sound does occur in English in lei*s*ure, plea*s*ure and in borrowed words like rou*g*e and gara*g*e. Essentially, it is very much like the sound of *j* in *Jack*, but without the [d] before it:

English	French
[dʒ]	[ʒ]
Jack	**Jacques**
[dʒak]	[ʒak]

5 [R] We have already mentioned the difference in quality of the **r** in French. You may find that, in addition to the standard [R] value, you will come across others. Do not be put off, stick to the standard one!

6 The [w] sound is the same as the one in *w*et and *w*ith. The [J] sound is the same as the one in *y*ear and *y*olk. The [ɥ] has no equivalent in English, but if while saying [i] you push your lips forward and round them, you may produce a sound close to it.

Vowels

[i]	le **lit**	*bed*	7
[y]	la **rue**	*street*	8
[e]	le pr**é**	*meadow*	9
[ø]	p**eu**	*little*	10
[ɛ]	la m**er**	*sea*	11
[ɛ̃]	la m**ain**	*hand*	12
[œ]	la p**eu**r	*fear*	13
[œ̃]	br**un**	*brown*	14
[a]	la p**a**tte	*paw*	15
[ɑ]	la p**â**te	*paste*	16
[ɑ̃]	gr**and**	*tall*	17
[ɔ]	le c**or**ps	*body*	18
[ɔ̃]	le coch**on**	*pig*	19
[o]	l'**eau**	*water*	20
[u]	la r**ou**e	*wheel*	21
[ə]	la premi**è**re	*the first*	22

Notes

7 [i] As mentioned in Rule 4 above, this [i] is close in value to the *ee* in *beef* or *meet*, but it is *shorter*.

8 [y] The tongue position is the same as for [i] but the lips are pushed outwards and rounded. This feature of lip-rounding plays a very important part in French. The purpose of it is to increase the volume of air contained in the mouth. This, as a result, changes the sound quite dramatically. It is important to master the lip-rounding technique because there are many pairs of words which are distinguished solely by that feature:

Compare:	la **v**ie [la vi] *life* (= spread)
and:	la **v**ue [la vy] *sight* (= rounded)
or:	la **b**iche [la biʃ(ə)] *doe* (= spread)
and:	la **b**ûche [la byʃ(ə)] *log* (= rounded)

It is very important that the *tongue position* should *not* be changed (see note 21 below).

9 [e] This sound is similar to that of the last section in words like health*y*, nutt*y*, part*y*, etc., as pronounced in standard English.

le nez [lə ne] *nose*

le bébé [lə bebe] *baby*

10 [ø] The tongue position is the same as for [e] but the lips are rounded—here again take great care to distinguish from [e]

Compare: le nez [lə nɛ] *nose*

and: le noeud [lə nø] *knot*

or: le dé [lə de] *die/thimble*

and: le deux [lə dø] *Second day of the month*

11 [ɛ] This sound is identical to the vowel sound in n*e*t, b*e*t, p*e*t:

le fait [lə fɛ] *fact*

le lait [lə lɛ] *milk*

12 [ɛ̃] The tongue position is the same as for 11, but this time some air escapes through the nose as well as through the mouth — this is known as nasalisation and is phonetically represented by [̃] placed above the sound concerned. Again, it is very important for you to master this nuance because, as in the case of lip-rounding, many word-pairs are distinguished by nasalisation alone.

Compare: le lait [lə lɛ] *milk*

and: le lin [lə lɛ̃] *linen*

or: fait [fɛ] *done*

and: fin [fɛ̃] *fine/thin*

13 [œ] This sound is similar to the vowel sound in f*i*r (*tree*) or in p*u*rr:

le coeur [lə kœR] *heart*

la soeur [la sœR] *sister*

14 [œ̃] The tongue and lip positions are similar to those used for 13 but, here again, there is an escape of air through the nose as well as through the mouth:

brun [bRœ̃] *dark-haired*/brown

un [œ̃] *a/one*

15 [a] As mentioned at the beginning of this chapter (Rule 3), this sound is roughly similar to that of the vowel in the Standard English words c*a*t, m*a*t, b*a*t, or in the Northern pronunciation b*a*th. Keep it distinct from the sound of 11: [ɛ]

la dame [la dam(ə)] *lady*

la flamme [la flam(ə)] *flame*

16 [ɑ] This sound is similar to the vowel sound in the English words c*a*r, d*a*rk and p*a*rk:

la pâte [la pɑt] *paste/dough*

le mât [lə mɑ] *mast*

17 [ɑ̃] The lip and tongue positions are similar to those required for 16 but, in addition, air escapes through the nose as in 12 and 14:

en [ɑ̃] *in*

lent [lɑ̃] *slow*

18 [ɔ] Very close to the vowel sound in the English words d*o*t, n*o*t and, sh*o*t:

la b**o**tte [la bɔt(ə)] *boot*

la n**o**te [la nɔt(ə)] *note/bill*

19 [ɔ̃] Similar tongue position to that in [ɔ]; lips slightly more closed and, here again, some air escaping through the nose as for 12, 14 and 17:

b**on** [bɔ̃] *good*

le p**on**t [lə pɔ̃] *bridge*

20 [o] This sound is 'half way' between [ɔ] and [u]–see 21:

l'**eau** [lo] *water*

b**eau** [bo] *beautiful*

21 [u] This sound is not very different from the vowel sound in English words b*oo*m, c*oo*l, l*oo*p, but the lips are pushed out and rounded:

le l**ou**p [lə lu] *wolf*

le c**ou** [lə ku] *neck*

22 [ə] This is a vowel with 'reduced value'. It never apppears in a stressed syllable (see below). The sound is not very different from that of vowel 13 [œ], and of the vowel sound in English *fi*rm, t*u*rn but the jaws are closer together. This sound is sometimes omitted from the pronunciation of certain words and some dictionaries will give it in brackets to indicate that fact:

la p**o**rte [la pɔRt(ə)] *door*

la b**ou**che [la buʃ(ə)] *mouth*

Warning: All French vowel sounds are *tense*. In other words, when you are saying them, your articulators — jaws, lips and tongue — should not change position at all.

Be aware of the sound difference between:

English	and	**French**
(a) note		**(une) note**
[nout]		[nɔt (ə)]

The vowels and consonants which we have seen in the first section of this chapter combine to form syllables, words, phrases and sentences, which make up the speech-chain. We shall now look at the most basic of those units: the syllable.

The syllable

Every word is made up of sections called syllables. Although there is a great deal of disagreement among specialists as to the definition of the syllable, it is generally agreed that it is a group of sounds composed of a central element-the vowel-and either no consonant at all or a limited number of consonants on each side of that vowel. The vowel is

essential but the consonant(s) may be absent in some syllables:
il a (*he has*) has 2 syllables [**il**/**a**] = VC/V

1 2

NB: Please be sure to distinguish between *letters* (written alphabet) and *sounds* (phonetic alphabet). The following examples in French will make the difference clear:

1   **exact** (*exact*) has 5 letters, 4 sounds [εgza] and 2 syllables[εg/za]

1 2

2   **comptons** (*let's count*) has 8 letters, 4 sounds [kɔ̃tɔ̃] and 2 syllables [kɔ̃/tɔ̃].   1234

1   2

3   **joli** (*pretty*) has 4 letters, 4 sounds [ʒɔli] and 2 syllables [ʒɔ/li].

1234   1 2

The vowel-vowel clash

The French language has a natural tendency to regularity and the pattern of syllables CV/CV/CV, etc. is preferred not only within one word but *between words* and an arrangement like CV/VC/etc. is avoided whenever possible. This point is very important because it explains many so called 'grammatical oddities' which are sometimes puzzling to the learner. For instance:

1   It explains why the difinite article **le** or **la** (*the*) loses its **e** or **a** if the next word begins with a vowel or a mute'h' (see 7 below for distinction between mute and aspirated 'h'). For example *le ami (*friend*) is *not* acceptable because the pattern is CV/V CV. So it becomes: l'ami. *la/auto (*car*) is, for the same reason, not acceptable either (CV/V CV), so it becomes:l'auto.

2   It also explains why some words add on a letter in certain cases:

*ce enfant (*this child*) ⟶ cet enfant

CV V CV   CVC VCV

3   It also explains why some masculine adjectives like **beau** (*beautiful*) and **nouveau** (*new*) change before nouns starting with a vowel or mute 'h' (see 7 below)

*le nouveau/ami (*the new friend*) ⟶ le nouvel/ami

   CV/VCV   CVC/VCV

*le beau/hôtel (*the beautiful hotel*) ⟶ le bel/hôtel

   CV / VC   CVC/ VC

4   It clarifies the reason why, when the 3 feminine possessives **ma, ta,**

sa (*my*, *your*, *his/her*) are followed by a word beginning with a vowel
or a mute 'h' they are replaced by the 3 corresponding masculines:
mon, **ton** and **son**:

    *ma/auto (*my car*) ⟶ mon/auto
    CV/V CV   CVC/V CV

    *ta/amie (*your friend*) ⟶ ton/amie
    CV/VCV   CVC/VCV

5   It explains why sometimes an 'intrusive' sound is put in between 2
words:

    *a-il? (*has he?*) ⟶ a-t-il?
    V/VC   V/C/VC

    *va-elle? (*does she go*) ⟶ va-t-elle . . ?
    CV/VCV   CV/C/VCN

6   It also sheds some light on the phenomenon of 'liaison' (= linking
2 words with a sound which, in normal circumstances, is not
pronounced; this phenomenon is more frequent in careful speech).
Compare: Il est content. *He is pleased.* [il ɛ kɔ̃tɑ̃]

and: Est-il content? *Is he pleased?* [ɛ t il kɔ̃tɑ̃]Here the **t** of **est**
            is sounded.

or: Vous travaillez. *You work.* [vu tRavaje]

and: Vous allez. *You go.* [vuz ale] Here the **s** of **vous** is
            sounded as [z].

7   It helps solve the mystery of the mute and aspirated 'h'. There are,
in French, a number of words beginning with 'h'. Before some of
these words, the article **le** or **la** (*the*), or other small words, lose their,
final vowel. (This only happens to 'lesser' words. You do not cut
vowels off nouns or verbs or adjectives!) But this is not the case with
the words in the list given below. These words start with an aspirated
'h'.

[In fact there is, in modern French, no sign of that 'h' in
pronunciation (but in old French, it used to be sounded, as it is in
English).Nevertheless, it is as if a 'ghost consonant' were still present,
thus preventing the vowel-vowel clash. So we say:

    l'hôtel (*hotel*) or cet horrible enfant (*this horrid child*) but:
    le hasard (*chance*) or **ce** héros (*this hero*)

    The following is a list of the words beginning with an aspirated 'h'
which you are most likely to encounter. There are others, but they are
less frequently used. In any case, a good dictionary will indicate
which words begin with an aspirated 'h' *either* by preceding the word

with an asterisk (*), *or* by beginning the phonetic transcription with an apostrophe (').

la hache *axe*	le héros *hero*
la haie *hedge*	le hêtre *beech*
le hall *hall*	le hibou *owl*
la halle *market hall*	la hiérarchie *hierarchy*
la halte *pause*	la Hollande *Holland*
le hameau *hamlet*	le homard *lobster*
la hanche *hip*	la Hongrie *Hungary*
le handicap *handicap*	la honte *shame*
le hangar *hangar*	le hoquet *hiccup*
le hareng *herring*	la horde *horde*
le haricot *bean*	la houille *coal*
le hasard *chance*	le houx *holly*
la hâte *haste*	le huit *eight*
la hausse *increase*	le hurlement *scream*
le haut *top/summit*	la hutte *hut*
le havre *haven*	

Stress (accentuation)

A section on phonetics would not be complete without a mention of stress (or accentuation). Stress is sometimes explained as the relatively greater force with which we pronounce some syllables. In English, there is stress on certain parts of important words (stressed syllables are printed in bold):

Paul went to the *door* and (he) *o*pened it. Total = 4 stresses

In French, the system is totally different. For the purpose of stressing, the speech-chain is divided into sense-groups, i.e. phrases having a meaning in themselves, and it is the last syllable of the sense-group *only* which will be stressed. (If the last syllable ends with an [ə] it does not count!)

Words on their own are treated as sense-groups. Compare:

1	*Paul!*	*Paul!*	
	Sense group		1 stress
2	Paul est allé à la **por**te.	*Paul went to the door.*	
	Sense group		1 stress
3	Paul est allé à la **por**te	et (il)l'a ouverte	
	Sense group	Sense group	2 stresses
	Paul went to the door	*and (he) opened it.*	

The temptation is great, particularly when words look the same in the 2 languages, to use the English system of stress and say:

*Il continue la démonstration. *He carries on with the demonstration.*

instead of:

Il continue la démonstration.

⟵——————————————————⟶

sense group

or

*Il a cessé ces activités. *He gave up these activities.*

instead of:

Il a cessé ces activités.

⟵——————————⟶

sense group

The above is the general rule. Sometimes, for the sake of emphasis, extra stresses are put in (particularly in radio and television reports).

Key points

1 French sounds are sometimes quite different from English ones.
2 There are 2 types of sounds: vowels [i, e, ɛ etc.] and consonants [p, t, m, etc.]
3 In the 'speech chain', the French avoid, as much as possible, a clash between two vowels by a variety of tricks.
4 French is not stressed in the same way as English. Only the last word of the sense-group carries the stress, so the rhythm of the two languages is quite different.

Appendix II
Accents and Other Signs;
Punctuation Marks

When writing French, it is necessary to make use of certain signs or marks. Those signs are important and must be used properly. They are introduced and explained below.

Accents

Accents are marks used in writing over certain letters. In French they are only found on **a**, **e**, **i**, **o** and **u**.
Note: These accents have a definite role to play and *cannot* be used at random.

There are 3 types of accents:

1 *The acute accent:´*. It can only be found on an **e**, and it changes the sound of that letter from [ə] to [e]. (See vowel list in Appendix I.)
Compare: Port**e**! [pɔRt(ə)] *Carry!*
and: port**é** [pɔRte] *carried*
or: Cherch**e**! [ʃɛRʃ(ə)] *Look (for)!*
and: cherch**é** [ʃɛRʃe] *looked (for)*

2 *The grave accent*: (`). It is found on **e**, and, much more rarely, on **a** and **u**.
(*a*) When over the **e**, it changes the sound of that letter to [ɛ]. (See vowel list in Appendix I.)
Compare: prot**é**g**é** [pRɔteʒe] *protected*
and: Prot**è**ge! [pRɔtɛʒ(ə)] *Protect!*
or: achet**é** [aʃ(ə)te] *bought*
and: Ach**è**te! [aʃɛt(ə)] *Buy!*
(*b*) When over an **a** or **u**, it does not change the sound of the letter, but it helps to distinguish between words which would otherwise look alike:
La voiture est **là**. *The car is there.*

Il **a** rendez-vous **à** cinq heures.   *He has an appointment at five o'clock.*

Jean **ou** Paul vont **où** ils veulent.   *John or Paul go where they like.*

3   *The circumflex accent:* (ˆ). It can be found on all five vowels: **a, e, i, o,** and **u**.
(*b*)   When over the **e** it changes the sound of that letter to [ε]. (See vowel list of Appendix I.)
Bête [bɛt(ə)]   *silly*
Être [ɛtR(ə)]   *to be*
(*b*)   On the other four vowels, it used to have the effect of lengthening the sound, but in modern French this is generally no longer the case. This accent also acts as an indicator that, in old French, the vowel used to be followed by an **s** which has now disappeared. (Often, however, this **s** is still present in the corresponding English words.) For example:
Un abîme   *an abysm*
La bête   *beast*
La côte   *coast*
La hâte   *haste*
Un hôte   *a host/guest*
Le mât   *mast*
La pâte   *paste/dough*

So, the letter most affected by accents is **e**; but there are certain circumstances where the sound of **e** changes to [e] or [ε] without the help of an accent. This is the case before geminated (i.e. double) consonants: **cc, dd, ff, ll, nn, ss, tt**, etc. For example:
Belle [bɛl(ə)]   *beautiful* (fem.)
Effacer [efase]   *to rub out*
Jette! [ʒɛt(ə)]   *throw!*
This is also the case when **e** is followed by two different consonants, provided the second one is *not* an **r** or an **l**:
Restons [Rɛstɔ̃]   *let's stay*
Le lecteur [lə lɛktœR]   *reader*
but: Réfléchir [RefleʃiR]   *to reflect*
La pègre [la pɛgR(ə)]   *the underworld*
Exception: If **e** is followed by the group of consonants **rl**, it does not take an accent:
La perle [la pɛRlə]   *pearl*
Le merle [lə mɛRlə]   *blackbird*

Apostrophe, cedilla, diaeresis and hyphen

1   *The apostrophe* (') is used to indicate that a letter, usually **e, a** or **i**, has been removed to avoid the vowel-vowel clash (see Appendix I). This is the written representation of the phenomenon called *elision*:

*Le arbre	⟶ l'arbre	*tree*
*La amie	⟶ l'amie	*girlfriend*
*Ce est	⟶ c'est	*this/that is*
*Quelque un	⟶ quelqu'un	*someone*

2   *The cedilla* (ˌ). It is placed under a **c** before **a, o** or **u**, to indicate that the **c** is to be pronounced [s]; if the cedilla were not there, the sound of **c** would be [k].

Compare: Recevoir [RəsəvwaR]   *to receive*
                Reçu [Rəsy]   *received*
                Reculer [R ə kyle]   *to go backwards*
                Celui-ci [səlɥisi]   *this one*
                Ça [sa]   *that thing*

Remember:
c = [s] before
     e or **i**
c = [k] before
     a, o, u

3   *The diaeresis* (¨). This mark is used in writing to indicate to the reader that two consecutive vowels *must* be pronounced separately, because they usually belong to two different syllables.

Compare: Oui [wi]   *yes*
and: Ouï [u/i]   *heard*

              1 2

or: (La) haie [ɛ]   *hedge*
and: Haïe [a/i]   *hated.* (fem.)

              1 2

4   *The hyphen* (-). Unlike the previous signs, it does not alter the sound of a word. It is simply used to link together words which are meant to form a whole:

     Celui-ci   *this one* (masc.)
     Quatre-vingt-dix   *ninety*
     Le porte-parole   *spokesman*

Punctuation

Broadly speaking, punctuation is the written representation of oral pauses and a marker for changes in voice pitch for the benefit of the reader:

1   The *full stop* indicates to the reader that he/she has come to the end of a sentence and that the voice must go down.

2   The *comma* signals the end of a sense-group but the voice must not go down.

3   The *semi-colon* indicates that a self-contained part of a sentence has ended, but that some more related information is to follow. The pitch should go down as for a full stop.

4   The *colon* indicates that direct speech is about to be reported or an explanation given. The voice should not go down, but the pitch at the beginning of the utterance which follows should be higher or lower than what preceded.

5   *Dots* (. . .) indicate that some things have remained unsaid. The voice should not go down.

6   The *exclamation mark* signals the end of a forceful statement. There should be an increase in volume and a change of pitch.

7   The *question mark* indicates a question has been asked. Generally, the voice will *either* go down if the question starts with words like **qui** (*who*), **où** (*where*), **quand** (*when*), **pourquoi** (*why*), etc. *or* go up with the other types of questions.

8   *Speech marks* (" ") are used to signal the beginning and end of sections of speech as uttered by the speaker (direct speech). The pitch of the voice at the start of the quotation should be markedly different (higher or lower) from that of the preceding section.

Key points

1   Accents have specific roles in French and they cannot be used indiscriminately. They are particularly important on **e**, because they change the sound of that letter.

2   The cedilla changes the sound of **c** from [k] to [s] before **a**, **o** and **u**.

3   The diaeresis warns that two consecutive vowels usually belong to two distinct syllables and should be pronounced separately.

4   Punctuation tells the reader that the pitch of the voice should go up, stay the same or go down, depending on the sign used, and that pauses should be inserted as appropriate.

French–English Vocabulary

The vocabulary list includes most of the words which have been used in the examples. It does not, however, include words which appear in lists or charts since in such cases the translation of each word has already been given. The meanings are those applicable in the context of the examples. The feminine of adjectives, when irregular, appears alongside the masculine.

Abbreviations

f = feminine	s = Singular
m = masculine	sthg = something
pl = plural	sbdy = somebody

à *at, to*
abandonner *to abandon*
d'abord *at first*
absence (f) *absence*
acceptable *acceptable*
accepter *to accept*
accident (m) *accident*
accord (m) *agreement*;
  d'—*OK*
accueillant *welcoming*
accuser *to accuse*
acheter *to buy, purchase*
achever *to finish*
acteur (m) *actor*
admirer *to admire*
adorer *to adore*
advenir *to occur*
affiche (f) *poster*
afin de/que *in order to*
Afrique (f) *Africa*
agent (m) *policeman*
agir *to act*
agréable *pleasant*
ah! *oh!*
aider *to help*
aigu, -ë *sharp, acute*
ailleurs *elsewhere*
aimé *loved*

aimer *to love*
ainsi *thus*
air (m) *air*
ajouter *to add*
aller *to go*
allô *hallo*
allumette (f) *match*
allusion (f) *allusion; faire — à*
  to allude to
alors *then;* - que *whilst*
Alpes (f. pl.) *Alps*
amasser *to gather*
ambitieux, euse *ambitious*
américain *American*
ami (m) *friend*
amusant *amusing*
an (m) *year*
ancien,-ne *former, old*
anglais *English*
Angleterre (f) *England*
animal (m) *animal*
année (f) *year*
annoncer *to announce*
août (m) *August*
apercevoir *to catch sight of*
s'apercevoir de/que *to notice*
  that
apéritif (m) *aperitif*

apparemment *apparently*
appeler *to call*
s'appeler *to be called*
applaudir *to clap, applaud*
apporter *to bring*
apprécier *to appreciate*
apprendre *to learn*
apprenti (m) *apprentice*
approcher *to bring near*
s'approcher *to approach*
après *after*
arbre (m) *tree*
argent(m) *silver, money*
arme (f) *weapon*
arrêt (m) *stop*; sans— *non-stop*
arrêter *to stop (sthg or sbdy)*
s'arrêter *to stop, to come to a standstill*
arrhes (f. pl) *deposit*
arriver *to arrive*
aspirateur (m) *vacuum cleaner*
(s')assembler *to gather, assemble*
(s')asseoir *to sit*
assez *enough*
assis *seated*
assurance (f) *assurance, insurance*
atteindre *to reach*
attendre *to wait*
attente (f) *wait*
attention (f) *attention*
attitude (f) *attitude*
au, à la *at the, to the*
aucun *none, no-one*
d'aucuns (m.pl) *some people*
au delà de *beyond*
aujourd'hui *today*
aussi *also, therefore*
autant *as much*
auto (f) *car*
automne (m) *autumn*
autre *other*
autrefois *in the past*
autrui (m. sing.) *other people*
aux *at the, to the*
avancer *to advance*
avant *before*
avec *with*

avenir (m) *future*
avertir *to warn*
avion (m) *plane*
avoir *to have*

bagages (m. pl) *luggage*
bague (f) *ring*
(se) baisser *to lower (oneself)*
bal (m) *dance, ball*
banque (f) *bank*
barbu *bearded*
bas, basse *low*
bateau (m) *boat*
bâtiment (m) *building*
battre *to beat*
se battre *to fight*
beau, belle *beautiful*
beaucoup *much, a great deal*
beaujolais (m) *Beaujolais wine*
béni *blessed*
bénin, bénigne *slight (illness)*
bénir *to bless*
besoin (m) *need;* avoir — *to need*
bête *silly, stupid*
bêtise (f) *silly mistake*
bien *well*
bien que *although*
bière (f) *beer*
bijou, -x (m) *jewel*
bizarre *peculiar, odd*
boire *to drink*
bois (m) *wood*
bon, bonne *good*
bonbon (m) *sweet*
bonhomme (m) *chap*
bonjour *Good day, hello*
boucher (m) *butcher*
boue (f) *mud*
bouger *to move*
bougie (f) *candle*
boulanger (m) *baker*
bourgogne (m) *Burgundy wine*
brave *kind, brave*
Brésil (m) *Brazil*
Bretagne (f) *Brittany*
brioche (f) *bun*

(se) brosser *to brush (oneself)*
brouillard (m) *fog*
bruit (m) *noise*
brun *brown*
bureau (m) *office, desk*

ça *that*
ça et là *here and there*
cacher *to hide*
cachet (m) *tablet*
cadeau (m) *gift*
café (m) *coffee, cafe*
calme *calm, quiet*
calmer *to calm down*
campagne (f) *countryside*
capitaine (m) *captain*
capitale (f) *capital city*
car *for*
car (m) *coach*
carte (f) *card; map;* — postale *postcard*
cassé *broken*
casser *to break*
cathédrale (f) *cathedral*
catholique (f) *catholic*
cause (f) *cause*
ce, cet, cette *this, that*
ceci *this*
céder *to give in*
cela *that*
célèbre *famous*
celui-ci, celle-ci *this one*
celui-là, celle-là *that one*
cendrier (m) *ashtray*
cent *hundred*
centaine (f) *a hundred or so*
centime (m) *centime*
cependant *meanwhile, nevertheless*
certain *certain*
certains (m. pl) *some people*
certes *indeed*
ces *these, those*
cesser *to cease, to stop*
c'est *it is*
ceux-ci, celles-ci *these*
ceux-là, celles-là *those*
chacun *each*

chaise (f) *chair*
chambre (f) *bedroom*
chance (f) *luck*
changement (m) *change*
changer *to change*
chanter *to sing*
chapeau (m) *hat*
charbon (m) *coal*
charmant *charming*
chasse (f) *chase, hunt*
chat (m) *cat*
château (m) *castle*
chauffeur (m) *driver*
chaussure (f) *shoe*
chauve *bald*
chemise (f) *shirt*
chêne (m) *oak*
chèque (m) *cheque*
cher *dear*
chercher *to look for*
cheval, chevaux (m) *horse(s)*
cheveux (m. pl) *hair*
chez *at the house of*
chien (m) *dog*
chimie (f) *chemistry*
choisir *to choose*
chose (f) *thing*
ciel (m) *sky, heaven*
cigare (m) *cigar*
ci-joint *herewith*
ciment (m) *cement*
cinéma (m) *cinema*
cinq *five*
cinquantaine (f) *about fifty*
cinquante *fifty*
clac! *slam!, bang!*
clair *clear*
classe (f) *class*
clef (f) *key*
client (m) *customer*
climat (m) *climate*
cloche (f) *bell*
cœur (m) *heart*
coffre-fort (m) *safe*
coin (m) *corner*
colère (f) *anger*
colis (m) *parcel*

collier (m) *necklace*
colline (f) *hill*
combien *how much*
commander *to order*
comme *as, like*
commencer *to begin*
comment *how*
complet *complete, full*
compréhensif, -ive *understanding*
comprendre *to understand*
compris *understood*
confiture (f) *jam*
connaître *to know*
consciencieux, -euse *conscientious*
conseil (m) *advice*
constamment *constantly*
construire *to build*
content *pleased*
continuer *to carry on*
contre *against*
corde (f) *rope*
cordial *cordial*
corrompre *to corrupt*
corrupteur, -trice *corrupting*
costume (m) *suit*
coudre *to sew*
coup (m) *blow*
(se) couper *to cut (oneself)*
courage (m) *courage*
courageux, -euse *courageous*
courir *to run*
course (f) *race*
court *short*
coûter *to cost*
craindre *to fear*
crâne (m) *skull*
cri (m) *scream, shout*
crier *to scream, to shout*
crime (m) *crime*
crise (f) *crisis*
cristal (m) *crystal*
croire *to believe*
cruel, -elle *cruel*
cuire *to cook*
curieux, -euse *curious, strange*

dame (f) *lady*

dans *in*
danser *to dance*
davantage *more*
débarquement (m) *landing*
débarquer *to land*
debout *standing*
décembre *December*
déchirant *heart-rending*
déchirer *to tear*
décider *to decide*
décision (f) *decision*
découvert *discovered, uncovered*
déçu *disappointed*
défaut (m) *fault*
déficit (m) *deficit*
dehors *outside*
déjeuner (m) *lunch*
déjeuner *to have lunch*
délinquance (f) *delinquency*
demain *tomorrow*
(se) demander *to ask (oneself)*
demi *half*
démonstration (f) *demonstration*
dent (f) *tooth*
départ (m) *departure*
dépense (f) *expenditure*
dépenser *to spend*
dépit (m) *spite;* en —
    de *in spite of*
depuis *since*
député (m) *member of parliament*
dernier, -ière *last*
derrière *behind*
des *some*
dès (que) *as soon as*
désastre (m) *disaster*
descendre *to go down*
désir (m) *desire, wish*
désirer *to desire, to wish*
destin (m) *fate*
détester *to hate*
deux *two*
devant *in front (of)*
devenir *to become*
devoir (m) *duty*
devoir *to have to*
diamant (m) *diamond*

dieu (m) *God*
difficile *difficult*
dimanche (m) *Sunday*
dîner *to dine*
(se) dire *to tell (oneself)*
directeur (m) *director*
discret *discreet*
discuter *to discuss*
disparaître *to disappear*
disparu *disappeared, missing*
se disputer to quarrel
disque (m) *record*
dix *ten*
dizaine (f) *ten or so*
docteur (m) *doctor*
donc *therefore*
donner *to give*
dont *whose, of which*
dormir *to sleep*
dossier (m) *dossier*
doué *gifted*
douleur (f) *pain*
doute (m) *doubt;* sans — *doubtless*
douter *to doubt*
doux, douce *soft*
douzaine (f) *dozen*
douze *twelve*
droit *right;* tout — *straight on*
dû, due *owed, due*
duquel, de laquelle *of which, of whom*
dur *hard*

eau (f) *water*
échapper *to escape*
écharpe (f) *scarf*
échouer *to fail*
éclatant *dazzling*
écouter *to listen*
écrire *to write*
édenté *toothless*
effectuer *to perform*
effet (m) *effect;* en — *indeed*
efficace *effective, efficient*
effort (m) *effort*
égal *equal*
égalité (f) *equality*

église (f) *church*
éléphant (m) *elephant*
élisabéthain *Elizabethan*
elle *she, her*
embouteillage (m) *traffic jam*
s'emparer de *to seize*
emploi (m) *employment*
ému *touched, moved*
en *in*
encore *again, still*
endormir *to put to sleep*
s'endormir *to fall asleep*
endroit (m) *place, spot*
enfant (m, f) *child*
s'enfuir *to flee*
énorme *enormous*
ensuite *then*
entendre *to hear*
entre *between*
entrée (f) *entrance, entry*
entrer *to enter*
entretien (m) *conversation*
envers *towards*
envoyer *to send*
épais, épaisse *thick*
épinards (m. pl) *spinach*
époque (f) *era*
épouser *to marry*
Espagne (f) *Spain*
espagnol *Spanish*
espérer *to hope*
espion (m) *spy*
essayer *to try*
et *and*
Etats-Unis (m. pl) *United States*
été (m) *summer*
été *been*
étoile (f) *star;*-filante *shooting star*
étonnant *astonishing*
étonner *to astonish*
étrange *strange*
étranger,-ère (m, f) *foreigner*
étranger (m) à l'— *abroad*
étude (f) *study*
eux, elles (m, f) *them*
s' évanouir *to faint*
événement (m) *event*

examiner *to examine*
excellent *excellent*
excepté *except*
excuser *to excuse*
exemple (m) *example;* par - *for instance*
exiger *to demand*
exister *to exist*
expérience (f) *experience*
exploiter *to exploit*
explosion (f) *explosion*
exprès *on purpose*
extra *extra*
extrêmement *extremely*

facile *easy*
facilement *easily*
faim (f) *hunger;* avoir - *to be hungry*
faire *to do, make*
falloir *to be necessary;* il faut que *it is necessary that*
famille (f) *family*
fané *wilted*
fatal *fatal*
fatigué *tired*
fatiguer *to tire*
faute (f) *mistake*
fauteuil (m) *armchair*
faux, fausse *false*
femelle (f) *female*
femme (f) *woman, wife*
fenêtre (f) *window*
ferme (f) *farm*
fermé *closed*
fermer *to close*
féroce *ferocious*
fête (f) *festival*
feu (m) *fire;* - rouge *traffic light*
fidèle *faithful*
fier, fière *proud*
figure (f) *face*
fille (f) *girl, daughter*
fillette (f) *little girl*
film (m) *film*
fils (m) *son*
fin (f) *end*

fini *finished*
finir *to finish, to end*
fixe *fixed*
flamme (f) *flame*
fleur (f) *flower*
fleurir *to bloom, to blossom*
flûte! *blast!*
fois (f) *time;* une — *once*
foncé *dark* (colour)
football (m) *football*
fort *strong, hard*
fou, folle *mad*
foule (f) *crowd*
fracture (f) *fracture*
frais, fraîche *cool, fresh*
frais (m. pl) *costs*
franc, franche *frank*
français *French*
France (f) *France*
frapper *to knock, to strike*
fraternité (f) *fraternity*
frère (m) *brother*
froid *cold;* avoir — *to be cold*
fromage (m) *cheese*
fruit (m) *fruit*
fumée (f) *smoke*
fumer *to smoke*
furieux, –ieuse *furious*

gaffe (f) *gaffe, blunder*
gagner *to earn, to win*
gant (m) *glove*
garçon (m) *boy, waiter*
garder *to keep, to guard*
gare (f) *station*
gâteux, -euse *senile*
gauche *left;* à — *on the left*
geler *to freeze*
général (m) *general*
généralement *generally*
genou (m) *knee*
gens (m. pl) *people*
gérant (m) *manager*
gifler *to slap (face)*
glisser *to slide, to slip*
gourmandise (f) *greed*
gouvernement (m) *government*

grand *tall, large, great*
grand-mère (f) *grandmother*
grand-route (f) *main road*
grand-tante (f) *great-aunt*
gris *grey*
gros, grosse *big, bulky*
guerre (f) *war*
guider *to guide*

(s')habiller *to dress (oneself)*
habiter *to dwell*
habitude (f) *habit;* d' — *usually*
haïr *to hate*
hasard (m) *chance;* par — *by chance*
haut *high*
herbe (f) *grass*
heure (f) *hour;* à l' — *on time*
heureux, -euse *happy*
hier *yesterday;* — soir *last night*
hiver (m) *winter*
Hollande (f) *Holland*
homme (m) *man*
honnête *honest*
honnêteté (f) *honesty*
honteux, -euse *ashamed*
hôtel (m) *hotel*
hôtesse (f) *hostess*
huit *eight*
hypersensible *hypersensitive*

ici *here*
idéal *ideal*
idée (f) *idea*
idiot *silly, stupid*
il *he*
ils *they*
imbécile (m, f) *fool, idiot*
impatient *impatient*
impatiemment *impatiently*
important *important*
importer *to be important, to import*
impressionnant *impressive*
incident (m) *incident*
incontestablement *unquestionably*
individualiste *individualistic*
information (f) *information*
ingénieur (m) *engineer*

inquiet, -iète *anxious*
inquiéter *to worry*
insulter *to insult*
insupportable *unbearable*
intéressant *interesting*
intervention (f) *intervention*
invité *invited*
invité (m) *guest*
inviter *to invite*
irritant *irritating*
isolé *isolated*

jamais *never*
jambe (f) *leg*
janvier *January*
Japon (m) *Japan*
jardin *garden*
jardinier (m) *gardener*
je *I*
jeter *to throw*
jeune *young*
joli *pretty*
jour (m) *day*
journal (m) *newspaper*
journaliste (m, f) *journalist*
juillet *July*
juin *June*
jusqu'à *until*

kaki *khaki*
kilomètre (m) *kilometre*

la (f) *the*
là *there;* — bas *over there*
lâcher *to release, to let go*
laisser *to leave, to let*
langue (f) *language, tongue*
(se) laver *to wash (oneself)*
le (m) *the*
lecture (f) *reading*
légume (m) *vegetable*
lentement *slowly*
le plus *the most*
lequel, laquelle (m, f s) *who, whom which*
les (m, f pl) *the*

lesquels, lesquelles (m, f pl) *who, whom, which*
les uns les autres *each other*
lettre (f) *letter*
leur (f) *their, to them*
lever *to raise*
se lever *to arise*
libérer *to free*
liberté (f) *freedom*
libre *free*
lire *to read*
lit (m) *bed*
livre (m) *book*
livre (f) *pound*
logique *logical*
Londres *London*
long, longue *long*
longtemps *a long time*
lorsque *when*
loup (m) *wolf*
loyer (m) *rent*
lu *read*
lui *(to) him, (to) her*
lundi (m) *Monday*
lutter *to fight*
lycée (m) *high school*

ma *my*
machine (f) *machine*
madame (f) *Madam, Mrs*
magasin (m) *shop*
magazine (m) *magazine*
magnifique *magnificent, splendid*
mai *May*
main (f) *hand*
mais *but*
maison (f) *house*
mal *badly, bad*
mal (m), maux (pl) *evil*
malade *ill*
malade (m, f) *sick person*
maladie (f) *illness*
mâle (m) *male*
malheureux, -euse *unhappy*
malin, maligne *shrewd*
maman (f) *Mum*
manger *to eat*

manifestation (f) *demonstration*
marche (f) *walk*
marché (m) *market*
marcher *to work, to function*
mari (m) *husband*
marine (f) *Navy*
mastic (m) *putty*
matin (m) *morning*
mauvais *bad*
me *(to) me*
méchant *unkind, nasty*
méchamment *nastily*
médecin (m) *doctor*
meilleur *better*
ménage (m) *housework, household*
menu (m) *menu*
mer (f) *sea*
merci *thank you*
mercredi (m) *Wednesday*
mère (f) *mother*
mètre (m) *metre*
mettre *to put*
midi *midday*
Midi (m) *South of France*
mieux *better*
milieu (m) *middle*
mille *thousand*
milliard (m) *thousand million*
minérale *mineral*; eau —*mineral water*
ministre (m) *minister*
minute (f) *minute*
moi *me*; —même *myself*
moindre *least*
moins *less*
mois (m) *month*
mon, ma, mes *my*
monde (m) *world*
monsieur (m) *Mr, Sir*
monter *to climb*
montre (f) *watch*
montrer *to show*
monts (m. pl) *mountains*; par—
et par vaux *always on the move*
monument (m) *monument*
morceau (m) *piece*
mordre *to bite*

mort *dead*
mort (m) *dead man*
mortel, -elle *deadly*
mot (m) *word*
mouchoir (m) *handkerchief*
mouillé *wet*
mourir *to die*
mousse (f) *foam*
mule (f) *mule*
mur (m) *wall*

naître *to be born*
néanmoins *nevertheless*
neige (f) *snow*
neiger *to snow*
ne . . . pas *not*
ne . . . plus *no longer*
ne . . . que *only*
net *neat, nett*
nettoyer *to clean*
neuf, neuve *new*
nez (m) *nose*
ni . . . ni *neither . . . nor*
Noël *Christmas*
noir *black*
noir (m) *darkness*
noisette (f) *hazel nut*
nom (m) *name*
nombre (m) *number*
note (f) *bill, note*
nous *we, us*
nouveau, nouvelle *new*
nouvelle (f) *piece of news*
nu *bare;* – tête *bareheaded*
nuit (f) *night*
numéro (m) *number*

obéissant *obedient*
œil, yeux (m) *eye, eyes*
œuf (m) *egg*
on *one, we*
s'opposer à *to oppose (sthg or sbdy)*
or (m) *gold*
orange (f) *orange*
ordre (m) *order*
oreille (f) *ear*

oser *to dare*
ou *or*
où *where*
oublier *to forget*
ouf! *phew!*
oui *yes*
ouvert *open*
ouvrier (m) *worker*
ouvrir *to open*

page (f) *page*
pain (m) *bread*
paire (f) *pair*
pâlot *wan, pale*
pantalon (m) *trousers*
papa (m) *Dad*
papier (m) *paper*
par *by*
paraître *to appear*
parce que *because*
pardon (m) *pardon*
parent (m) *parent*
paresse (f) *laziness*
paresseux, -euse *lazy*
parler *to talk*
parmi *among*
parole (f) *word*
part (f) *part;* de ma – *on my behalf*
parti *gone*
partir *to go*
partout *everywhere*
pas (m) *footstep*
(ne . . .) pas *not*
passeport (m) *passport*
passer *to pass*
se passer de *to do without (sthg or sbdy)*
patience (f) *patience*
patrie (f) *home country*
patron (m) *owner, manager*
pauvre *poor*
pauvreté (f) *poverty*
payer *to pay*
péché (m) *sin*
peindre *to paint*
peler *to peel*
pelouse (f) *lawn*

penser *to think*
(se) perdre *to lose (oneself)*
perdu *lost*
père (m) *father*
période (f) *period*
périr *to perish*
permettre *to allow*
Pérou (m) *Peru*
Perse (f) *Persia*
personne (f) *person*
personne *nobody*
petit *small*
petit-déjeuner (m) *breakfast*
pétrole (m) *petroleum*
peu *little*
peur (f) *fear;* de – que *for fear that*
peut-être *perhaps*
photo (f) *photograph*
pièce (f) *coin, room, piece, play*
pied (m) *foot;* à – *on foot*
pierre (f) *stone*
pincée (f) *pinch*
pipe (f) *pipe*
pis *worse, worst;* tant — *too bad*
place (f) *place, square*
placer *to place*
plage (f) *beach*
plaindre *to begrudge, to pity*
se plaindre *to complain*
plainte (f) *complaint*
plaisir (m) *pleasure*
plan (m) *plan*
plante (f) *plant*
planter *to plant*
plat *flat*
pleurer *to cry*
pleuvoir *to rain*
pluie (f) *rain*
plus *more*
plus . . . plus *the more . . . the
   more*
plusieurs *several*
plus tard *later*
poche (f) *pocket*
poignée (f) *handle;* — de main
   handshake
(ne . . .) point *not*

police (f) *police*
politicien (m) *politician*
pomme (f) *apple*
pommier (m) *apple tree*
ponctuel, -elle *punctual*
porte (f) *door*
portefeuille (m) *wallet*
porter *to carry, to wear*
Portugal (m) *Portugal*
poterie (f) *pottery*
poudre (f) *powder*
pour *for*
pour que *so that*
pourquoi *why;* — pas? *why not?*
pourtant *however*
pouvoir *to be able to*
prairie (f) *meadow*
pré (m) *meadow*
préférer *to prefer*
premier, -ière *first*
prendre *to catch, to take*
(se) préparer *to prepare (oneself)*
près *near*
présenter *to present*
président (m) *president*
prêt *ready*
prétendre *to pretend*
prêter *to lend*
prévoir *to forecast*
prière (f) *prayer;* —
   de . . . *please . . .*
prix (m) *price*
problème (m) *problem*
prochain *next*
professeur (m) *professor, teacher*
promenade (f) *walk, outing*
se promener *to go for a walk*
prometteur, -euse *promising*
propre *own, clean*
protéger *to protect*
prudent *cautious*
prudemment *cautiously*
public, -ique *public*
public (m) *public*
puis *then*
puissance (f) *power*
Pyrénées (f. pl) *Pyrenees*

quai (m) *quay, platform*
qualité *quality*
quand *when*
quant à *as regards*
quatre *four*
que *whom, which, that*
quel, quelle, quels, quelles *what, which*
quelque *some*
quelque chose *something*
quelquefois *sometimes*
quelques *several*
quelqu'un *someone*
qui *who*
quiconque *whoever*
quitter *to leave*
quoi? *what?*
quoi que *whatever*
quoique *although*

réagir *to react*
recevoir *to receive*
refaire *to do (sthg) again*
(se) refermer *to close again*
refuser *to refuse*
regard (m) *look, glance*
regarder *to look at*
regretter *to regret*
reine (f) *queen*
remarque (f) *remark*
remède (m) *remedy*
remercier *to thank*
rencontre (f) *meeting*
rencontrer *to meet*
rendez-vous (m) *meeting*
rendre *to give back*
rentrer *to return home, to go back in*
renvoyer *to send back*
réparation (f) *repair*
repas (m) *meal*
répondre *to answer, to reply*
réponse (f) *answer, reply*
reposant *restful*
se reposer *to rest*
république (f) *republic*

réputation (f) *reputation*
rescapé (m) *survivor*
restaurant (m) *restaurant*
rester *to stay*
retard (m) *delay;* en — *late*
retour (m) *return*
retourner *to return*
se retourner *to turn round*
réunion (f) *meeting*
réussir *to succeed*
rêve (m) *dream*
réveiller *to wake (sbdy) up*
se réveiller *to wake up*
revenir *to come back*
rêver *to dream*
revoir *to see again;* au — *goodbye*
rhume (m) *cold*
riche *rich*
richissime *extremely rich*
ridicule *ridiculous*
rien *nothing*
rigoureux, -euse *harsh, rigorous*
rire *to laugh*
rivière (f) *river*
robe (f) *dress*
rocher (m) *rock*
roman (m) *novel*
rouge *red*
rougir *to turn red, blush*
rouler *to drive along, to roll*
route (f) *road*
rue (f) *street;* grand- — *main street*

sa *his, her, its*
sable (m) *sand*
sac (m) *bag*
samedi (m) *Saturday*
sandwich (m) *sandwich*
satisfait *satisfied*
savoir *to know*
scandale (m) *scandal*
scandaleux, -euse *scandalous*
scrupules (m. pl) *scruples*
sec, sèche *dry*
sel (m) *salt*
selon *according to*

semaine (f) *week*
sembler *to seem*
sentiment (m) *feeling*
sentir *to feel, to smell*
sept *seven*
servir *to serve*
seul *alone*
sévère *strict, severe*
si *if, yes*
siffler *to whistle*
signer *to sign*
silence (m) *silence*
simple *simple*
simplement *simply*
situation (f) *situation*
six *six*
sœur (f) *sister*
soi *oneself*
soif (f) *thirst*
soin (m) *care*
soir (m) *evening*
soirée (f) *evening*
soldat (m) *soldier*
soleil (m) *sun*
solitude (f) *solitude*
solution (f) *solution*
sombre *dark, gloomy*
son, sa, ses *his, her, its*
sonner *to ring*
sorte (f) *sort*
sortir *to go out*
sot, sotte *silly, stupid*
souci (m) *care, worry*
soudain *suddenly*
souffrant *suffering, ill*
souffrir *to suffer*
souhaitable *desirable*
souhaiter *to wish*
soupe (f) *soup*
sourire *to smile*
souris (f) *mouse*
souvent *often*
spectateur, -trice (m, f) *spectator*
stock (m) *stock*
stylo (m) *pen*
suite (f) *follow-up;* tout de — *at once*

suivant *following, next;* au — !
   next!
suivre *to follow*
superbe *superb*
sur *on*
sûr *sure*
surprise (f) *surprise*

ta *your*
table (f) *table*
tableau (m) *picture*
Tamise (f) *Thames*
tant *so much;* — pis! *too bad!*
tapis (m) *carpet*
tard *late;* trop — ! *too late!*
taureau (m) *bull*
taxi (m) *taxi;* chauffeur de — *taxi
   driver*
te *(to) you*
téléphoner *to telephone*
temps (m) *time, weather*
tendre *tender, soft*
tenir *to hold*
se tenir *to behave*
tension (f) *tension*
terminer *to finish, to end (sthg)*
terrible *terrible*
tête (f) *head*
têtu *stubborn*
toi *you*
toit (m) *roof*
tomber *to fall*
ton, ta, tes *your*
tort *wrong;* avoir — *to be wrong*
tôt *early*
toucher *to touch*
toujours *always, still*
tour (m) *turn*
tour (f) *tower*
touriste (m, f) *tourist*
tourner *to turn (sthg)*
se tourner (vers) *to turn (towards)*
tous *(pl) all*
tousser *to cough*
tout *everything, quite*
tout à coup *suddenly*
train (m) *train*

tranquille *calm, quiet*
travail (m) *work*
travailler *to work*
travers: en travers *across*
trentaine (f) *thirty or so*
trente *thirty*
très *very*
triste *sad*
tromper *to deceive*
se tromper *to make a mistake*
trop *too, too much*
trouver *to find*
tu *you*
tuer *to kill*

un, une *a, one*
uniforme (m) *uniform*
union (f) *union*
université (f) *university*
urgent *urgent*
usine (f) *factory*
utiliser *to use*

vacances (f. pl) *holiday*
vache (f) *cow*
vague (f) *wave*
vaillamment *bravely*
vaisselle (f) *washing up, crockery*
valise (f) *suitcase*
vase (m) *vase*
véhémentement *vehemently*
vendeur (m) *salesman*
vendre *to sell*
venir *to come*
vent (m) *wind*
vérifier *to check*
vers *towards*
vert *green*
veste (f) *jacket*
viande (f) *meat*
vice (m) *vice*
victime (f) *victim*
vieille (f) *old woman*
vieux, vieille *old*
vieux (m) *old man*

villa (f) *villa*
village (m) *village*
ville (f) *town*
vin (m) *wine*
vingt *twenty*
vingtaine (f) *twenty or so*
violemment *violently*
visa (m) *visa*
visite (f) *visit*
visiter *to visit*
visiteur, -euse (m, f) *visitor*
vite *fast*
vitesse (f) *speed*
vitrail, -aux (m) *stained glass
    window*
vive . . . ! *long live . . . !*
vivre *to live*
voici *here is, here are*
voilà *there is, there are*
voir *to see*
voisin (m) *neighbour*
voiture (f) *car*
voler *to fly, to steal*
volet (m) *shutter*
votre, vos *your*
vôtre (m, f) *yours;* à la — ! *your
    health!*
vouloir *to want, to require*
voulu *wanted, required*
voyage (m) *travel*
voyager *to travel*
voyageur, -euse (m, f) *traveller*
vrai *true*
vraiment *truly*
vu *seen*
vu que . . . *considering that . . .*
vue (f) *sight, view*

y *there*
y compris *included*
yeux (m, pl) *eyes*

zéro *nought, zero*
zoo (m) *zoo*
zut! *blast!*